This book
the date

Jniversity

Rethinking Contemporary Feminist Politics

Gender and Politics series
Series editors: Johanna Kantola, University of Helsinki, Finland and Judith Squires, University of Bristol, UK

This timely new series publishes leading monographs and edited collections from scholars working in the disciplinary areas of politics, international relations and public policy with specific reference to questions of gender. The series showcases cutting-edge research in Gender and Politics, publishing topical and innovative approaches to gender politics. It will include exciting work from new authors and well-known academics and will also publish high-impact writings by practitioners working in issues relating to gender and politics.

The series covers politics, international relations and public policy, including gendered engagement with mainstream political science issues, such as political systems and policymaking, representation and participation, citizenship and identity, equality, and women's movements; gender and international relations, including feminist approaches to international institutions, political economy and global politics; and interdisciplinary and emergent areas of study, such as masculinities studies, gender and multiculturalism, and intersectionality.

Potential contributors are encouraged to contact the series editors: Johanna Kantola, (johanna.kantola@helsinki.fi) and Judith Squires (judith.squires@bristol. ac.uk)

Series Advisory Board:
Louise Chappell, University of Sydney, Australia
Joni Lovenduksi, Birkbeck College, University of London, UK
Amy Mazur, Washington State University, USA
Jacqui True, University of Auckland, New Zealand
Mieke Verloo, Radboud University Nijmegen, the Netherlands
Laurel Weldon, Purdue University, USA

Titles include
Jonathan Dean
RETHINKING CONTEMPORARY FEMINIST POLITICS

Gender and Politics Series
Series Standing Order ISBNs 978–0–230–23917–3 (hardback)
and 978–0–230–23918–0 (paperback)

You can receive future titles in this series as they are published by placing a standing order. Please contact your bookseller or, in case of difficulty, write to us at the address below with your name and address, the title of the series and the ISBNs quoted above.

Customer Services Department, Macmillan Distribution Ltd, Houndmills, Basingstoke, Hampshire RG21 6XS, England

---

Rethinking Contemporary Feminist Politics

Jonathan Dean
Teacher in Political Theory, Department of Government, University of Essex, UK

First published 2010 by
PALGRAVE MACMILLAN

Palgrave Macmillan in the UK is an imprint of Macmillan Publishers Limited,
registered in England, company number 785998, of Houndmills, Basingstoke,
Hampshire RG21 6XS.

Palgrave Macmillan in the US is a division of St Martin's Press LLC,
175 Fifth Avenue, New York, NY 10010.

Palgrave Macmillan is the global academic imprint of the above companies
and has companies and representatives throughout the world.

Palgrave® and Macmillan® are registered trademarks in the United States,
the United Kingdom, Europe and other countries.

ISBN 978–0–230–23892–3   hardback

This book is printed on paper suitable for recycling and made from fully
managed and sustained forest sources. Logging, pulping and manufacturing
processes are expected to conform to the environmental regulations of the
country of origin.

A catalogue record for this book is available from the British Library.

A catalog record for this book is available from the Library of Congress.

Printed and bound in Great Britain by
CPI Antony Rowe, Chippenham and Eastbourne

Contents

List of Table   vii

Acknowledgements   viii

Introduction   1
  Mapping the 'New Feminist Politics'   2
  Outline of the book   5

1 Current Developments in Feminist Politics   9
  Feminist temporalities 1: Decline and
    deradicalisation   10
  Feminist temporalities 2: 'New feminisms' and
    feminist re-emergence   15
  Feminist temporalities 3: Post-feminism   19
  Feminist spatialities 1: Transnational feminisms   21
  Feminist spatialities 2: State feminism   26
  Feminist radicalities   31

2 Rethinking Feminist Radicalism   36
  Why radicalism?   36
  Mapping the terrain: 'Post-foundational'
    challenges to politics   38
  Laclau: The role of articulation and equivalence   42
  Arendt and Zerilli on politics and 'the social'   47
  Feminism and political imagination   52
  Synthesising Laclau and Zerilli   57
  Discourse theory and (feminist) political analysis   59
  Conclusion: Rethinking 'radicality'   61

3 The Fawcett Society: The End of the Road
  for Equality Feminism?   64
  'A jolly good chat': Fawcett's ethos and
    historical background   65
  The question of women's political participation
    and representation   71
  The politics of childcare and work-life balance   76
  Fawcett's rebranding and its aftermath   82
  Theorising Fawcett's rebranding   93

Fawcett's new feminist agenda: Some critical remarks   96
Conclusion   98

4   Women's Aid: Professionalised Radicalism?   100
    Women's Aid: Origins and historical background   101
    The present-day Women's Aid: A brief overview   103
    Women's Aid: Success and professionalisation   105
    Domestic violence, immigration and anti-racism   113
    Domestic violence as a 'figure of the newly thinkable'   115
    Critical assessments: A drift towards the
        'new managerialism'?   121
    Conclusion   125

5   The F-word: Cultural Politics and Third-Wave Feminism   127
    Feminism and the Internet   129
    The F-word: Diversity, inclusiveness and reasserting
        feminism   130
    Cultural politics and feminist individualism   135
    Anger, affect and resistance: Contesting feminist
        depoliticisation   141
    Negotiating the third wave   150
    Generational disidentifications, or, who's afraid
        of third-wave feminism?   157
    Concluding reflections and critical comments   160

Conclusion: The Consequences of Optimism   163
    Contemporary feminism and political optimism   164
    Optimism, pessimism and 'post-politics'   166
    Theorising political optimism   169
    The (re)turn to Gramsci   177

Notes   184

Bibliography   197

Index   218

List of Table

3.1 Shifts in Fawcett Society discourse, before and
     after 2005 rebranding   95

Acknowledgements

I'd like to start by acknowledging my debt to four books which I have found consistently inspiring throughout the project, namely, Ernesto Laclau and Chantal Mouffe's *Hegemony and Socialist Strategy*; Judith Butler's *Gender Trouble*; Linda Zerilli's *Feminism and the Abyss of Freedom*; and Angela McRobbie's *The Aftermath of Feminism*. My debt to all these texts cannot be overstated.

I would like to thank the Economic and Social Research Council for funding both my research at Essex and at the LSE Gender Institute. Extra special thanks are due to Jason Glynos and Anne Phillips for their expertise and always good-humoured support. I would like to thank all my research participants – too numerous to mention by name – without whom this project simply would not have been possible.

Special thanks are also due to Angela McRobbie and Aletta Norval – for their feedback and encouragement; Lasse Thomassen, David Howarth and Vicky Randall – for their ever detailed and helpful comments on earlier drafts of chapters; Hazel Johnstone, without whom the LSE Gender Institute would grind to a halt; and Sean Nixon, for fun diversions encompassing the academic, the cultural and the ornithological.

I have benefited from immensely helpful feedback on earlier drafts of chapters from a broad range of people. These include, at Essex: Paul Bou-Habib, and various participants in the Ideology and Discourse Analysis graduate programme at Essex between 2003 and 2007, with particular thanks to Jo Gadegaard, Jenny Gunnarsson-Payne, Peter Bloom and David Payne. Thanks also to Eamonn Carrabine, Nick Allen and my conference-organising colleagues Michael Strange and Laura Glanc. And a very big thank you to Jackie Pells – for her unrelenting helpfulness and good humour. At the LSE Gender Institute, Clare Hemmings, Sadie Wearing, Sumi Madhok, Mary Evans, Kim Hutchings, Anna Feigenbaum, Marsha Henry and Ania Plomien not only provided detailed feedback on my work, but have helped make the GI an exceptionally rewarding and enjoyable research environment. I am especially grateful to Christina Scharff who not only welcomed me into the social and academic fabric of the gender institute, but also provided many engaging hours of discussion about our shared intellectual concerns.

I am hugely grateful to my editors at Palgrave MacMillan who have been efficient and helpful throughout. The following people also provided invaluable comments, feedback or help, and I am extremely grateful to all of them: Members of the History of Feminism network (especially Jeska Rees, Marc Calvini-Lefevbre, Esme Cleall, Angela Grainger and Naomi Hetherington); Kate Kenny, Kathy Jones, Malin Rönnblom, Ulrika Dahl, Nina Lykke, Cynthia Cockburn, Cristina Santos, Kristin Aune, Katherine Rake, Nicola Harwin, Sarah Browne and Anna Rogers.

Very big thanks also to the 'genderlicious' crew – Christina Scharff, Deborah Finding, Natasha Marhia, Patrizia Kokot, Amy Hinterberger, Carolyn Williams, Carolyn Pedwell, Joanne Kalogeras, Maria do Mar Pereira, Marina Franchi, Rebekah Wilson and Gwendolyn Beetham – for helping make my year at the GI so enjoyable. Thanks also to my 'international friends' – Angeliki Alvanoudi, Mia Liinason, Malena Gustavson and Cheryl Auger – who helped make conferences in Örebro, Stockholm and Utrecht so memorable. On a personal note, I would like to thank my parents and all my lovely friends in London and Scotland. Finally, I'd like to thank Maria: no amount of appreciative discourse could adequately convey my gratitude. Beijinhos.

An earlier version of Chapter 2 was originally published as 'Feminist Purism and the Question of "Radicality" in Contemporary Political Theory', *Contemporary Political Theory* 7 (3): 280–301, 2008, while parts of the discussions of third-wave feminisms in Chapters 1, 3 and 5 have been reproduced from 'Who's Afraid of Third Wave Feminism: On the Uses of the "Third Wave" in British Feminist Politics', *International Feminist Journal of Politics* 11 (3): 334–52, 2009. I am grateful to Palgrave Macmillan and Routledge respectively for permission to reproduce material from these articles.

Introduction

This book emerges at an interesting time for feminist activism in the UK and Western Europe.[1] It responds to a sense among the feminist activist community that 'something' is happening with regards to feminist politics, certainly in the UK, and possibly elsewhere, and that this 'something' has thus far gone largely unexamined within academic circles. This 'something' refers to how, in the UK, the mid- to late 2000s have witnessed significant increases in influence, visibility and popularity of a range of autonomous feminist practices, through groups and events such as The Fawcett Society, Object, Ladyfest, Reclaim the Night marches and numerous others. A critical examination of the existing literature on feminist political practices is therefore timely, not least because there has been 'surprisingly little research' into the state of feminist politics in Britain in recent years (Mackay, 2008: 17).

In addition to these empirical questions, the book is also driven by a sense that these current developments in feminist politics might be productively analysed through dialogue with new theoretical insights concerning the nature of 'politics'. Specifically, this book takes inspiration from contemporary strands of post-structuralist and post-Marxist political theory which offer a challenge to what we might call dominant *topographical* understandings of politics – that is, a conception of politics as a specifically delimited domain of social life. Very broadly speaking, these perspectives argue that politics is not an activity confined to specific types of spaces or institutions, but is, rather, a mode of action, unpredictable and impossible to fully master or domesticate. Such arguments – articulated in various ways by authors such as Ernesto Laclau, Linda Zerilli and Jacques Rancière – share certain resemblances to, and are in some cases informed by, feminist challenges to dominant understandings of politics, in that they emphasise how political action can emerge suddenly and unexpectedly in a diverse range of spaces. This book's central concern is to ask how a combination of new empirical developments in feminist activism, and new theoretical challenges to dominant understandings of politics, might prompt a rethinking and a re-evaluation of established narratives about contemporary feminist politics, particularly with regard to their spatial and temporal assumptions. It does this through a combination of theoretical analysis and empirical research, the latter consisting of three case studies of contemporary UK-based feminist groups (The Fawcett Society, Women's Aid and the F-word).

Mapping the 'New Feminist Politics'

I want to suggest that it might be helpful to use the designation the 'New Feminist Politics' to signify these new empirical developments in contemporary feminism. This might at first seem to be a potentially problematic formulation. But the appeal to a notion of a *New* Feminist Politics is not so much intended to designate a profound temporal break. Rather, I use it as analogous to what Butler, in her recent work, has referred to as the 'New Gender Politics', which, for her, signifies 'a combination of movements concerned with transgender, transexuality, intersex, and their complex relations to feminist and queer theory' (Butler, 2004: 4). Again using Butler's terminology, the 'New Feminist Politics' designates a series of performative citations of feminist politics, which – in their character as citational – exhibit elements of continuity with earlier feminisms. However, in their 'new' spatial and temporal context, those citations of necessity entail elements of rearticulation.

The 'newness' of the 'New Feminist Politics' signifies an increasing *visibility* of substantive, activist feminist politics in recent years. But what is specific about this new visibility? In very general terms, it refers to how several works on contemporary feminism published in the 1990s seem to have had to actively *look for* feminist politics, as if it weren't immediately visible. Books such as Natasha Walter's *The New Feminism* (1998) and Baumgardner and Richards' *Manifesta* (2000) were primarily in dialogue with a set of imagined interlocutors: the media commentator proclaiming the 'death of feminism' and the young woman denouncing feminism as old-fashioned and irrelevant. Consequently, such works were devoted to either showing that feminism *is* still relevant and topical, or to finding feminist politics in practices or cultural productions (single mothers' support groups, TV shows such as *Buffy the Vampire Slayer*) that are not obviously or overtly *political*.

The 'New Feminist Politics' designates a change in the terrain of the debate: that is, it is now more or less indisputable – within Anglo-American contexts – that there *are* instances of feminist politics taking place. It indicates that the primary question of 'does feminist politics still exist?' has been answered affirmatively, such that the focus has moved to the question of 'how can we characterise the currently existing instances of feminist politics?' Thus, there is undoubtedly a qualified optimism running through this book. Crucially, this optimism is grounded not so much in a naïve celebratory relation to the cases analysed but, rather, in the relieved sense that the more primary question of whether feminist politics still exists is no longer a relevant or pressing question. Therefore, it is a cautious optimism not grounded in a (necessarily) affirmative response to the question of whether new feminist political practices are radical, progressive and transformative, but, rather, in the fact that we are able to pose such questions in the first place. To put it flippantly, if one's goal is to highlight how claims about the 'death of feminism' are constatively inaccurate and performatively unsuccessful, one no longer has to make tenuous feminist readings of cultural productions such as *Buffy* or *Xena: Warrior Princess* to make the point.

Among the more prominent elements within the purview of the 'New Feminist Politics' in the UK are the London Feminist Network, which has a very active email list and does regular activism (usually around the issues of sexuality and pornography), the re-establishment of the Reclaim the Night marches against sexual violence (spearheaded by the London Feminist Network), the Million Women Rise march against violence against women, Feminist Fightback (an explicitly socialist feminist group), the Feminist Activist Forum, Object (which campaigns against the objectification of women in the media), the FEM conferences in Sheffield (which bring together activists working on a range of issues), Ladyfest events (feminist events focussing on women's art and creativity) and a whole host of new feminist 'zines' (that is, small circulation, independently produced, printed publications). Also, the Internet has facilitated a spread of feminist 'blogging' and the establishment of links between disparate feminist groups and individuals (Rowe, 2008): for instance, the UK feminist action Yahoo email list has, in recent years, received numerous posts by people across the UK starting, or hoping to start, local feminist groups.

In very general terms, there is a sense that these new modes of feminist political activity have emerged in response to a perceived gap between the mainstreaming of feminist concerns and the liberal democratic promise of gender equality, on the one hand, and the existence of unequal gender relations, on the other. There is a significant level of mobilisation around a collective sense that 'the battle has not been won', and that there is still significant work to do. Indeed, this dimension of affectivity is enhanced by a shared opposition to those hegemonic post-feminist discourses which structure modes of feminist (dis)identification (Scharff, 2010).

In terms of their more substantive aspects, many of these new forms of activism are centred on issues such as women's sexuality, violence against women, beauty and pornography. Questions relating to pornography and violence against women seem particularly recurrent within current feminist activism and the feminist 'blogosphere'. However, the focus on these issues is by no means unanimous: to a large extent, these new forms of activism around pornography and violence against women could be read as new iterations of 'traditional' radical feminist concerns. In tension with these strands are groups such as Feminist Fightback, a prominent London based feminist activist group which is explicit in its identification as socialist feminist, and also, in contrast to much current UK feminist activism, is forthright in its defence of sex-workers' rights. In a number of respects, one could say these fault lines map onto the 'classic' tripartite division of radical/socialist/liberal, reworked into the contemporary conjuncture (with groups such as The Fawcett Society and the Women's Budget Group representing the liberal end). However, the following chapters disrupt such a mapping, in large part by problematising dominant understandings of 'radicalism' within feminist discourse.

In addition to the emergence of new forms of autonomous feminist mobilisation, the same period has also seen ongoing work and activism by more established groups such as the National Alliance for Women's Organisations (NAWO), the Women's Resource Centre, Rights of Women, Justice for Women, Southall Black Sisters and the Newham Asian Women's Project.[2] Of particular note, according to a comprehensive overview by Predelli et al. (2008), is that the past few years have witnessed something of a reconciliation, so to speak, between ethnic minority and ethnic majority women's groups. While divisions between women's groups along ethnic and racial lines still persist, Predelli et al. draw attention to, for example, the longstanding alliance between Southall Black Sisters and Justice for Women concerning the legal treatment of women who kill abusive partners, and the campaign relating to the impact of the 'no recourse to public funds' rule for victims of domestic violence with insecure immigration status (which involved numerous organisations but was also spearheaded by Southall Black Sisters).

Outline of the book

Against this backdrop of an apparent proliferation of feminist activism across the UK, the bulk of the book is devoted to an analysis of how the current empirical and theoretical developments alluded to above might occasion a rethinking of established narratives about the state of contemporary feminist politics. In so doing, I take issue with two main sets of narratives about the recent – by which I mean post-1960s – history of feminist politics. First, I interrogate accounts which frame the recent feminist past as one of decline, demobilisation, institutionalisation and deradicalisation. However, I also cast a critical eye over more optimistic narratives of feminist re-emergence (often pitched in terms of 'new' or 'third-wave' feminisms). The central argument put forward is that the bulk of these diverse accounts rest upon problematic understandings of feminist *radicalism*: consequently, the book's theoretical intervention is to articulate a post-structuralist reading of feminist radicalism, which we can then use productively to critically intervene in existing discussions about the state of feminist politics, and to conduct empirical analysis of current feminist practices. For the most part, my reformulated notion of feminist radicalism leads me to claim that most accounts of the feminist present underestimate the vibrancy and radicalism of contemporary feminist politics. Importantly though, this line of argument seeks to resist the temptation of an overcelebratory account which the strong critique of narratives of feminist decline might give rise to, as I aim to show how a number of both pessimistic *and* optimistic narratives rest on problematic understandings of feminist politics, and of dynamics of continuity and change.

The empirical dimension of these arguments consists of three detailed case studies. The first of these will be *The Fawcett Society*. The Fawcett Society is a long running organisation which claims to be the leading voice fighting for gender equality in the UK, and is, in some senses, the 'most institutionalised' of my three cases. It is relatively large, well structured, well organised and has strong links with the media and government. Furthermore, its roots are in Suffragist-influenced liberal feminism, and as such the organisation has traditionally adopted a relatively optimistic view of engagement with a range of state institutions. My second case study is *Women's Aid*, the UK's national domestic violence charity. Like The Fawcett Society, Women's Aid is large, well organised, and has a high profile in the media and in government. Unlike The Fawcett Society, however, Women's Aid's roots are in the more 'autonomous' dimensions of second-wave feminism. My final case study looks at an Internet feminist magazine called *The F-word*, although I also focus on its 'real' offshoot, the London Thirdwave Feminists. Unlike the previous two groups, The F-word is an Internet 'zine', and seems to be the largest and best maintained of the various Internet-based feminist groups and publications in the UK. While it does not specifically engage in campaigning activity, it nonetheless provides a forum for young British feminists to exchange ideas and information. It therefore very much seems to have its finger 'on the pulse' of grass-roots feminism, and as such it remains entirely autonomous from the British state. When analysing the cases, I pose the following questions:

- What are their key aims and objectives?
- What types of political strategies are used? How are these political strategies discursively framed, accounted for and justified? How might we, as political analysts, characterise their political strategies?
- What specific hegemonic discourses are contested, and which are complied with (intentionally or otherwise)?
- What is the role of the signifier 'feminism'? How is it used and understood?

My research consisted of exhaustive analyses of the three groups, using a combination of archival research, participant observation and semi-structured interviews with key actors within the various groups. The interviews included a mixture of face-to-face interviews, group interviews (focus groups) and email correspondence.[3]

Despite the diversity of the three cases, I make no claims that these three can be seen as in some sense 'representative' of contemporary UK feminism as a whole, although they are all undoubtedly key players in the current feminist scene. Rather, my aim is to provide some snap-shots of how engagement with specific cases might provide insights that challenge, or run counter to, existing narratives about British feminism. While I note that the context is entirely British, throughout I shall remain alert to how the British case links into debates about the transnational within contemporary feminism. I do this by looking at how, if at all, UK feminists are engaged in the articulation of feminist demands across and above national borders, and by highlighting how attachments to particular UK-based narratives may, perhaps inadvertently, reproduce certain Anglo-American hegemonies within contemporary feminist history.

I note that there are other biases perpetrated by my case selection. For one, the nature of the case selections perhaps risks bracketing out activism focussed on the intersections of race, gender, sexuality and other identity categories. However, discourses of diversity and intersectionality are constantly negotiated by the groups involved (particularly The Fawcett Society and Women's Aid), particularly in light of new equalities legislation,[4] while The F-word has played host to a number of discussions around race and sexuality. All these issues will be addressed in the context of the cases.

I also acknowledge that there is undoubtedly an English and indeed London/Home Counties bias to the cases. Thus, my use of the term UK feminism is something of a misnomer: English feminism would be more apt, especially considering that feminist activism in Scotland has arguably remained more vibrant than in England (Mackay, 2008; Lovenduski and Randall, 1993: 359), and considering my use of Kantola's work on the Scottish case to expose the English bias of narratives of decline and depoliticisation. However, the findings presented here will enable fruitful comparisons with ongoing research on feminism in Scotland, such as Sarah Browne's (2008) work on the contemporary history of feminism in Scotland and Lesley Orr's (2008) work on Scottish Women's Aid. More broadly, the findings presented here on British feminism in the transnational context will contribute to a broader conversation about the state of feminist politics. Key issues I explore in the British context – the relationship between feminism and the state, the question of generational relations, the intersections between feminism and other progressive political agendas, the implications of web-based activisms – are being tackled not only by feminists in Western democracies but also elsewhere. Consequently, the theoretical and empirical explorations presented over the following chapters open up lines of enquiry that may contribute to a broad rethinking of feminist politics in the UK, in other national contexts and transnationally.

Overall, my intention is to resist the temptation to characterise in excessively general terms the state of contemporary feminism, and to caution against a too-strong adherence to unitary narratives about feminist politics. Partly drawing inspiration from Clare Hemmings' (2005) work on temporal dynamics in feminist theory, my aim is not to posit a totalising alternative narrative, but to expose the exclusions and often unarticulated assumptions that make particular narratives possible, and, more substantively, to draw attention to the existence of certain practices which risk being underplayed or overlooked altogether from the perspective of current dominant feminist narratives. Taking inspiration from post-structuralist political theory, I intend to show how contemporary feminism, in the UK and elsewhere, is a site of a diversity of intersecting and often conflicting 'logics' which resist subsumption under any particular account.[5]

Chapter 1 assesses current literatures on contemporary feminism, with particular attention paid to problematising dominant assumptions about the spatial and temporal dynamics of feminist politics. In Chapter 2 I draw upon contemporary post-structuralist theorisations of radical politics to enable a more critical and complex assessment of contemporary feminism, before using these theoretical developments to analyse my three empirical case studies (Chapters 3, 4 and 5). In the Conclusion, I revisit the question of political optimism within feminist, post-structuralist and post-Marxist political theory, exploring ways in which the analysis of feminist politics presented here prompts a critique of notions of cynicism and heroism which circulate within these theoretical discourses.

1
Current Developments in Feminist Politics

This chapter assesses academic narratives about the recent history of feminist political practices, and raises a number of critical questions. There are two relevant sets of narratives I wish to call into question. The first is a set of broadly (though by no means entirely) melancholic narratives that describe a burgeoning feminist movement in the 1970s which is then presented as having gone into decline, and/or lost a degree of its vitality and energy due to a series of shifts in feminist political practices. Here, notions such as fragmentation, decline, institutionalisation, depoliticisation and deradicalisation are key recurrent terms. I explore the assumptions that underpin these narratives by asking what kind of attachments and political orientations drive them and in what ways these might lead to a selective reading of contemporary feminist politics. More specifically, I contend that these various narratives suffer from what we might call a 'political deficit', in which the complexities of feminist politics are somewhat obfuscated amidst excessively broad accounts of decline, fragmentation and institutionalisation. In particular, I argue that authors tend to reproduce, often inadvertently, versions of what we might usefully call the 'deradicalisation' thesis, by virtue of the existence of varying degrees of attachment to a specific modality of 'seventies' feminist politics. I outline how many authors, whose portrayals of the contemporary feminist scene are quite balanced, nonetheless often implicitly or explicitly invoke a 'proper place' for a (radical) feminist politics, in a way that obscures aspects of continuity and change in recent feminist history and perhaps underestimates the radicalism of certain contemporary feminist practices.

The second set of narratives I interrogate are those more celebratory accounts which claim that recent years have seen a re-emergence of a dynamic feminist movement. These have come from a variety of perspectives, but include accounts framed in terms of 'new feminism', 'third-wave feminism' and, in some instances, accounts of feminism transnationally. While these accounts are helpful in that they refuse the pessimism and melancholy of the first set of narratives, they are often insufficiently alert to dynamics of continuity and change, and perhaps risk overlooking the ambiguities and complexities of contemporary feminist politics.

In exploring these narratives, I pay particular attention to their constructions of feminist temporality and spatiality. I begin with the temporal dimension, focussing on narratives of decline, fragmentation and re-emergence in relation to literature on contemporary feminist history, third-wave feminism, new feminism and 'post feminism' (the latter three of which are often concerned with the relationship between feminism and popular culture). Following that, I shift to the literature on the spatial dynamics of contemporary feminist politics, by looking at recent debates concerning 'transnational feminism' and 'state feminism', which both deal largely with changes in feminist political space. Towards the end of the chapter I assess the ways in which specific conceptions of 'radicalism' within feminist politics still haunt a number of these accounts in ways which reproduce certain problematic narratives about declining vibrancy and radicalism of feminism.

Feminist temporalities 1: Decline and deradicalisation

Until recently, it was persistently reiterated that the autonomous feminist movement, within an Anglo-American context at least, had declined, fragmented and fizzled out. While, as we shall see, there has recently been a proliferation of less pessimistic accounts, linear narratives of decline still hold considerable sway.[1] Notions of loss, fragmentation and decline are often invoked alongside an implied melancholic longing for a return to a specifically 'seventies' mode of feminist politics. I use 'seventies' in inverted commas to capture the ways in which feminism in that decade is – in the present – retroactively constituted as having certain qualities (such as radicalism, purity and authenticity) as opposed to referring to 'actually existing' feminism from the 1970s (Hemmings and Brain, 2003). In the UK context, the tone of such accounts is also typically predicated on a sense of looking back, as if we are retrospectively analysing a particular entity (British feminism) whose time has passed. This view is partly premised upon the cessation of the British Women's Liberation Movement annual conferences in 1978, which is frequently read as symptomatic of the break up or fragmentation of the movement more generally (Coote, 2000: 6; Coward, 1999: 2–3). Frequently, one finds overtly melancholic statements bemoaning the absence of a clearly visible critical feminist lobby, as encapsulated by Angela McRobbie's reflections where she asks:

> Is there a group challenging old feminism in order to create something new? There is certainly no new organised lobby. There have been no campaigns or demonstrations by young women, no new magazines, and barely a handful of explicitly feminist books by younger women. That passion and energy is surely gone.
>
> (McRobbie, 2000: 212)

This implicitly evokes a time when there was a clearly identifiable feminist lobby, which was assumed to be vibrant, active and dynamic. In this vein, Paul Byrne, writing in 1996, claims that in the UK 'the autonomous women's movement has largely disappeared' (Byrne, 1996: 69). Elsewhere, Lynne Segal describes how feminism 'grew rapidly as a mass social movement, peaking in the mid-1970s before dissolving as a coherent organisation by the end of the decade' (Segal, 1999: 9). Such accounts, albeit perhaps unintentionally, tend to reproduce a melancholic attachment to a particular mode of feminist politics prior to its 'mainstreaming' within politics, popular culture and the academy (see Hemmings, 2005: 127).

Other authors, even when cautioning against excessively melancholic or simplistic narratives of feminist decline, nonetheless employ a discourse of feminist death or paradigm break, as if they were writing a post-mortem of feminism, rather than an account of its continued existence. For example, Jane Pilcher, while acknowledging the presence of feminism in some quarters, nonetheless invokes the death of feminism as an 'active, campaigning political movement' (Pilcher, 1998: 111). Similarly, Sheila Rowbotham has observed that 'though there was not [by which, in context, she means 'no longer'] a single identifiable "women's movement" in either Britain or the US [in the 1990s], sexual politics continued in women's activism around, for example, health groups, campaigns to decriminalize prostitution and agitation against inequalities in the treatment of breast cancer' (Rowbotham, 1997: 568–9). Again, this draws an uneasy distinction between a 'single identifiable women's movement', on the one hand (implicitly temporally situated in the 'seventies'), and 'continuing sexual politics', on the other. Also, Paul Bagguley argues that British feminism is a movement in 'abeyance', that is, one which empirically has declined in visibility but holds on to a latent potential to reassert itself (Bagguley, 2002), while Hollows and Moseley (2006) frame a discussion of contemporary feminism in popular culture around a narrative of the women's movement's declining visibility.

There are a number of ways in which these accounts are problematic. At a basic empirical level, Elizabeth Meehan correctly asserts that such a view 'underestimates what was going on before the 1960s and what still continues' (Meehan, 1990: 189), as well as overestimating the unity and coherence of feminist politics in the 'seventies' (Rowe, 1982; Toynbee, 2002; Grey and Sawer, 2008). However, more fundamental is the way in which contemporary feminist activism is, in these accounts, thought *in terms of* 'seventies' feminism. Thus, a particular reading of autonomous 'seventies' feminism is invoked as *the* paradigm of feminism *per se*. This has the effect that contemporary feminist activism is not investigated in its complexity but is, instead, subsumed under a narrative of movement decline which, although it may have some sound empirical grounding, risks doing an injustice to the vibrancy, dynamics and specificities of more recent feminist activism.

While these narratives of decline are sometimes pitched as a simple quantitative reduction in the number of feminist activists, often they are also given a more qualitative thrust through linking notions of 'decline' to shifts in feminist practice and priorities. These narratives work with a presumption that 'seventies' feminism was – despite its internal divisions – at least partially predicated upon a consensus that values such as autonomy and purity were fundamental, and that the movement's radicalism in large part derived from its adherence to these values (Rowbotham, 1989: 123; Gelb, 1989: 4; Lovenduski and Randall, 1993; Bouchier, 1983; Chester, 1982; Squires, 2007: 123; Predelli et al., 2008: 22; Byrne, 1996: 61). In the British context, the emphasis on autonomy was also, at least in part, a consequence of feminism's often close connections to the libertarian strands of radical class politics (Lovenduski, 1995: 128; Bouchier, 1983: 61). Martin Pugh provides perhaps the clearest outline of these core values, and is worth quoting at length. He writes:

> The hallmark of women's liberation consisted in avoiding the formal, hierarchical structures typical of male politics. The alternative took the form of communes which were self-contained, all female units. Since communes proved difficult to sustain, a more common expedient was to create spaces from which men were excluded and in which women felt less intimidated; with their democratic and co-operative approach and absence of formal leadership, these groups sometimes verged on

anarchism. But they offered an ideal means of allowing women to share their experiences of sexism, a technique known as 'consciousness-raising' which became a central part of the movement.

(Pugh, 2000: 319)[2]

However, there is a consensus that at least some of this early autonomy and radicalism has been lost due to a series of shifts in feminist political practice. The post-1970s feminist scene is typically characterised as one of institutionalisation (Lovenduski and Randall, 1993; Walby, 2002; Nash, 2002: 313), fragmentation (Squires, 2007: 120–5; Hollows, 2000: 6) and deradicalisation (Bouchier, 1979), or a combination of all of these (Byrne, 1996). The notion of 'fragmentation' may be linked to a sense of feminist politics taking on a less coherent, more erratic character: for instance, Judith Squires notes that 'the idea of a singular movement has been eclipsed by a series of provisional alliances or loosely coupled networks' (Squires, 2007: 124). Alternatively, it is often linked to the critique – primarily articulated by non-white feminists and emphasising racial hierarchies – of a notion of feminist politics as motivated by a shared sisterhood of women with broadly convergent political concerns (Lovenduski and Randall, 1993; Byrne, 1996: 59; Predelli et al., 2008: 98).[3]

By contrast, narratives of institutionalisation and deradicalisation often claim (or imply) that aspirations to large-scale change via autonomous mobilisation and a distrust of mainstream political institutions gave way to a more compromising, reformist stance (although it is important to note that these authors are by no means of necessity hostile to these shifts).[4] In the British context, this can be accounted for through a combination of increased opportunities for 'moderate' feminist influence in the Labour Party during Neil Kinnock's leadership (Lovenduski and Randall, 1993: 138–40; Bagguley, 2002); the establishment of women's committees by the Greater London Council and in other urban centres (Gelb, 1989: 84–8); feminist involvement in the implementation of equal opportunities legislation (Charles, 2000: 104); the development of links between feminist NGOs, pro-feminist MPs and women's policy agencies (Lovenduski, 2007); the institutionalisation and professionalisation of feminism in the university system (Warwick and Auchmuty, 1995); and the emergence of new political opportunity structures at the supranational level (Walby, 2002).

This apparent decline of an autonomous, relatively unified yet non-institutionalised feminist movement is summarised by Banaszak, Beckwith and Rucht, who note that

[w]omen's movements in West Europe and Canada with radical and even revolutionary antecedents transformed their feminist policy concerns and their relationship with the state. They have moved from an early radicalism, autonomy and challenge to the state in the 1970s, to a more moderate, state-involved, and accommodationist stance by the 1990s.

(Banaszak, et al.: 2003: 2)

These accounts undoubtedly capture something crucial about recent shifts in feminist practices. However, they suffer from a number of problems. For one, Banaszak et al. (2003) equate feminist radicalism with autonomy and 'challenge to the state'. Such a view invites the question of whether this exhausts the ways in which a feminist politics might be described as 'radical', and whether such a claim might exaggerate the extent to which feminist politics can be said to have lost much of its dynamism and radicalism (an issue explored more fully later in this chapter). Furthermore, these narratives of decline tend to – with regard to the British context at least – overestimate the extent to which feminism in the 1970s was antagonistic towards the state. Indeed, campaigns for, and provision of, state-funded services were an integral component of socialist feminism in the UK throughout the late twentieth century (Coote and Campbell, 1987: 94). As such, these narratives risk exaggerating the discontinuities between an alleged 'anti-statist' past and a 'statist' present (Nash, 2002: 319; McRobbie, 2009: 154).

To frame the argument in more general terms, narratives of decline, fragmentation, institutionalisation and deradicalisation risk constituting 'seventies' feminism as authentic and unitary in a manner that blinds us to key aspects of both the feminist pasts and the presents. Indeed, in the quote above, Squires rather tellingly invokes the 'idea' of a singular movement (as opposed to the actual empirical existence of a unitary feminism). Does this perhaps suggest that the division between the 'unified' and 'pure' feminist seventies and the 'fragmented' and 'institutionalised' feminist present says more about the biographical trajectories and affective investments of the individual authors than it does about what feminist activism in the 1970s or in the present 'really' looks like? Clare Hemmings writes that 'such apocalyptic feminist positions expect the present to resemble the past. When it does not, a radical break is imagined and the future abandoned, leaving only the cultivation of memory' (Hemmings, 2005: 128). Although Hemmings is writing about academic feminist theory, I think we can reasonably claim that a similar instantiation of feminist temporality is at work in some of these accounts of feminist activism, whereby a radical break from the feminist 'seventies' is imagined and the present seen as somehow lacking and inauthentic.

As shall become clear, a key – albeit broad – empirical claim I make over the following chapters is that contemporary instances of feminist politics exhibit elements of continuity and discontinuity with earlier modes of feminism in ways which these narratives of decline (or in some cases death) often fail to adequately grasp. By invoking notions such as decline, movement demise or even something less melancholic such as 'abeyance', one risks ridding oneself of the responsibility of a more detailed assessment of contemporary feminist practices. Such assertions are not usually empirically justified but tend to operate as the very ground upon which claims about contemporary feminist practices are made. This, along with the unacknowledged Anglo-American partiality of the narratives (addressed below), curtails the usefulness of these diverse narratives of loss for the understanding of contemporary feminist politics.

Feminist temporalities 2: 'New feminisms' and feminist re-emergence

In the 1980s and 1990s, narratives of decline were very much to the fore in literature on the contemporary history of feminist activism. By contrast, the period from the late 1990s onwards has seen a number of more optimistic accounts of the emergence of a range of new feminist practices. Such accounts are articulated in diverse ways, although a common rhetorical strategy is to invoke notions of break or paradigm shift from a moribund older form of feminism, to a new, lively and vibrant contemporary feminism. Here, notions such as 'new feminism' or 'third-wave feminism' are commonly invoked in the service of celebratory narratives of re-emergence. Although such accounts might at first seem to be in opposition to narratives of decline, they nonetheless converge in their emphasis on a feminist paradigm break between qualitatively different old and new feminisms. In so doing, both sets of narratives arguably over-emphasise break and discontinuity over continuity across time.

Importantly, a number of texts proclaiming the arrival of a 'new' feminism have been aimed at a popular rather than academic audience. In a British context, arguably the most important among these was Natasha Walter's *The New Feminism* (1998), written partially in counterpoint to the increasing number of pronouncements of the 'death of feminism' across the popular media. Walter's argument is essentially twofold: first, she draws attention to the widespread adherence to feminist principles on the part of young women (even if they are not explicitly named as feminist). Second, she argues that despite the apparent decline of the women's movement in coherent organisational terms, there continues to exist a wide variety of campaigns and organisations with goals sympathetic to feminism. Walter's assertions on these issues are expressed in a distinctly forthright tone, which is helpful to the extent that it refuses a melancholic account of the trajectory of second-wave feminism. However, Walter adopts an almost wholly uncritical stance towards the feminist practices she describes, a problem exacerbated by her championing of what might be seen as an individualised 'power feminist' sensibility which lacks a critical political awareness (see Segal, 1999: 228–9).[5]

Less overtly celebratory variations on the same theme include McRobbie's (1999) 'popular feminism' which describes a proliferation within the popular media of modes of female subjectification which encourage assertiveness and a 'fun-seeking' sensibility,[6] and Kate Nash's (2002) 'micro-politics of everyday life'. While both allude to the individualisation and partial depoliticisation of feminist precepts, according to Nash, this 'need not be a pessimistic account'. She writes that while such activities 'may not amount to a social movement in any precise, sociological sense ... the "micro-politics" that are undoubtedly the legacy of the women's may be better understood as a social revolution rather than as a new wave of the women's movement' (ibid.: 325–6).[7] Such accounts are undoubtedly helpful, but tend to be insufficiently attentive to the constraints placed upon 'popular feminist' discourse, and are unclear about the ways in which the spread of such discourse may enable and/or restrict the possible emergence of more critical, less individualised forms of political practice (but see Viner, 1999).[8]

More overtly celebratory narratives of feminist re-emergence crop up in several recent publications coming under the rubric of 'third-wave feminism'. The notion of a 'third wave' is worth exploring in detail. It originally gained currency in the late 1980s at a time when post-structuralist and postmodernist critiques of hegemonic feminist conceptions of womanhood and subjectivity were becoming increasingly prevalent. These theoretical developments also coincided, and to a large extent overlapped, with critiques from black, 'third world' and postcolonial feminist perspectives of the parochialism of dominant conceptions of feminist politics and subjectivity (Gillis et al., 2004: 3; Dicker and Piepmeier, 2003: 14; Bulbeck, 1998: 14; Mohanty, 2003; Arneil,

1999: 186–223). In this context, the 'third wave' refers to a specific theoretical position that problematises a monolithic or 'essentialist' conception of female/feminist subjectivity. And indeed, the notion of a 'third wave' as indicating a theoretical position that opens up a space for a relativising of white Euro-American feminist perspectives remains attractive to a diversity of feminists (Chakraborty, 2007; Darraj, 2003). However, the period since the late 1990s seems to have witnessed a gradual shift away from a postcolonial/post-structuralist conception of the 'third wave' towards a sedimenting of what we might call the 'generational paradigm', in which the notion of a third wave signifies, above all else, a specifically 'young' feminist subjectivity (Eisenhauer, 2004: 82).[9]

The sedimentation of the 'third wave' as signifying a specifically young feminism is grounded upon the claim that young feminists are today faced with an altogether different set of concerns than those faced by second-wave feminists, brought about by a series of shifts in hegemonic gender relations over recent decades. According to Baumgardner and Richards' (2000) classic third-wave text *Manifesta: Young Women, Feminism and the Future*, third-wave feminism is closely tied to the ways in which certain feminist precepts today have a popular purchase which was lacking for previous generations. They contend that 'for anyone born after the early 1960s, the presence of feminism in our lives is taken for granted. For our generation, feminism is like fluoride. We scarcely notice that we have it – it's simply in the water' (Baumgardner and Richards, 2000: 17–18). They claim that the 'third wave' is of necessity a little amorphous, capturing a diversity of modes of feminist activity ranging from full-scale lobbying of political institutions to 'girlie' feminist reclamations of conventional femininity. They thus resist the claim that the 'third wave' is merely apolitical and superficial by claiming that it is part of a broader radical agenda tied up with other concerns such as environmentalism, anti-capitalism and peace movements (ibid.: 303–4).[10] Furthermore, they argue that the 'third wave', and the feminist generational shift it performatively instantiates, is intended to resolve the anxieties around feminism and femininity which they regard as being particularly pressing for many younger feminists and would-be feminists (Baumgardner and Richards, 2004).

While, as with Walter, their work is useful in that it resists the melancholy that pervades some accounts, one may argue that the inclusion of such a broad range of practices under the rubric of 'third-wave feminism' diminishes its critical or political awareness. Furthermore, one may claim that the generational framing of 'third-wave feminism' and its valorisation of normative femininity further suggests an adherence to a mindset largely complicit with individualist and consumerist logics (Dicker and Piepmeier, 2003: 17–18; Taft, 2004: 71; Drake, 1997: 107). However, I would qualify this argument a little by noting that while much work under the 'third-wave' banner is certainly guilty of a rather crass cultural populism,[11] my critique should not be read as a dismissal of all forms of feminist engagement with the 'popular'. Indeed, a strong case can be made that the centrality of popular culture and media in the delineation and maintenance of hegemonic understandings of gender normativity is such that feminist engagements with the popular cultural domain take on an immediate and pressing political significance (Heywood and Drake, 2004: 14; Munford, 2004: 144; Levy, 2005).

A more acute problem when thinking about the notion of a 'third wave' than accusations of cultural populism is that the generational framing of the second and third waves is ill-equipped to grasp the temporal dynamics of contemporary feminism. As indicated above, it is often used in a manner that over-emphasises break at the expense of continuity, and risks a complicity with a hegemonic repudiation of the figure of the (second-wave) feminist, who is framed as old, ugly, unattractive and threatening (Henry, 2003; Dean, 2009; McRobbie, 2009: 156–9). Furthermore, the lexicon of generational waves, in more general terms, risks reproducing a specifically Anglo-American feminist genealogy as hegemonic (Dean, 2009), and is thus of limited analytical use.

Finally, with regard to the broader framing of these debates, there is something troubling about the way 'third-wave feminism' is discussed by both supporters and critics. Most of the literature focusses on attempting a teleological movement towards some level of closure of the meaning of the signifier 'third wave', by addressing questions such as 'what is the third wave?' or 'what does the third wave mean to me/us?'. Thus, 'third-wave feminism' is generally presupposed to refer constatively[12] to a feminist agenda or subjectivity that is taken to already be in existence. By contrast, I want to suggest that it would be more productive to develop an approach to the study of third-wave feminism that looks at how it is taken up and *used* in different contexts. We presently lack a thorough empirical analysis of how the term has been used politically by feminist activists (although this will be attended to in the case studies. See also Dean, 2009; Rogers, 2008). In addition, the theoretical frame developed in the Chapter 2 will provide a route through which to critically evaluate singular uses of the signifier 'third wave', as opposed to trying to devise general statements or rules about the character of 'third-wave feminism' in toto.

Feminist temporalities 3: Post-feminism

While, as we shall see in the case studies, there are diverse ways in which the signifier 'third wave' can be used politically, it remains problematic as a tool for the characterisation of contemporary feminist practices, both in Anglo-American and international contexts. Potentially more promising in this regard is the advent of a range of literatures dealing with the question of 'post-feminism'. Discourses around post-feminism resonate with third-wave feminisms given that both are concerned primarily with the intersections between feminism, femininity and popular culture. Post-feminism is understood in numerous different ways (see Projansky, 2001: 67–8 for a typology). While some have used 'post-feminist' as a form of self-identification to refer to a 'new' modality of (quasi) feminist politics (Whelehan, 2000: 90–3; Gamble, 2001: 42–5; Genz, 2006), it is most useful when it describes an ambivalent set of hegemonic discourses around gender, feminism and femininity. As such, analyses of post-feminist discourse are only indirectly concerned with the state of feminist activism, but they nonetheless throw up several key questions for the task at hand. In contrast to melancholic accounts of a pervasive anti-feminist 'backlash' (Faludi, 1992; Whelehan, 2000), those works that characterise the hegemonic gender regime as specifically 'post-feminist' reject any simple relation of externality between pro and anti-feminist discourses. Rather, 'post-feminism' seeks to capture a complex and ambivalent set of discourses which serve to blur the feminist/anti-feminist distinction (Walby, 1997; Gill, 2007; Tasker and Negra, 2007).

This conception of post-feminism is given its most systematic explication in Angela McRobbie's recent work. She uses the concept of a 'post-feminist gender regime' to describe the multiple ways in which feminism has been mainstreamed and 'taken into account' across a wide variety of domains, but whereby this very 'taken into account-ness' occasions the *undoing* of feminism by invoking it as something no longer relevant and necessary. Referring primarily to the UK, she writes: 'my own account of post-feminism is equated with a "double movement", gender retrenchment is secured, paradoxically, through the wide dissemination of discourses of female freedom and (putative) equality. Young women are able to come forward on the condition that feminism fades away' (McRobbie, 2007a: 720).[13] Thus, although certain aspects of liberal feminism assume the character of a Gramscian common sense (McRobbie, 2004: 256), feminism is nonetheless 'almost hated' to such an extent that the performative denunciations of feminism have 'consolidated into something closer to repudiation than ambivalence' (ibid.: 247). McRobbie suggests that for (predominantly young) women to assume a viable female subjectivity, it is imperative that they affirm neoliberal, individualising notions of self-management, regulation and consumption. Such a move was only made possible by the sedimenting of the values of women's autonomy drawn from second-wave feminism, but the latter must be denounced, as it is constituted as being at odds with the individualised economic and sexual agency required to be an intelligible feminine subject. More generally, these new discourses of female individualisation, self-management and success operate, she argues, as a 'substitute for feminism', so as to ensure that a new women's movement 'will not re-emerge' (McRobbie, 2009: 1).

McRobbie's overview of the interplay between invocation and repudiation of feminism within hegemonic gender discourses is, for the most part, convincing. However, while accounts of post-feminist discourses describe an interplay between invocation and repudiation – implying something other than an across-the-board hostility to, and squeezing out of, feminist politics – it is, particularly in McRobbie's work, unclear exactly where, when and how feminist politics is able to emerge within the public sphere. Despite her subtle analysis of appropriations of feminist discourse in the mainstream media, McRobbie is curiously emphatic in her denial that feminist politics is afforded any space in mainstream public discourse, through repeated use of tropes such as feminism 'fading away' or unqualified assertions such as 'there is no longer any place for feminism in contemporary political culture' (McRobbie, 2009: 55). Even when acknowledging the emergence of new forms of feminist cultural politics such as The F-word website and Ladyfest, McRobbie writes, 'let us not get carried away too quickly in this respect ... they [these new feminist subcultural practices] are almost instantly tracked, charted, documented and publicised through practices of corporate theft' (ibid.: 121). While she offers a glimmer of hope in acknowledging the political possibilities of feminism in the academy (ibid.: 151), overall McRobbie exaggerates the extent to which the current gender regime is predicated upon the demise of feminist politics.[14]

Hollows and Moseley allude to this in their assertion that 'what McRobbie calls the "cultural space of post-feminism" cannot simply be equated with a denunciation of, and non-identity with, feminist politics' (2006: 15), while Projansky writes that 'feminism continues to exist not only as a discursively defined thorn in the side of post-feminist popular culture but also as a complex and varied social movement' (2001: 88). In addition, Hollows and Moseley also steer a path between melancholia and celebration in their account of 'popular feminist' cultural productions (such as the films *Pretty Woman* and *Working Girl*) which appropriate and disavow elements of second-wave feminist discourse, but in a manner that is not quite so vehemently repudiative as suggested by McRobbie (see also Stacey, 1992). Elsewhere, while one might agree with Stephanie Genz's argument that post-feminist discourse both opens up and closes down possibilities for new feminist political articulations, her equation of these political possibilities with a Blairite/Giddensian Third Way seems highly problematic given the conservative elements that permeate New Labour discourse on gender (Levitas, 1998; Annesley, 2001; Benn, 2000; Phillips, 2000). So while these interventions are helpful in that they open up a space for a less 'repudiative' conception of post-feminist discourse than that offered by McRobbie, they still don't provide much of a sense, beyond mere signposts, of the relationship between affirmations of feminism, feminist politics and post-feminist discourse.

More generally, there is a shortcoming concerning the theorisation of feminist politics which permeates almost all the literature on feminism and popular culture (whether it is framed in terms of new, third-wave or post-feminism). Such texts often seem to find feminist politics everywhere (e.g. new and some third-wave feminisms) or nowhere (e.g. McRobbie's post-feminism). Some recent texts have articulated a more even-handed analysis of the feminism/popular culture relation (e.g. Hollows, 2000; Hollows and Moseley, 2006; and especially Gill, 2007), but there is still scope for a more detailed theoretical and empirical analysis of current feminist political practices in and against popular culture. My intention is that, after the rethinking of radical feminist politics I propose Chapter 2, we might be able to steer a course between the twin extremes of feminist politics as everywhere/nowhere, and thus articulate a more balanced appraisal of the contemporary feminist scene.

Feminist spatialities 1: Transnational feminisms

While the narratives of feminist re-emergence referred to above partly derive their efficacy from the mere assertion of the existence of a new feminism, performatively instantiating something of a temporal break, a slightly different set of rhetorical strategies can be found in the recent proliferation of literature dealing with 'transnational' forms of feminist mobilisation. Here, the emphasis is less on instantiating new modes of feminist temporality, and more on shifts in the type of institutional and indeed geographical spaces in which feminist politics takes place.[15]

The literature dealing with the question of transnational feminist mobilisation tends to operate with the presumption that the past few decades have witnessed a shift from local and national feminist concerns towards an increase in mobilisation across national borders. The emphasis on the 'transnational' is generally intended to signify the fluid, unpredictable and shifting nature of feminist politics, and is thus in opposition to any notion of a unified set of 'women's interests' or a 'global sisterhood' (Mohanty, 2003: 17–42). In Valentine Moghadam's words, transnational feminism consists of new 'network-based' mobilisations, that is, 'structures organised above the national level that unite women from three or more countries around a common agenda, such as women's human rights, reproductive health and rights, violence against women, peace and antimilitarism, or feminist economics' (2005: 4).

This has been made possible and precipitated by, for example, technological advances, responses to critiques of Western bias in feminist theory and practice and the emergence of new political opportunity structures linked to new forms of supranational governance (including the UN and regional bodies). In most instances, the UN Fourth World Conference on Women in 1995 in Beijing is treated as a turning point, a key moment in which new forms of transnational feminist mobilisations emerged. Most recent literature is thus very much geared towards assessing the current state of feminist politics 'post-Beijing'. Within these parameters, I will make clear that various authors disagree profoundly about the implications of new forms of feminist mobilisation: some are almost unreservedly celebratory, while others are more attuned to the limitations, constraints and hierarchies that permeate instances of transnational feminist politics.

In very general terms, the literature on transnational feminism makes visible how narratives of decline, deradicalisation and re-emergence are generated by investments in quite specific national (or at best regional) feminist contexts. As Aili Mari Tripp points out, rather than understanding new forms of feminist activity in the global South as simply emulating earlier developments in Europe and North America, it would be more pertinent to understand late twentieth-century feminism as undercut by complex multidimensional influences whereby 'feminist movements globally have learnt from one another but have often had quite independent trajectories and sources of movement' (Tripp, 2006: 51–2). A related but more forthright assertion of Western bias in contemporary histories of feminism is put forward by Nira Yuval-Davis (2006) who argues that the emphasis on autonomy and separatism characteristic of 'seventies' feminist identity politics is/was undercut by racism and parochialism. In opposition to this, she argues for a 'transversal' feminist politics geared towards the creation of linkages (or what in Chapter 2 I shall call 'equivalences') between feminist mobilisations across issues and national borders. Thus, Yuval-Davis is resolutely opposed to even a residual equation of 'radicalism' with separatism and/or autonomy.

A number of authors working on the issue of transnational feminism also emphasise the potential radicalism of 'transversal' modes of action, and thus refuse the terms set out by Anglocentric narratives of decline and deradicalisation. However, at times this can lead them to become a little caught up in the excitement of these new forms of feminist politics, by articulating somewhat over-celebratory narratives of re-emergence which in many respects resemble the Anglo-American narratives of new/third-wave feminist re-emergence discussed above. Valentine Moghadam, for example, is emphatic in her account of the capacity of transnational feminist networks to enable a bridging of the North-South divide in feminism and to make links between feminism and other progressive struggles around, for example, the environment, anti-capitalism and anti-racism. She also maintains that such networks help bridge the gap between the injustice of hierarchical forms of organisation and the ineffectiveness of leaderless organisational structures (Moghadam, 2005: 102). And she sees the advent of the Internet and the UN conferences of the 1990s as integral to these new possibilities (ibid.: 9).

Similarly, and despite offering a brief cautionary note expressing anxiety about 'low mobilization of the women's movement in the global North' (Snyder, 2006: 48), Margaret Snyder paints an extremely upbeat picture of a strong growth of women's movements across the world in the 1990s and early 2000s, working alongside the UN to 'build new institutions to sustain the movement women were creating' (ibid.: 45). Furthermore, Sylvia Walby presents an unremittingly positive picture of the ways in which the increasing sedimentation of a global human rights discourse has rendered supranational institutions as fruitful terrains for feminists to effect change (Walby, 2002: 159). Elsewhere, Melinda Adams (2006) paints a highly favourable picture of the facilitating role of the African Union in the emergence of a regional transnational feminist agenda in Africa, while Mona Lena Krook (2008) discusses how campaigns around gender quotas constitute part of a new global women's movement.

In a rather different vein, some more critical voices have cautioned against adopting a celebratory stance towards the apparent increase in transnational forms of feminist politics. They have pointed out how shifts from the local/national to the transnational can create and reinscribe uneven power relations and may place new risks and constraints upon feminist political action. For instance, Manisha Desai advocates a cautious approach towards feminist activism centred on the UN, on the grounds that the UN still adheres to a neocolonial discourse of development and also demands that participation by non-state actors be confined to registered NGOs, 'furthering the NGOisation and depoliticisation of movements' (Desai, 2005: 323; see also Lang, 1997). Desai also alerts us to how transnational activism is predicated upon expert knowledge, professionalisation, cross-border travel and familiarity with information technology in a manner that privileges those with the necessary cultural and material resources (ibid.: 327). A similar set of arguments are made by Breny Mendoza who, writing with regard to Latin American feminisms, notes that the emergence of transnational feminism has brought about a 'decontextualisation' of feminist struggle, and a concomitant 'depoliticisation, deradicalisation and fragmentation' (note that these are the exact words she uses, Mendoza, 2002: 308).[16] She also – I think correctly – highlights how academic discourse around 'transnational feminism' often entails a rather naïve and sometimes patronising romanticising of political activism by third-world women in a manner that does nothing to contest power imbalances between feminist actors (ibid.: 309).

A similarly cautionary analysis of the present situation with regard to transnational feminism is provided by Chandra Mohanty in 'Under Western Eyes Revisited' (Mohanty, 2003: 221–51). She alerts us to a number of ways in which the radicalism and vitality of specifically anti-racist feminist politics has declined. However, it should be noted that Mohanty at no point equates that lost radicalism with a decline in autonomous and/ or separatist feminist practices. Rather, she links it to trends such as increasingly technocratic forms of management in the US higher-education sector and the global intensification of capitalist relations of production. She writes that 'although the context for writing "Under Western Eyes" in the mid-1980s was a visible and activist women's movement, this radical movement no longer exists as such' (ibid.: 236). Instead, she argues that the feminist movement has now been eclipsed by the anti-globalisation movement as the key site of progressive political mobilisation, such that a political priority is for the anti-globalisation movement to more fully incorporate concerns related to gender justice (ibid.: 249).

However, Mohanty's work, along with much of the other literatures referred to above, is geared towards a general assessment of the current state of 'the' transnational feminist movement. My intention here is not to adjudicate between the optimists and the pessimists (perhaps 'critics' would be more generous), but to ask what implications these accounts might have for the theorisation of contemporary feminist politics, and whether it might be possible to steer a course between the twin extremes of 'post-Beijing euphoria', on the one hand, and a more pessimistic account of the NGOisation and depoliticisation of transnational feminism, on the other.

The more celebratory accounts risk exaggerating the 'newness' of contemporary modes of transnational feminism (indeed many strands of Anglo-American second-wave feminism were heavily invested in the transnational dimension). Also, they tend to reproduce a version of feminist temporality centred around a break, implicitly assumed to have taken place in the late 1980s or early 1990s, in such a way as to preclude a complex understanding of the dynamics of continuity and change across the decades. Also, in their altogether rather general – and subsumptive – account of feminist re-emergence, we often have an inadequate grasp of how these logics of re-emergence (if they do actually exist) might impact differentially across contexts. Indeed, it is perhaps no surprise that those works that are focussed more on specific cases tend to be more even handed and less celebratory in tone (as we shall see later in the chapter). Furthermore, as Angela McRobbie has argued in a biting critique of Sylvia Walby's piece, Walby (and others) fails to acknowledge the punitive conditions under which these new modes of feminist practice are allowed to emerge within supranational governmental institutions (McRobbie, 2009: 152–4). However, the more pessimistic accounts also suffer from a not unrelated set of problems. Again, they tend to be excessively broad in their scope, and we are left with only the most general sense of how logics of NGOisation impact upon the actual discourse and practices of feminist activists 'on the ground'. We would benefit from further analysis of the extent to which specific modes of feminist engagement might lead to depoliticisation and deradicalisation, and we may ask what sorts of practices might offset the potential depoliticising dynamics of transnational feminism. And how might these processes manifest themselves unevenly in different contexts?

Several works do provide tentative, contextual answers to these questions. Myra Marx Ferree and Aili Mairi Tripp's edited collection *Global Feminism* is particularly useful here. Several contributions to this volume highlight the ambiguity and double-edged nature of much transnational feminist practice. In the introduction, Ferree (2006) frames transnational feminism in terms of 'political opportunity structures', alluding to how new forms of supranational governance open up new political possibilities, but acknowledging that how these are used will always be a contextual, empirical question. In the same volume, McBride and Mazur (2006) hypothesise that the emergence of transnational feminism might lead to a degree of cross-national convergence in terms of feminist practice and policy issues, but find that there was no obvious pattern and that levels of cross-national convergence need to be explored issue by issue. And Yakin Ertürk (2006) and Hilkka Pietilä (2006) discuss the progressive political possibilities of feminist appropriations of rights-based discourses in Turkey and Finland respectively, without lapsing either into an overt optimism or pessimism.[17] These texts point towards a framing of contemporary transnational feminisms and women's human rights as neither necessarily emancipatory (as Walby and Moghadam would have it) or unambiguously depoliticising (as McRobbie and Mohanty seem to claim). Rather – and it seems a banal point – transnational feminism is by definition a shifting, uneven set of political processes about which it is difficult to generalise.

However, two points which are absolutely central to my overall argument emerge from my engagement with the literature on transnational feminism. First, the literature brings to light the parallel existence of a diversity of feminist temporalities and spatialities in a manner that exposes the rather parochial nature of the narratives of loss and re-emergence that I referred to in previous sections. In particular, these multiple feminist temporalities and spatialities draw attention to how the investments that drive narratives of loss are investments rooted in a very specific national (as well as temporal) context. This prompts us to investigate continuity and change across contexts in both space and time, bringing to light the limitations of the generalisations that permeate many Anglo-American histories of feminism. Second, we saw earlier (and will see again in greater detail later) that there is a tendency to equate the radicalism of a feminist politics with a notion of being 'outside' particular types of institutional space. However, in opposition to this, the literature on transnational feminism draws attention to a conception of radicality based more on 'transversality' rather than separatism or autonomy. As I shall argue in Chapter 2, this is potentially a very useful resource to explore the character of radical feminist politics.

Feminist spatialities 2: State feminism

While the literature on transnational feminism is focussed on reconfigurations of feminist politics beyond the space of the nation state, the 'state feminism' literature refers to the emergence of new forms of feminist or pro-feminist practice within the institutions of the local, national and supranational state (Mazur and Stetson, 1995a: 1; Lovenduski, 2005: 4). 'State feminism' can thus encompass some or all of the following: (1) feminist civil society organisations working *with* state institutions, to promote a feminist agenda (such that the relation is not necessarily antagonistic); (2) feminists or people with pro-feminist sympathies working within state institutions such as through women's policy agencies; and (3) the state behaving in 'pro-feminist' ways (e.g. through the passing of anti-discrimination legislation). In the sections on decline and deradicalisation I briefly referred to mechanisms of increasing feminist engagement with state institutions, but a more comprehensive assessment of the literature on 'state feminism' is absolutely crucial if we are to think about how to conceptualise a range of contemporary feminist political practices.

Much early work on feminism and the state was sceptical of the political effectiveness and desirability of feminists working amicably with state institutions which were perceived to be antagonistic to feminist demands (Gelb, 1989; Charles, 2000; Ferguson, 1984; Halford, 1992; Cockburn, 1991; Schirmer, 1982). However, for many, the notion of a somewhat monolithic state hostile to feminist demands did not ring true. Feminists from the Nordic countries have been particularly vocal in this regard: for some of them, the 'woman friendly' welfare state (Hernes, 1987: 15) has provided a fruitful terrain for feminist practice (Kantola, 2006; Jónasdóttir and van der Fehr, 1998; Borchorst and Siim, 2008). Taking inspiration from Nordic pro-state feminisms, Amy Mazur and Dorothy McBride Stetson's *Comparative State Feminism* (1995) marks the emergence of the 'state feminism' literature. Their starting point was to analyse, in cross-national comparative terms, the workings of a 'less monolithic state as a potential ally to women's diverse interests' (Mazur and Stetson, 1995a: 6). Broadly speaking, they painted a generally favourable picture, noting that the furthering of feminist demands through the formalised institutions of women's policy agencies is more likely to be successful when accompanied by widely supported autonomous feminist organisations (Mazur and Stetson, 1995b: 290). Despite appealing to a notion of a 'less monolithic state', their conclusions were still grounded on a fairly neat separation between 'autonomous radical groups' outside the state and 'moderate reform groups' inside the state (ibid.: 290).

More recent work on state feminism, however, has seen a more explicit problematisation of a simple inside/outside dichotomy. This is partly a consequence of an increasing engagement with forms of multilevel governance, which have provided new openings both at regional level within states, and through supranational institutions such as the EU and the UN (Outshoorn and Kantola, 2007a; Banaszak et al., 2003; Squires, 2007).[18] This in turn has led to a cautious optimism permeating much recent state-feminism work.

Outshoorn and Kantola – whose *Changing State Feminism* (2007) is explicitly concerned with updating the findings of *Comparative State Feminism* – note that state feminism is now much stronger in 6 out of the 12 countries studied, and identify regionalisation as the key driving force behind this success (Outshoorn and Kantola, 2007b: 273–4). Furthermore, in Kantola's (2006) book *Feminists Theorise the State*, she draws attention to the Scottish context as an example of new feminist openings amid new forms of multilevel governance. She notes that since the onset of devolution a 'new politics' discourse has prevailed, making newly devolved state institutions more accessible to feminist lobbyists, particularly on the issue of domestic violence. Kantola writes, '[I]n some ways, England and Scotland experienced parallel institutional changes in terms of access, legislation and funding. However, each of these was more far-reaching in Scotland, because there was no fundamental institutional shake-up in England' (2006: 140). Fiona Mackay also makes a very similar argument: in relation to the Scottish Zero Tolerance campaign against violence against women, she writes, '[T]his campaign provided a shorthand symbol of the radical possibilities of coalitions between the women's movement and the local state in the context of oppositional politics' (Mackay, 2008: 25).

Kantola and Mackay's work on the Scottish context is helpful in two main respects. First, it further highlights the partiality of narratives of decline and deradicalisation, in that they are scarcely applicable to the UK as a whole, let alone more widely. Second, it draws attention to how feminist engagements with state institutions are predicated upon the specific constitutive discourses that operate in any given context, such that the 'new politics' discourse that circulates in post-devolution Scotland enabled new feminist political articulations to be made and heard.

Much of the state feminism literature is thus invaluable in that it provides detailed empirically grounded analyses of contemporary gender equality politics that avoid the sorts of nostalgic melancholy that one sometimes finds in more historical accounts. While many of the assessments of specific national contexts in *Changing State Feminism* do describe narratives of feminist decline, the overall picture is diverse: Amy Mazur (2007), for instance, paints a positive picture of new feminist political articulations emerging in France, while Spain, Belgium, Germany, Sweden and Finland are all presented as having more established and effective women's policy machineries than in 1995 (Bustelo and Ortbals, 2007; Celis and Meier, 2007; Lang, 2007; Bergqvist et al., 2007; Holli and Kantola, 2007). Notably, the state feminist scene in Great Britain emerges as one of the most favourable. Here, Joni Lovenduski (2007) draws attention to a range of policy changes which have provided openings for successful feminist engagement at national state level (Lovenduski, 2007). This includes the establishment in 2007 of a single equalities body, the Commission for Equality and Human Rights, in which state feminists were consulted extensively. Furthermore, Lovenduski draws attention to the successful establishment in the UK of a network of MPs, women's policy agencies and feminist NGOs which have been able to successfully push for pro-feminist change at national state level across a range of issues. Finally, she notes that the sedimentation of 'diversity' as a policy priority has facilitated an increasing awareness of the intersections of gender and other identity categories. However, Lovenduski mentions that these advances are partially offset by a significant over-representation of white women in the women's policy machinery, and the fact that 'women's movement demands are incorporated into agency activity through a filter of government priorities' which tend to favour business interests (ibid.: 161).

Despite this, there are some troubling dimensions to the work on state feminism. For one, there is a very strong emphasis on policy outcomes. State feminist practices are analysed in terms of *effectiveness*, focussing on the outputs arising from women's policy agency activity. This has the rather curious consequence that the actual role of feminist movements is somewhat under-examined. We are not given much of a sense of the types of discourses and practices that are put to use by feminists working within state institutional apparatus. Questions of how they articulate their demands towards particular actors, and what types of practices are employed, are left unanswered. We are also given little sense of the subjective self-understandings of the feminist actors involved: we don't know how they make sense of their own actions and political priorities, and how they negotiate the institutional milieu in which they operate. Thus, while it is certainly legitimate to explore state feminism in terms of policy outcomes, the picture will, of necessity, be incomplete if unaccompanied by a more discursive and ethnographic examination of how the actors understand and negotiate these new spaces for feminist practice.

In addition, when issues related to the women's movement *are* dealt with, they tend to be framed by a set of problematic tropes about the decline, institutionalisation or fragmentation of the women's movement. Let me provide a few examples. Stetson (2001: 279), writing about abortion politics, claims that 'by the end of the 1980s in most countries the women's movements had declined or disappeared'. Outshoorn and

Kantola (2007a: 16) frame their analysis in the context of an 'increasingly fragmented' women's movement, as do Bustelo and Ortbals (2007: 215) and Guadagnini and Dona (2007: 176). Kantola writes (about the UK), 'by 1978, the initial unity of the women's movement had already been lost and the movement was fragmenting' (2006: 74). Elsewhere, Lang (2007) and Celis and Meier (2007) both allude to the 'institutionalisation' of the feminist movement.

I do not mean to suggest that these accounts are of necessity 'wrong' in any profound sense, but I do worry about the discursive work that notions such as 'institutionalisation' and 'fragmentation' are charged with. In the above examples, these are not mere unimportant asides, but are central framing devices for the whole analysis, as it is (at least in part) the alleged demise of the women's movement proper that renders state feminism important and interesting. Consequently, I fear that, as with the narratives of decline we looked at earlier, notions such as fragmentation and institutionalisation performatively instantiate the unquestioned notion that the women's movement 'proper' no longer exists, and is thus not in need of investigation. One may legitimately ask a host of questions, such as historically, what did the women's movement look like prior to 'fragmentation'? What do the 'fragments' now look like? How do they operate? Indeed, perhaps it was always already 'fragmented'. And beyond a few fleeting gestures towards the coexistence of autonomous and institutionalised strands of feminist politics (e.g. Randall, 1998; Sauer, 2007) we don't get much sense of what kinds of discourse and practice sustain that coexistence, or that might traverse or subvert the boundaries between them.[19]

Furthermore, these accounts, when speaking directly about the feminist or women's 'movement', implicitly work with an understanding of the 'women's movement' as tied to notions of public visibility, separatism and radical protest. A curious consequence of this is that the role of hierarchical, professionalised feminist groups, which nonetheless remain autonomous (I am thinking here of groups like The Fawcett Society, Rights of Women or Women's Aid in the UK), is afforded disproportionately little attention. However, Kantola's (2006) work on Women's Aid – which provides insights into the dynamics of professionalised yet largely autonomous feminist groups – is a notable exception.

Finally, I note that Kantola's argument converges with mine in other important ways: she is absolutely unequivocal in her aversion to any notion of a monolithic or unitary state, or a simple inside/outside the state dichotomy, and her use of post-structuralism for the analysis of political practices is very close to my own. However, in employing tropes of 'fragmentation', I fear that she lets an essentialism in through the back door by employing the same problematic feminist temporality that I have been putting into question. In general terms, though, Kantola's deconstructive approach to feminism and the state is enormously helpful in thinking through a more balanced approach to contemporary feminist politics. When taken to its logical conclusion, Kantola's insights suggest that any a priori assumptions about feminist temporality, the recent history of the feminist movement or the relationship between feminism and the state should be resolutely abandoned.

Feminist radicalities

I have argued that in much of the relevant literature, despite the emphasis on diversity and ambiguity, a certain set of assumptions often re-emerges, in a manner which reproduces problematic conceptions of feminist temporality and spatiality. In this section, I want to specify a little more clearly the content of these assumptions.

My concern is that tropes such as fragmentation, decline, institutionalisation and deradicalisation are framed through an unexamined discursive linking of notions such as autonomy, authenticity, purity and radicalism. Even those works described above which often take a positive view of 'state feminist' practices, nonetheless typically equate 'radicalism' with 'autonomy'. This is an understandable move, given the genealogy of Anglo-American feminism, but it tends, perhaps inadvertently, to reproduce certain temporal and spatial dynamics within feminism that might be open to question. The equation of radicalism with autonomy tends to be haunted by the notion that this autonomy has largely disappeared, and has been replaced by other feminist practices perhaps more geared towards engagement with the state. Consequently, 'genuinely' radical, authentic feminist politics still has as its paradigm a very specific spatial and temporal context: autonomous feminist spaces, typically in the UK, in the 1970s. This throws up a set of questions: What if feminist 'radicality' were to be separated from a notion of 'autonomy'? What if the radicalism of a feminist politics might inhere in some other form(s) of discourse or practice?

Before I attend to these questions, let me briefly highlight several instances of the sorts of rhetorical strategies that instantiate these notions of feminist radicality. Martin Pugh, in a detailed account of the UK women's movement in the twentieth century, writes, '[F]eminism could indeed become part of mainstream politics and in the process expect to lose some of its revolutionary potential, or it could keep its distance and preserve its integrity; certainly some feminists reacted by becoming more suspicious of conventional politics and by seeking a more radical agenda' (2000: 332). This explicitly links 'radicalism' to an avoidance of mainstream political channels. Recall also the quotes referred to earlier where Mazur and Stetson distinguish between 'autonomous radical feminist groups' and 'moderate reform groups', and where Banaszak et al. equate radicalism with 'autonomy' and 'challenge to the state', while Stetson's work on abortion politics refers to 'autonomous radical feminist groups' (2001: 279). Elsewhere, Joyce Gelb asserts that 'rather than becoming bureaucratized and less radical, the British movement has retained its ideological fervour and commitment and has continued to seek new alternative structures' (1989: 181–2). Here, Gelb equates 'becoming bureaucratised' with becoming 'less radical'. Even Baumgardner and Richards write, 'legislation by itself is clearly not enough, which is why we advocate activism on a very grassroots scale to support the formal structures of equality …. Here are radical, not reformist, approaches to women's oppression' (2000: 303–4), reinscribing analogous binaries such as inside/outside, reformism/radicalism, legislation/grassroots activism.

While not explicitly invoking notions of radicality and/or autonomy, similar sentiments can be found in many relevant works on contemporary feminist politics. Nickie Charles, discussing the implications of feminist attempts to oversee the implementation of equal opportunities legislation, writes, 'this was a move away from the autonomous women's movement, which has operated largely on the basis of networks and small groups … and into the state, albeit at a local rather than national level. It could be argued that this marked the first stages of the institutionalisation of feminism' (2000: 104). Similarly, R. Amy Elman writes:

> After years of selecting to be 'outside the system' it is seemingly incongruous that, relative to their Swedish counterparts, [British and American feminists] have assumed a more prominent position in the state's adoption, execution and the monitoring of policies and programmes for battered women. The significance of movements is no longer discerned in their ability to marshal visible demonstrations against the state or business communities, but instead as carriers of ideas that influence states to alter their agencies in ways that make such protest unnecessary.
>
> (Elman, 2003: 113)

Although not using the lexicon of radicalism and autonomy, these arguments still instantiate a particular temporality that situates a noisy, radical 'autonomous' women's movement temporally at some point in the past and spatially 'outside' the state. This is further exacerbated by the tendency to frame 'radical' and 'liberal' feminism as mutually constitutive, whereby they are often assumed to be in an antagonistic relationship by virtue of them mapping onto a notion of 'outside' and 'inside' respectively (Walby, 1990: 3; Waylen, 1998: 5; Eisenstein, 1981; Ferguson, 1984; Harne, 1996; Coppock et al., 1995: 183; Mueller and MacCarthy, 2003: 229).

Consequently, my concern is that many authors, irrespective of whether they self-identify as 'radical feminist' or not, nonetheless implicitly work with an equation of radicality with autonomy and outsider status. This, I argue, is a consequence of the genealogy of the signifier 'radical' within Anglo-American feminist theory and practice. We may say that this *topographical* conception of feminist radicality arises from the view that radical feminist theory derives its radicality from its perceived uncovering of the 'roots' of specific social relations which are only analysed superficially from other, 'less radical' perspectives (Bell and Klein, 1996: xix; Bryson, 1992: 181; Allwood and Wadia, 2001: 163; Millett, 1977).[20] Furthermore, when substantively identifying the 'root' of systemic gender-based subordination, radical feminist theory has tended to identify the domains of sexuality, pornography and sexual violence as key (MacKinnon, 1989; Dworkin, 1981, Leeds Revolutionary Feminist Group, 1982: 64).

This gives us some indication of what it means for a feminist political action to be 'radical'. But to clarify the nature of the problem, I want to draw a tripartite distinction between radical feminist principles, radical feminist analysis and radical feminist practices. Here, the principles include, for example, autonomy, empowerment and self-determination for women. Indeed, these are sound principles that one would suppose everyone of a feminist disposition would support. However, specific to radical feminism is its analysis of gender relations in the idiom of patriarchy as a pervasive, all-encompassing and ontologically primary system. The emphasis on the all-encompassing character of patriarchy is such that radical feminist practices – as we have seen – are typically grounded in an autonomous feminist anti-statism, historically often in the form of small group 'consciousness-raising'. In presenting it in these terms, we can say that 'seventies' autonomy-based feminism was in fact a historically specific and contingent response to a specific analysis of the entrenched character of gender inequality in Anglo-American contexts in the 1970s.

However, somewhere along the line, this one specific mode of feminist practice ended up becoming the very principle, the ontological ground, of feminist conceptions of radicality. Here, one specific mode of feminist practice became ossified *as* radicality, confining 'radicality' to a specific topos for feminist politics, such that a historically contingent mode of practice came to be seen as having a necessary relation to the signifier 'radical' (see Chester, 1982: 61). Thus, my intention is in some senses very simple: to explore ways of dismantling the necessity of the relation between radicality and autonomous anti-statism such that we can claim that feminist practices that might merit the qualifier 'radical' can and do emerge in contexts other than autonomous anti-statism.

Let me clarify some points. I do not wish to claim that autonomous feminist practices are in any fundamental sense 'not radical'. Rather, my point of divergence concerns the nature of that radicalism. I suggested above that 'seventies' feminist women-only consciousness-raising is frequently presented as the ground of feminist radicality. By contrast, as we shall see in Chapter 2, I argue that there is nothing intrinsically radical about a group of women meeting up in a women-only space. Rather, the radicalism of those consciousness-raising efforts inhered not in some essence of consciousness-raising practices, but in the way they were constituted: that is, they were radical because they provided new configurations of, for example, the public/private distinction, women's sexuality and the relation between the personal and the political.

While in this section I have fixated somewhat on the notion of 'radicalism', I hope to have shown that the discursive linking of radicalism with autonomy poses a number of problems for conceptualising contemporary feminist politics. For one, it both reflects and reinstantiates a particular feminist temporality in which genuine radicalism is situated in an imagined 'seventies' feminist past and as such has now declined, fragmented, become institutionalised or disappeared altogether. It thus remains complicit with a paradigm of the history of feminism that situates a profound break at some point, possibly in the 1980s. Furthermore, it leads to a somewhat parochial reading of feminist temporality: the autonomy and separatism that is perceived to have underpinned the radicalism of 'seventies' feminism is less applicable to transnational feminisms, in which arguably a 'transversal' conception of radicality is more apt. In more general terms, thinking radicalism in the idiom of autonomy and separatism gives rise to the question of whether we might characterise different sorts of feminist practices as radical. If we move beyond the assumption that genuinely 'radical' feminist practices ended in the 1980s, then we might be able to get a better sense of the *diversity* of feminist practices both transnationally and in different sorts of relationships to state institutions. This in turn might allow for a more nuanced reading of the complex dynamics of continuity and change across time and space.

This book therefore refuses point-blank to accept any notion of decline, fragmentation, institutionalisation or deradicalisation as an a priori starting point for its analysis. Rather, whether a given feminist practice has (not) declined, fragmented or lost its radicalism can only be discerned through empirical analysis informed by theoretical insights. By the same token, neither does this book take as its starting point a more celebratory notion of feminist re-emergence. While there do appear to be new forms of feminist activism emerging both in the UK and elsewhere, I do not automatically assume that this necessarily renders established narratives invalid. Rather, these new forms of activism provide an opportunity for detailed critical analysis, not simple celebration.

However, to go about this task we will need to develop a theoretical perspective that facilitates the following: an understanding of 'radicality' not tied to any one specific spatial or temporal context; an engagement with the complexities of feminist politics, such that feminist politics is not seen to exist everywhere or nowhere, or of necessity only in specific spaces; a sensitivity to context, and an analysis of the complex dynamics of continuity and change across time and space. In Chapter 2, I draw on several recent developments in post-structuralist political theory, in particular the work of Ernesto Laclau and Linda Zerilli, in a bid to retheorise (radical) feminist politics in a manner more amenable to the task at hand. I shall link these theoretical concerns to key insights from both the literatures on state feminism (drawing primarily on Kantola) and transnational feminism (mainly using Mohanty and Yuval-Davis' work). In addition to the core tasks, such a perspective enables us to begin to address supplementary questions such as how might we better think about the varying relations between feminism and state institutions? What are the potential opportunities and dangers opened up by discourses of 'third-wave' feminism? And, how might we characterise the intersections between feminism and popular culture?

2
Rethinking Feminist Radicalism

Why radicalism?

The theoretical task at hand here is in many respects a difficult one, for it casts its critical eye towards two divergent perspectives: one that sees feminism as having lost much of its radicalism, vitality and visibility, and another that celebrates its (apparent) current ascendancy. In opposition to both of these, my intention is to articulate an understanding of feminist politics as something which both emerges and disappears in a diversity of contexts in a manner resistant to subsumption under either narratives of decline/deradicalisation, or re-emergence.

To assist such a task, this chapter seeks to reformulate our understanding of 'radicalism' in relation to feminist politics, by drawing on a series of strands of contemporary post-structuralist political theory. I propose a reworked conceptualisation of 'radicalism' in feminist politics through which one can interrogate the dominant narratives in the existing feminist literature. This will provide a basis to avoid either of the problematic accounts identified in Chapter 1: first (and arguably most significantly), it avoids the tendency to see the radicalism of feminist politics as tied to a very specific set of spaces and practices, and, second, it avoids seeing any affirmation of feminism as intrinsically radical and progressive. It therefore enables a more balanced mapping of the feminist terrain, and enables us to see contemporary feminism as riddled with various modes of radical critique (often in unexpected places), but without this occasioning a complacent celebratory stance.

But why, one might reasonably ask, focus on notions of 'radicalism/radicality'? This is a reasonable objection. Often, notions of radicalism become subjects of rather aimless language games, invoked to give one's own position a positive normative force – 'I am more radical than you'.[1] This then gives rise to the question of whether there is any mileage in seeking to use the term as a tool for rigorous evaluation of political practices. At one level, one could certainly say that the rather vacuous character of the term is such that we should resign ourselves to the fact that it is simply used within language games among theorists and activists, and nothing more. However, I want to make the rather less defeatist claim that if it is operationalised in a systematic manner (although acknowledging its essentially contestable character), it may become a useful tool for critically evaluating a range of political practices, with quite specific implications for how we might characterise the empirics not only of feminism but also a range of oppositional political movements.

Indeed, perceptions of changes in the radicalism of social movements (both feminism and others), implicitly or explicitly inform narratives about their changing nature, and notions of 'radicalism' can be read as indicative of the movement's vibrancy, energy and critical capacities more generally. For an avowedly oppositional political project such as feminism, self-perceptions of 'radicalism' are often crucial to the movement's self-understanding. As intimated by Ferree and Pudrovska, 'the term 'feminist' is generally seen as a radical frame for wanting change in the position of women. Internationally, 'I'm not a feminist, but ...' is a common way to endorse the resonant aspects of specific women's movement claims while distancing oneself from this radical identity' (2006: 250). While, arguably, this moves a little close to the terrain of regarding any affirmation of feminism as by definition 'radical', it does suggest the importance of some notion of, or some investment in, 'radicalism' as crucial to feminist politics. Admittedly, this can lead to the problematic terrain of judging who is 'more radical' than others, and with it the risk of delegitimising perspectives that are characterised as 'less radical'. But this is a risk I am willing to take. After all, the reformulation of radicalism advanced here is in many respects intended to relegitimise a range of feminist practices that would be regarded as normatively suspect from the perspective of more orthodox understandings of feminist radicalism.

To go about reworking the notion of radicalism, I draw on a series of strands of contemporary post-structuralist (or 'post-foundationalist') political theory to flesh out a specifically *non-topographical* conception of radical politics: that is, one that avoids seeing 'radicality' as *logically* and *necessarily* tied to particular, contextual spaces, practices or signifiers. I shall argue that the *radicality* of a politics describes the character of a political action (implying contextuality and relationality), rather than an inherent quality of an object or subject. More specifically, I want to claim that the radicality of a feminist politics inheres not in specific types of political practice, but in its 'world-building' capacity, its capacity to bring into existence new frames of thought and action. Crucially, I argue that no specific site for feminist engagement can be seen as ontologically more amenable to the emergence of radical practices than others.

To begin, I contextualise the above theoretical claims by mapping out the general contours of post-structuralist challenges to topographical understandings of politics. However, as shall become clear, this is a broad terrain and can lead to divergent political and analytical positions. Consequently, my rearticulation of radical (feminist) politics will need to be narrowed down. In so doing, I begin by drawing on the work of Ernesto Laclau (and his early collaborations with Chantal Mouffe), who at various points in his work has sought to address the question of how we might think the radicality of a politics after the deconstruction of Marxism. I argue that their effort to link the notion of 'radicalisation' to the process of constructing equivalential linkages between disparate demands constitutes an essential element of a reconfigured notion of radicality, but is insufficient. Laclau's work, I argue, underplays the role of creativity and imagination in oppositional political practices, and so I supplement his work with insights drawn from recent attempts by Linda Zerilli and other neo-Arendtian feminist theorists to tackle questions of freedom and imagination in (feminist) politics. Foregrounding the notion of equivalence in Laclau, I then seek to articulate this with Linda Zerilli's reworking of the concept of political imagination. This, I believe, furnishes us with a conception of radicality that is sufficiently fluid to allow for radical practices to be identified in a diversity of contexts, while remaining sufficiently rigorous to cast certain feminist practices as more or less 'radical' than others. This new conceptualisation of radicality might point towards an altogether different reading of contemporary feminism to that found in the feminist literature referred to in Chapter 1, the implications of which will be articulated during the course of this chapter.

Mapping the terrain: 'Post-foundational' challenges to politics

The reformulation of feminist 'radicality' proposed here arises out of a specific theoretical genealogy. It is situated within the broader context of what, after Oliver Marchant, we might refer to as 'post-foundational' political thought. This refers to the general trend towards a 'radicalisation' of political theory in the aftermath of the Second World War. Post-foundational political theory is premised upon the problematisation of 'metaphysical figures of foundations – such as totality, universality, essence and ground' (Marchant, 2007: 2). It thus makes the ontological claim that contingency – that is, the absence of *a priori* substantive constituent elements of society – is irreducible. This radical notion of contingency means that the notion of 'the political' ceases to refer to a given set of institutions, but, rather, captures how *any* and *all* social practices are, in some sense, constituted in and through political struggle. Thus, all domains of the social – not just those we regard as 'political' in an everyday sense – are products of contingent contestations and moments of institution. Fundamentally, my argument – along with that of post-foundationalism more generally – is that politics is a specific mode of action and not something with an inherent, necessary link to particular types of social space, and that 'radicality', likewise, cannot be seen as restricted to a specific topos for (feminist) politics.

As Marchant puts it, 'the issue at stake here is that no particular ontic politics can ever be grounded within the ontological realm of the political, but will always have to be articulated within the space opened by the play of the political difference' (ibid.: 159). In invoking the Heideggerian ontic/ontological distinction,[2] Marchant's point is that no specific contextual politics (such as autonomous women-only feminist mobilisation in the 1970s) can ever successfully occupy the *ground* of politics in general. In Chapter 1, I argued that a very contextually specific mode of feminist practice has, in many cases, become ossified as *radical* feminist politics *in toto*. This would, therefore, be an example of an ontic politics constituting itself as an ontological grounding for feminist politics. While, as Judith Butler (1995) argues, some provisional 'grounds' for our understandings of the social world are unavoidable, politics emerges where and when these 'grounds' are contested and/or reconfigured (Dyrberg, 2004). Thus, to overlook or deny the contestations and negotiations surrounding the gap between the ontic and the ontological (or the specific and the general) is a depoliticising gesture that risks placing a gag on the vibrancy – and indeed radicality – of both earlier and contemporary feminist contestations.

I note that these might seem like rather sweeping philosophical gestures, and one might reasonably ask what this has to do with our analysis of feminist politics. To shed some light on this, it may be helpful to situate the emergence of 'post-foundational' political thought within the contextual events of the late twentieth century (and earlier).

One may argue, with Laclau and Mouffe, following Claude Lefort, that the period following the French Revolution has been characterised by the 'dissolution of the markers of certainty', rendering an ever-expanding range of domains of the social open to political contestation and intervention (Laclau and Mouffe, 2001; Lefort, 1988).[3] This in turn has served to challenge notions of politics as having a necessary link to either specific bodies (such as the king), or to specific institutional spaces (such as the parliament). This challenge, one may argue, has intensified since the Second World War. Politically, the so-called new social movements of the late 1960s onwards created new sites of antagonism around, for example, environment, gender, race and sexuality in ways not reducible to a notion of politics as linked to the taking of decisions in formal political institutions. And theoretically, works by, for example, Foucault (1977, 1978) and Lukes (1974) argued that power is not necessarily something that is possessed or exercised but, rather, is productive and ubiquitous, meaning that struggles for power are not restricted to tussles over who occupies positions at the top of legal, economic and (conventional) political hierarchies. Thus, post-foundational political theory claims that these developments have made more apparent something that was always already latent, yet largely unacknowledged: namely, that politics – conceived in terms of the contestation and institution of social life – has never had a necessary link to any particular domain of the social. And, to (finally) return to the question of feminism: one may argue that feminist activism and scholarship played a crucial role in these reconfigurations of politics. Second-wave feminism, at least as much as any other late twentieth-century political and theoretical strand, served to create new sites of antagonism in spaces hitherto regarded as grounded in natural and immutable laws. Despite the rather predictable inattention of many of the leading male post-foundational theorists to questions of gender and the contribution of feminism, I want nonetheless to place feminism at the forefront of post-foundational political thought and the decentering of conventional political institutions within political theory. Indeed, the popular second-wave feminist slogan 'the personal is political' resonates strongly with the post-foundational notion that politics can and does take place in spheres hitherto regarded as beyond the purview of the political.

This will suffice for now as a general mapping of the theoretical terrain in which we are operating. However, one must acknowledge that the map is broad, and a number of divergent positions may follow from the post-foundational problematisation of conventional notions of politics. As Marchant (2007: 3) points out, in contrast to liberal and/ or conservative thinkers such as Michael Oakeshott and Richard Rorty, we are operating here in a specifically *left* post-foundationalism. And yet, even within left post-foundationalism, there are multiple possible positions one can adopt. One potential consequence of the decentering of (conventional) political institutions is that one might say that 'everything' is in some sense political. This in turn could lead to a naively celebratory position that conceives all social practices as 'political'. Indeed, this is a position that critics have attributed to Judith Butler's (post-foundational) promulgation of subversive citations of gender (Nussbaum, 1999; Benhabib, 1995). While I would take issue with such a reading of Butler, this, as I shall argue in greater detail later, is a position one would want to avoid. However, I would also look to avoid adhering to the opposite extreme: that is, the view that politics 'proper' can only be said to refer to those irregular moments in which the social fabric is profoundly disrupted. The most hard-line proponent of this perspective is Alain Badiou, for whom authentic politics is of the order of the 'event', instigated by a militant political subject heterogeneous to the logic of the 'situation'. The latter refers to a given state of things or a social order, which is implicitly assumed to be relatively static: for example, he uses the designation 'capital-parliamentarianism' for the contemporary political 'situation' (Badiou, 2005: 84). The 'event', on the other hand, refers to a supplement which 'can neither be named nor represented by referring to the resources of the situation (its structure, the established language naming its terms, etc)' (Badiou, 1992: 36–7). Consequently, Badiou's political orientation rests primarily upon his advocacy of a fidelity to the singularity of an 'event' that radically disrupts the logic of the 'situation' (Hallward, 2004: 2). While not quite as hard line as Badiou, Jacques Rancière similarly restricts authentic moments of politics to those rare moments in which the emancipatory political subject – the demos – interrupts the 'natural' order (the 'distribution of the sensible', as Rancière calls it) by speaking out of turn, by unsettling their allocated roles within the 'police' order (Rancière, 1995; 1999).[4]

While Rancière provides an innovative post-foundational slant on how we might conceptualise emancipatory egalitarian politics, and – potentially at least – avoids regarding specific spaces and subjects as having a necessary relation to an emancipatory (that is, radical) politics, my worry is that both he and Badiou restrict politics to too narrow a range of practices. In contrast to authors such as Badiou, the conception of radical politics advanced here resists an excessive reliance on dramatic moments of political rupture that radically reconfigure the social order.

Such an approach – which one arguably finds in the works of a range of authors on the Lacanian Left – is imbued with what Simon Critchley has called (referring to Badiou) a 'heroism of the decision', whereby there is an excessively strong affective investment in dramatic moments of radical discontinuity with the status quo (Critchley, 2000: 13; see also Norval, 2007: 138–9).[5] A 'heroic' conception of radical politics would seem to run the risk of delegitimising a range of critical practices as not sufficiently political, and seems to lead to rather melancholic narratives about the absence of emancipatory modes of politics. The rest of this chapter will be situated within post-structuralist/post-foundational challenges to 'the political', and will seek to rethink radicality in a manner which avoids either seeing radical feminist political practices almost everywhere, or as happening only very infrequently.

Laclau: The role of articulation and equivalence

One of the most rigorous theorisations of (radical) politics from a post-structuralist/post-foundational perspective is provided by Ernesto Laclau (sometimes in collaboration with Chantal Mouffe). In line with the basic contours of post-foundationalism described above, and in contrast to either a Marxist conflation of politics with class struggle, or a liberal conflation of politics with arbitration between 'interests', Laclau and Mouffe maintain that one cannot determine in an *a priori* fashion the character of social and political relations in a given context. Instead, they emphasise the importance of the contingent examination of competing discourses that vie to become 'hegemonic' (Mouffe, 2000; Laclau and Mouffe, 2001). Consequently, from a Laclauian perspective, as Howarth and Glynos argue, 'politics is about taking decisions in a contingent and undecidable terrain, which involves radical acts of power and institution' (Glynos and Howarth, 2007: 114). In view of the impossibility of simple determinism, social and political identities are seen as always potentially open and subject to what they call rearticulation. Against this backdrop, the main argument of their opus *Hegemony and Socialist Strategy* is, as Mouffe puts it,

> that social objectivity is constituted through acts of power. This implies that any social objectivity is ultimately political and that it has to show the traces of exclusion which govern its constitution. The point of convergence – or rather mutual collapse – between objectivity and power is what we [Laclau and Mouffe] meant by 'hegemony'. This way of posing the problem indicates that power

should not be conceived as an external relation taking place between two preconstituted identities, but rather as constituting the identities themselves.

(Mouffe, 2000: 99)

Drawing on these perspectives, I take feminist politics to be a delicate and contested process involving the construction of discursive totalities via the articulation of elements which have no necessary link. Rather than claiming that 'everything is political', such a view maintains, instead, that everything is *potentially* open to (radical) politicisation, but that such a politicisation requires specific types of action and agency, on the part of individuals and groups (Honig, 1995b: 147). Consequently, from a Laclauian perspective, no domain of the social can be seen as ontologically resistant to radical politicisation: the question of where or how a radical politics will emerge will inevitably be a conjunctural empirical question, rather than something that can be deduced in abstraction.

But this leaves unanswered the question of what sorts of practices need to be effected if an action, or set of actions, is to count as politically *radical*. It is here that the notion of equivalence comes into play.[6] Laclau and Mouffe describe how political agendas are often formed through processes of establishing linkages between various political demands that have no necessary or inevitable relation with one another. A 'chain of equivalence' refers to the (relatively) unified system of elements arising from the construction of these linkages, such that the particularity of each of the elements assumes less importance than its equivalence to other elements (Laclau and Mouffe, 2001: 128). For example, the chain of equivalences in Thatcherite discourse included elements such as the free market, a strong state and a traditional morality. Consequently, we can say that any given political demand could potentially become part of a radical agenda if it is inscribed within a (pluralistic) counter-hegemonic chain of equivalence, although we cannot know in advance the precise mode of political practice or the type of political space in which the construction of the chain will take place.

A further important point here is that chains of equivalence derive their unity partly through the production of what Laclau has called 'empty signifiers', privileged signifiers that condense a series of disparate political demands into a relatively cohesive agenda. For example, signifiers such as 'Solidarnosc' in Polish politics, 'the personal is political' in feminism and 'New Labour' in 1990s UK politics all became 'emptied' as they came to assume the function of condensing a diversity of issues into a relatively stable political project. It should be clear that no signifier is intrinsically 'empty': the question of which precise signifiers serve this function will always be empirical and historically contingent. Furthermore, it is, of course, nonsensical to claim that a signifier can be *entirely* emptied of meaning. Rather, certain signifiers *become* empty as they come to assume the function of anchoring together an increasing number of political demands. In so doing, (tendentially) empty signifiers have a strong performative function, in that, in the process of naming, they bring into existence political agendas that only tenuously existed before (Laclau, 1996: 36–46). Therefore, the radicality of a politics in Laclau and Mouffe's schema inheres in the moment of newness and inauguration brought about by the performative constitution of chains of equivalence.

More specifically, for Laclau and Mouffe a political demand becomes radical at the point at which it becomes incorporated into a broad counter-hegemonic equivalence, rather than simply being addressed in its particularity (Laclau, 2005a: 117–18). As Glynos and Howarth argue, drawing on Laclau, a political demand becomes *radical* when it contests a fundamental norm of a regime or set of institutional practices (2007: 115). However, it seems that a 'fundamental' challenge to a set of norms will require specific modes of equivalential articulation between grievances. To illustrate, a woman may experience sexual harassment at work, and may complain to her bosses who may then (if she is very lucky!) take disciplinary measures against the offending individual. Given that her grievance is solved within the existing institutional structures of the company, she has no need to formulate a radical agenda – she can simply 'carry on as normal'. If, however, her grievance is not addressed, she may then alert her colleagues to the injustice she has suffered, which may serve as a starting point for the construction of a broader struggle against the company's practices. Drawing on Laclau and Mouffe, we can say that the moment of *radicalisation* occurs at the point where linkages – equivalences – are established between her grievance and other grievances with the company's practices. This is the point at which the social space becomes dichotomised into two factions with divergent interests. In this case, however, the moment of radicalisation is further heightened by the political valence in the woman's decision to constitute her grievance specifically as 'sexual harassment' (which relies on an implicitly feminist analysis of the situation) as opposed to, for example, 'bad behaviour' or 'rudeness' on the part of the boss. The use of the feminist lexicon of 'sexual harassment' thus implicitly establishes equivalential linkages between her constitution of the situation as 'sexual harassment' and other implicitly or explicitly feminist claims of discrimination in the workplace or elsewhere. Crucial, however, is the notion that one does not have to substantively specify the content of these demands (although I have done so here purely for the purposes of illustration): the moment of 'radicalisation' is a formal process inasmuch as it has no necessary relation to any specific content.

This characterisation of 'radicality' is invaluable as it avoids seeing the radicality of a politics as inhering in particular types of social space: a radical equivalential chain, for instance, may cut across different types of institutional and non-institutional space. These interventions have a number of interesting consequences for the literature on spatial dynamics in contemporary feminism referred to at the outset. For one, the emphasis on the contextuality of specific types of institutional space (such as the national state) resonates with the state feminism literature's emphasis on the emergence of new modes of gender governance and opportunities for feminist intervention at the level of the state. While Pringle and Watson (1992) provided early signposts in the direction of the productive use of Laclau and Mouffe for feminist state theory, Kantola's (2006) use of post-structuralism to conceptualise the state as 'differentiated', as a site of overlapping and contradictory forms of discourse and practice, also militates against *a priori* assumptions about the character of particular state institutions. Thus, while patriarchal and anti-feminist logics do operate within the state, it cannot be seen as *fundamentally* patriarchal given the existence of areas where such logics are weak or non-existent.[7] This is a relatively simple point, but it is crucial as it points towards a view of radicality as entailing a politics which aims at bringing about new forms of political articulation, but without necessarily restricting these transformative efforts to the realm of civil society. In the context of a more normative excursus in *Hegemony and Socialist Strategy*, Laclau and Mouffe make the case for theorising radical politics as potentially *cutting across* the state/civil society distinction. They write,

> In recent years much has been talked about the need to deepen the line of separation between state and civil society. It is not difficult to realise, however, that this proposal does not furnish the Left with any theory of the surface of the emergence of antagonisms which can be generalised beyond a limited number of situations. It would appear to imply that every form of domination is incarnated in the state.
>
> (Laclau and Mouffe, 2001: 179)[8]

For example, a women's policy agency[9] may operate in a purely advisory role, and thus remain simply a 'non radical', institutionalised part of the state apparatus. Alternatively, it could radicalise its agenda by explicitly linking certain policy aims to demands articulated by, for example, other women's organisations, feminist academics, journalists, bloggers or other progressive political movements. The simple key point is that, we, as feminist political analysts, cannot make *a priori* assumptions about the radicality or otherwise of, for example, a women's policy agency. Assessing the radicalism of a feminist group, actor or action is always an empirical question and cannot be assumed on the basis of the type of institutional space in which the action under investigation takes place.

A further, arguably more interesting, resonance between the Laclauian notion of oppositional politics as the construction of equivalential demands and the literature analysed in the Chapter 1, relates to the implied notion of equivalence in Mohanty and Yuval-Davis's accounts of transational feminist mobilisation. Mohanty's early work, for instance, resists the conventional (radical) feminist emphasis on sisterhood as the ground for feminist resistance, with its privileging of gender over other social cleavages. In opposition to this, she promulgates a politics based on solidarity between oppositional political struggles, a solidarity which is not given but needs to be created through imaginative articulations across contexts (Mohanty, 2003: 7–8). For Mohanty, the radicality of a feminist politics is thus not given in an *a priori* privileging of gender-based struggles, but in its ability to foster articulations between struggles around race, gender and the critique of capitalism (ibid.: 46; 54–5). Mohanty and Laclau thus both reject from the outset what we might call a 'politics of purity', that is, a notion that radical politics has a proper place or object that must be adhered to if the dangers of compromise or blunting are to be avoided. For both, compromise is integral to an oppositional politics. Mohanty argues that no 'noncontaminatory' or pure feminism is possible or desirable (ibid.: 63): feminist demands are constantly articulated in and through specific contexts that militate against notions of purity. Similarly, Laclau's notion of articulation (which emphasises how elements in a discourse are by definition altered in the moment of articulation) along with the critique of Marxism's politics of purity, foregrounds the tentative, messy and contaminatory nature of radical politics. A similar argument is made by Nira Yuval-Davis, who advances a 'transversal' conception of feminist politics in opposition to one based on identity. As with Mohanty and Laclau, Yuval-Davis resists a politics of purity based on separatism, which she regards as potentially racist and apolitical (2006: 289), and also highlights the centrality of compromise and negotiation in the construction of politics. She writes, 'transversal politics is not only a dialogue in which two or more partners are negotiating a common political position, but it is a process in which all the participants are mutually reconstructing themselves and the others engaged with them in it' (ibid.: 286).

In different ways, all these perspectives thus counterpose a politics based on the contingent articulation of demands to one based on essentialist notions of identity or purity. They are also opposed to the hardline post-foundational thesis that genuine moments of politics are rare. Rather, they claim that various and complex modes of political contestation are likely to be ongoing at any given time, but nonetheless hold on to a notion of the specificity of politics in a way that avoids lapsing into either a belief that 'everything' is political, or that any affirmation of feminism is by definition radical and transformative. The emphasis on the construction of equivalences and the logic of hegemony more generally thus shares with critics such as Wendy Brown (2000) and Stuart Hall (1988) an antipathy towards a pervasive left melancholia in the aftermath of the deconstruction of Marxism, but without this occasioning a naïve celebratory position.

Laclau's work is thus not only of value in itself, but provides a theoretical lens through which to characterise a number of themes that recur within the literatures that I draw upon, enabling a theorisation of how we might begin to evaluate the 'radicalism' or otherwise of contemporary feminist practices. Despite this, to articulate a satisfactory operationalisation of feminist radicality we will need to look beyond Laclau's work. In Laclau there is a sense that the distinctiveness of a counter-hegemonic politics arises primarily, perhaps even purely, from its being in opposition to a further element. His focus on the reactive and oppositional dimensions of political action under-theorises the creative, performative and imaginative processes that go into creating both oppositional political formations and new ways of being within the world. To fully flesh out an 'imaginative' notion of radical politics we will require a more thorough explication of the role of imagination and creativity in contemporary radical politics.

Arendt and Zerilli on politics and 'the social'

Several recent works have attended to the essentially imaginative, creative and aesthetic character of political theory *in toto* (Panagia, 2006;

McManus, 2005). However, while interesting, in highlighting the creative and fictive characteristics of the political theory canon, they do not really address the role of creativity and imagination in oppositional political *practices*.[10] More useful for the task at hand here, however, are recent works that take inspiration from Hannah Arendt. Arendt is, in many respects, an anomalous figure, both within feminist theory and post-foundational political theory. Despite her emphasis on politics as rooted in action, judgement and unpredictability, we may argue that she nonetheless retained a *topographical* notion of politics, by invoking a neatly circumscribed realm in which political practices take place (see Honig, 1993, especially p.94).[11] Furthermore, in seeking to articulate a 'neo-Arendtian' approach to feminism, one does of course open oneself up to the charge that Arendt was no feminist, and was in many respects hostile to the 'woman question', seeing it, to some degree, as irretrievably condemned to the realm of 'the social'.[12]

Despite these problems, Arendt's appeal lies in her rigorous theorisation of a notion of 'politics' that affords a centrality to notions of imagination and creativity. Thus, from a post-foundationalist perspective, Arendt's insights prove invaluable, so long as we seek to radicalise some of her claims in order to avoid the rather conservative republican tendencies that permeate much of her work.[13] This part of the argument takes inspiration in particular from Bonnie Honig's *radicalisation* of Arendt which seeks to weaken the rigidity of Arendt's distinction between the public and the private, articulating a conception of the public realm as signifying the possibility for the spontaneous emergence of a range of political spaces, rather than treating it as a definitively fixed topos (Honig, 1993: 224; see also Glynos and Howarth, 2007: 115). In different ways, Honig and also Adriana Cavarero (2002) have drawn on Arendt to argue against conceiving politics as a problem of order, pertaining to the stable organisation of objects and institutions. By contrast, politics, they argue, consists in moments of unpredictability, fissure and destabilisation of order, and thus cannot be contained within any given set of spaces.[14]

Proceeding with a 'non-topographical' reading of Arendt, in the rest of the chapter I seek to flesh out an understanding of the role of imagination and creativity in radical politics by linking insights from Laclau and the post-foundationalists with recent feminist interpretations of Arendt, particularly the recent work of American political theorist Linda Zerilli. Zerilli advances a reading of Arendt from what we might term a post-foundational perspective (although she doesn't explicitly frame it as such: she proceeds as if Arendt was always already deconstructed). In so doing, Zerilli (2005a) highlights the importance of political freedom as action, as a worldly experience, such that specific substantive issues or political spaces are not seen as having any intrinsic or necessary attachment to radical political freedom.

This radical reading of Arendt advanced by Zerilli (and indeed Honig and Cavarero) foregrounds a specifically Arendtian notion of plurality, which refers not to plurality as pluralism, in the sense of a diversity of sociological groups (such as gender, race, class), but to the fact that, following Arendt, 'Men' rather than 'Man' inhabit the earth, such that political freedom is bound up with an emphasis on individuals speaking and acting collectively. As Arendt points out – musing approvingly on the question of freedom in Ancient Greek city states – 'freedom was understood as being manifest in certain, by no means all, human activities, and that these activities could appear and be real only when others saw them, judged them, remembered them. The life of a free man needed the presence of others' (Arendt, 1963: 24).[15] Furthermore, for Arendt freedom is/was 'a tangible, worldly-reality, something created by men to be enjoyed by men rather than a gift or a capacity' (Zerilli, 2005a: 120). A radicalisation of the notion of 'plurality' would suggest that freedom is tied to worldly, contextual processes of contestation and negotiation with others, in contrast to a traditional feminist emphasis on purity and unity as the precondition for a radical feminist subjectivity.

Zerilli's intervention thus shares with Laclau – and indeed Mohanty and Yuval-Davis – a critique of a politics based on identity and separatism, and affirms a notion of politics as grounded, messy and unpredictable. Such a perspective takes issue with both a politics of purity and separatism, and a more mainstream liberal notion of politics as arbitration between pre-given interests. This is because both entail the domestication of politics to 'the social' (ibid.: 3–7). This logic of domestication, as outlined by Zerilli, is reflected in the widespread view of politics as entailing arbitration between political demands for the social advancement of particular groups, such that politics becomes analogous to 'housekeeping', leading to normalisation and conformism (Arendt, 1958: 39; Zerilli, 2005a).[16]

In discussing these issues, a case could be made that Arendt herself was excessively forthright and uncompromising in her disdain for a range of social issues, in particular those related to the questions of poverty and material want (Arendt, 1963: 16–17). On this matter, Zerilli notes that this is indeed a legitimate concern, but argues that 'a more generous reading' would 'suggest that she does not in fact exclude social concerns from politics but warns against the introduction of the instrumentalist attitude that such concerns often carry with them' (Zerilli, 2005a: 3). It is this latter sense of the 'social' that I wish to carry forward here, such that the 'social' is not an inherent property of particular issues but is instead what Zerilli calls an 'antipolitical sensibility', that is, a specific mode of responding to and dealing with particular issues (ibid.: 4). Taking this latter approach also provides an outlet for moving beyond Arendt's notoriously rigid public/private distinction (see Arendt, 1958: 22–78; 1963: 86) and thinking more in terms of how specific 'private' issues might be taken up politically. Furthermore, thinking of 'the social' in this mode enables us to avoid Arendt's tendency to use metaphors that invoke 'the social' as an active, devouring and irresistible force (what Pitkin (1998: 3–4) refers to as 'the social as 'Blob', alluding to the 1950s science-fiction film *The Blob*).

Using this revised conception of 'the social', Zerilli argues that the domestication of politics to 'the social' is manifest in, for example, the tendency in much American feminism to view the formal conferral of rights as sufficient for substantive freedom to be realised. Zerilli claims that the 'deeply juridical and institutional orientation of much contemporary feminism, like that of American society at large, shows how we have lost track of the idea of political freedom which the radical claim to rights once encoded' (2005a: 120). Consequently, 'we tend to become invested in securing them [rights] as such, rather than in maintaining our investment in the sometimes less stable practices that created them in the first place .... Freedom does not consist, not as such, in the political representation that follows from the successful institutionalization of such a demand' (ibid.: 120).

Here, Zerilli is not denying struggles for rights *tout court*. Rather, she highlights how efforts must be made to ensure that the institutionalisation of a right (such as women's rights to equal participation in political institutions) does not lead to a situation in which assimilation to dominant logics becomes necessary. For instance, the question of freedom becomes radically sidelined if assimilation to a masculinist framework becomes a precondition for women to be taken seriously in political institutions: the institutionalisation of a right thus by no means guarantees that political freedom will follow from that institutionalisation. To give an example, we may say that the processes of post-feminist (dis)identification, as described by McRobbie and outlined in the Chapter 1, are partly predicated upon the belief that the institutionalisation of certain elements of feminist struggles render feminism out of date and no longer necessary: thus, such logics are, in some respects, predicated upon a broader hegemonic acceptance of the domestication of politics to the social. Of course, the critique of the domestication of politics to the social advanced here is not a dismissal of all modes of feminist engagement with the state, but, rather, a critique of one particular mode of 'state feminism'. It is a critique of the process whereby demands are articulated in their particularity, such that their more transformative potential remains unrealised. It does not claim that feminist engagement with state institutions *necessarily* leads to this particular mode of political practice.

The domestication of the political to the social is also manifest, according to Zerilli (2005a: 9–16), in the foregrounding of what she calls the 'subject question' in much contemporary feminist theory and practice. The subject question pertains to the feminist preoccupation with the question of subjectivity, and with it the fantasy of a unified category of 'woman', with its concomitant presumption of unity, mastery and purity, underwritten by a view of freedom conceptualised in terms of negative liberty and mastery of, or escape from, the contingencies of *collective* political action (ibid.: 9). In contrast to this, Zerilli contends, after Arendt, that political deeds, once done, inevitably have effects beyond the doer's control (ibid.: 13–14), and thus cannot be explained with reference to a sovereign conception of political agency.

For Zerilli, a prime example of the subject question's domestication of politics to the social can be found in the proliferation in Anglo-American feminism during the 1980s of an identitarian conception of feminist politics. Here, Zerilli is critical of the ways in which the critique of the white, middle-class dominance of feminist politics at times led to a preoccupation with sociological identity categories (black women, straight women, disabled women) rather than an engagement with the possible political consequences of that critique. Other examples of the 'subject question' might include the overdetermination of feminism by the 'wave' metaphor, with its fixation on discreet generational subjectivities, and the tendency for 'radical feminism' to be framed primarily as a mode of feminist subjectivity, rather than as an evaluative or analytical term. These examples of somewhat reductive formulations of feminist subjectivity all, in different ways, could be read as indicative of an attachment to a sovereign conception of political agency, whereby feminist subjectivity needs to be unambiguously delineated prior to political engagement, rather than being constituted in and through political struggle. In opposition to this, Zerilli claims that such a view restricts and constrains from the outset the radical possibilities of a feminist engagement, resonating strongly with Butler's (1995, 1999) critique of the will to unity and transparency in the construction of feminist subjectivity.

While Zerilli's intervention is extremely helpful, there is undoubtedly a sense in which she exaggerates the extent to which feminist theory and practice has been guilty of domesticating the political to the social. Furthermore, and I think more fundamentally, Zerilli presents what is in essence a critique of *particular* forms of feminist subjectivity as a critique of subjectivity *in toto*. As we shall see, a post-foundational theorisation of radical politics entails a dialectic between desubjectification and subjectification, enabling us to draw a distinction (which Zerilli seems reluctant to draw) between reductive, sovereign conceptions of feminist subjectivity, on the one hand, and constructions of feminist subjectivity that leave room for contingency and openness, on the other.

Despite this, her framing of the problem nonetheless helps shed light on the tendency within feminism to operate with sedimented categories – such as thinking in terms of generational 'waves' or taking the radical/liberal/socialist distinction as axiomatic – and the ways in which such an approach diminishes scope for a reflexive and critical feminism that is alert to the contingencies of political action. I take from Zerilli not a belief that contemporary feminists are guilty of presupposing a strongly essentialist conception of, for example, the feminist subject or the category of woman, but that there is a latent essentialism in the way in which understandings of particular forms of feminist politics and subjectivities are formulated.

Feminism and political imagination

The above sections emphasised the usefulness of Laclau's work for the task at hand, and set out the basic contours of Zerilli's intervention. In this section, I want to begin to more substantively bring these perspectives together so as to formulate an alternative, more productive understanding of feminist radicality. This new formulation of 'radicality' must be sufficiently fluid to be applicable to a diversity of different contexts and to be able to affirm the dynamism and complexity of feminist politics, while not being so vague as to be useless for the purposes of critical analysis of specific instances of feminist practice. Having already drawn on the Laclauian notion of equivalence, my claim is that if this is supplemented with the notion of political imagination from Zerilli's work, we can formulate a notion of radicality that enables a critical engagement with contemporary feminist practices without lapsing into insufficiently nuanced accounts of decline and deradicalisation.

I shall begin by sketching out what I understand by the notion of 'political imagination', after which I will show how, when used in conjunction with Laclau, it can advance our understanding of feminist radicality. Crucial to a specifically *political* conception of imagination is that our ability to make judgements is not subsumptive or determinate, but is world-building and creative. Judgement, for Zerilli, is not to be thought in epistemological terms (knowledge based on the inherent properties of objects), but rather, in political terms. For Zerilli, the former concerns 'the application of concepts to particulars and the rational adjudication of knowledge/truth claims', whereas the latter concerns 'opinion formation and practices of freedom' (2005a: 146). In this sense, political judgement is not grounded in the universal nature of an object, but on a sense of contingent opinion formation: as Zerilli likes to point out, to claim that a rose is beautiful is not to make a claim grounded in the universal quality of roses, but is a contingent judgement about a specific, particular rose (ibid.: 133). Likewise, the notion of imagination, 'when it is considered in its freedom ... is not bound to the law of causality, but is productive and spontaneous, not merely reproductive of what is already known, but generative of new forms and figures' (Zerilli, 2005b: 163). A non-determinate conception of imagination is grounded in the 'poetic, rhetorical and world-creating capacity of language' (ibid.: 166; see also Norval, 2007: 101).

According to this perspective, the vibrancy and radicality of a feminism is not grounded upon – at least not only upon – the articulation of knowledge claims or upon any particular mode of feminist politics, but on the extent to which a feminism seeks to create what Cornelius Castoriadis (1997: 267) has called 'figure of the newly thinkable', that is an ungrounded, radically inaugurative figure or model with which to instantiate new modes of understanding of particular objects or phenomena.[17] An imaginative, freedom-centred politics, Zerilli argues, is a 'world-building exercise' whereby political actors act *together* in ways which bring into existence things and ideas which did not exist before.

This position is most cogently expressed in Zerilli's discussion of intersexed bodies: that is, bodies showing intermediate sexual characteristics. She claims that citing evidence of the existence of bodies which do not fit within a two-sex frame is not sufficient to challenge that frame, as such bodies continue to be subsumed under the 'rules' of the binary sex system. What is additionally required, she argues, is the capacity to *imagine* new frames which go beyond the binary sex system: imagination, she argues, 'allows us to think the possibility of something beyond the epistemic demand of deciding the true and the false' (Zerilli, 2005a: 9). She notes that

> If the exception to the rule rarely disrupts our tendency to subsume all bodies under the rule of sex difference, that may be because what we lack is not an appropriately denaturalised position from which to doubt what we think we see but an alternative figure of the thinkable with which to organize anew the very experience of seeing, that is, of meaning'.
>
> (Ibid.: 62)

While Zerilli is certainly not alone in highlighting the potential instability of the binary gender system, her intervention brings to light how binary gender norms need not necessarily be challenged by the empirical existence of intersex bodies. To more substantially problematise binary gender norms, something more than mere empirical examples is required: that is, the capacity for processes of political imagination that can offer insights into new modes of understanding political relations.

Let us provide a further example. Aletta Norval advances a reading of Wollstonecraft's politicised use of the appellation 'women' (as opposed to 'ladies') as a moment of radical feminist political imagination. This is in contrast to the standard liberal interpretation of Wollstonecraft. The liberal interpretation, Norval argues (2007: 142), is only possible following the long-term sedimentation of the liberal paradigm of rights claims. This risks overlooking how the designation 'women' – with its concomitant reworking of hegemonic understandings of gender and the public/private divide – was a radically inaugurative move, rather than a mechanistic extension of existing political discourses.[18] That said, if, as Norval argues, the designation 'woman' marks the place of a dispute within the existing order, then, in contrast to Zerilli's seemingly unqualified dismissal of the question of subjectivity: this would suggest that imaginative political action – potentially at least – entails a dialectic of disidentification and subjectification. Norval argues, drawing on Rancière, 'the irruption of politics is always a matter of subjectification through *dis*identification, a removal from the naturalness of place, rather than one of identification' (2007: 142, italics in original). Indeed, in this sense, one could read the emergence of second-wave feminism as a paradigmatic example of a 'removal from the naturalness of place'.[19]

We may also argue that the radicality of Anglo-American second-wave feminist politicisations of hitherto non-political domains derived not from the inherent politicality of particular spaces, but from the way in which empty signifiers such as 'the personal is political' imaginatively brought previously disparate elements together into an equivalential chain (such as housework, the sexual division of labour, reproductive issues, sexual autonomy, the democratic discourse of equality). We can say such a move was *radical* in that it brought together these disparate elements in a way which was inventive and imaginative, that is, it could not have been foreseen in any mechanistic way, or simply read off from the character of the elements that were brought together.[20]

These examples all show how no political articulation is intrinsically new or imaginative: the radicality or a political action can only be discerned by a careful empirical analysis of the action in relation to the hegemonic context. This is a broad claim, but it has a number of consequences. For one, it suggests that no affirmation of feminism is of necessity intrinsically radical and transformative, but, by the same token, it also suggests that certain types of feminist practice are not by necessity non-radical or complicitious. For instance, Norval's reading of Wollstonecraft above engenders a sensitivity to context when examining 'liberal' feminist claims. Similarly, as Karen Zivi argues in a piece on rights and Butler's notion of performativity, it highlights the potentially radical and creative dimensions of rights claims. She writes, 'in saying "I have a right" I am not simply describing an already existing reality, but bringing into being a set of relationships or ways of being that may not have existed prior to my speaking' (2008: 166). This is a crucial point, as it reinforces my claim that a radical articulation need not necessarily be restricted to autonomous political mobilisations beyond the state, but may seek to engage and challenge a range of state institutions through the imaginative articulation of certain types of rights claims.

Zerilli's account of the creative and imaginative character of political action is, for the most part, convincing. However, her framing of the problem in such terms as to counterpose a freedom-centred, imaginative politics *against* one based on knowledge claims is, I think, misleading, and her hostility towards what she terms the 'epistemological turn' in feminism is excessive. As Jon Simons has pointed out, 'Zerilli seems to collapse all forms of epistemology into foundationalism, urging us to give up on epistemology altogether' (2000: 274). However, in response to Simons' article, Zerilli (2000) appears to shift a little towards framing the issue in terms of the insufficiency, rather than the total illegitimacy, of knowledge claims for feminism. Thus, while Zerilli's intervention can at times come across as an unqualified hostility to knowledge claims *per se*, I read it as a critique of a consideration of knowledge claims as sufficient for, or foundational to, a feminist politics. It would thus be nonsensical to regard knowledge production as anathema to a (radical) feminist politics.

Despite these problems, Zerilli's (and others) neo-Arendtian feminist theory helps theorise the performative, creative and imaginative dimensions of an oppositional politics which are, arguably, under-theorised in Laclau. In some senses, both Ernesto Laclau and Linda Zerilli highlight the irreducibly creative character of political action: politics here is conceptualised as involving the imaginative construction of relationships between things which have no intrinsic or necessary link. Political relations are thus 'external to their terms: they are not given in objects themselves, but are a creation' (Zerilli, 2005a: 23); politics is thus concerned with 'the ability to see or to forge new connections' (ibid.: 162). In contrast to a feminist politics of purity, no particular issue, object or space can be seen as having a necessary relation to radical politics. As Zerilli puts it,

> There is nothing intrinsically political about, say, housework ... the word *political* signifies a relation between things, not a substance in any thing. Housework becomes political when two things that are not logically related, say, the principle of equality and the sexual division of labour, are brought into a relationship as the object of a dispute, that is, as the occasion for the speech and action with which people create the common world, the space in which things become public, and create it anew.
>
> (Ibid.: 23)

Thus, the radicality of a politics is given in the process of imaginatively constructing new ways of seeing the world, rather than being given in the objects themselves. To continue with the housework example, one could say that there are two ways one might conceptualise the second-wave feminist 'politicisation' of housework. One possible angle would be to say that housework was in some way always already political, in that it was grounded in a gendered power differential. Alternatively, one may argue that housework was 'politicised' through – as Zerilli says above – the creative linking together of elements that have no necessary relation. I want to firmly side with the latter perspective. The former would require one of two moves. On the one hand, one could extend the argument to say that 'everything is political', a move which either leads to a naively celebratory approach, or robs politics of any of its specificity (Jodi Dean, 2006; Fraser, 1989: 76). On the other hand, one could draw a division between things that are political in some fundamental sense, and things that are ontologically resistant to politicisation. However, this would be a curious move to make from a feminist perspective: it would profoundly curtail the inventive and imaginative dimensions which have been so important to feminist politics, and would risk imposing limits on the types of issues that could be brought into a feminist politicisation. As Bonnie Honig points out, 'the impulse to secure, foundationally, the division between the political and the non-political is articulated as a concern for the preservation of the political but is itself an antipolitical impulse' (Honig, 1993: 122). It is thus largely nonsensical to imply that (radical) feminist politics has a 'proper place' in specific (non) institutional sites.

Synthesising Laclau and Zerilli

We can now, finally, bring Zerilli's and Laclau's insights together more substantially. If, for Laclau, a radical politics entails the construction of counter-hegemonic linkages between demands that have no necessary relation, then implicit in Laclau is the belief, explicitly articulated by Zerilli, that politics requires *imagination* (Norval, 2007: 103). Thus, although expressed in slightly different theoretical idioms, the moment of radicalisation in Laclau (think of the example of the woman who becomes radicalised after experiencing sexual harassment) falls within the frame of Zerilli's emphasis on imagination and inauguration. The example of the character of the woman's *response* to the experience of sexual harassment in the workplace is certainly a moment of radical political freedom in at least two senses. First, there is an experience of newness and unpredictability at the point where linkages between her grievance and other grievances are established. Second, there is a moment of freedom as imagination: the lack of a *necessary* link between her grievance and other concerns is such that imagination is required in the process of articulation and the construction of a frontier.

Furthermore, Laclau's emphasis on the performative character of empty signifiers chimes heavily with Zerilli's use of Castoriadis's notion of 'figures of the newly thinkable': the latter, for Zerilli, is a figure which opens up political possibilities which were previously lacking. In much the same way, Laclau's concept of an empty signifier captures the processes by which new political configurations are created via the condensation of a diversity of elements into an empty signifier which is charged with the task of embodying and making possible the emergence of new political possibilities. Furthermore, Zerilli has elsewhere highlighted how Laclau's critique of the One of classical universalism chimes strongly with Arendt, with its eschewal of truth criteria and a subsumptive mode of rule-following, and its emphasis on contingent practices of opinion formation (Zerilli, 2004: 92). Thus, Zerilli sees an affinity between critical judging in Arendt and the operation of hegemony in Laclau based on the latter's emphasis on 'the reinscription (not the sublation) of particulars into chains of equivalence through reference to the universal as an empty place (ibid.: 93).

Let us clear one thing up. My emphasis on contingency, 'boundlessness' and things lacking a 'necessary relation' could be taken to indicate a voluntarism of sorts, a belief that 'anything is possible'. As Stuart Hall (1996: 146) writes of Laclau and Mouffe: '[I]n [*Hegemony and Socialist Strategy*] there is no reason why anything is or isn't potentially articulable with anything. The critique of reductionism has apparently resulted in the notion of society as a totally open discursive field' (Hall, 1996: 146). However, there is an interesting tension in Hall's argument. The first sentence – that anything is *potentially* articulable with anything else – is true, so long as the qualifier *potentially* is acknowledged. The key point is that political struggle – difficult, unpredictable and messy – will be necessary for this potential to be realised, and that certain hegemonic contexts will always present obstacles to particular types of articulations being made. And, indeed, these 'obstacles' will themselves be products of earlier political struggles. Therefore, it does not logically follow from the notion of potential articulability that we operate in a 'totally open discursive field'. Notions such as boundlessness and unpredictability are not intended to claim that 'anything is possible', but that we cannot know or master in advance of a political action what the consequences of that action might be. Perhaps, if we were to be polemic, we could in fact say that 'nothing is (intrinsically) impossible', but with the qualification that certain articulations will be a good deal more possible than others. In many respects, this is where Laclau's and Zerilli's works overlap most fundamentally, as both take the view that no political articulation is always necessarily impossible (a view shared with several other post-foundationalists).

To summarise the argument so far, my claim is that the radicality of a feminist politics inheres not in the extent to which it adheres to an abstracted model of feminist separatism and autonomy, but in its capacity to imaginatively bring into existence new ways of seeing and understanding the world via the construction of equivalential linkages. This alternative theoretical perspective offered here might lead us to a different, or at least more complex, picture of contemporary feminism in the UK than that offered either by melancholic narratives of decline and deradicalisation, and more optimistic narratives of feminist re-emergence.

The former often presents the radicality of a feminism as linked to the question of autonomy, such that it is taken as given that more institutionalised feminist organisations are likely to be at the 'less radical' end of the feminist spectrum. The latter risks portraying any affirmation of feminism as by definition radical and progressive. However, in opposition to this, the perspective offered here claims that ascertaining the radicality of a feminist group would require close empirical examination of the character of its political practices.

Discourse theory and (feminist) political analysis

In this final section, I shall provide some further indications of how the post-structuralist/post-foundationalist understandings of politics advanced in this chapter might assist the empirical sections that follow. In very general terms, as suggested above, empirical research informed by post-structuralist political theory is grounded in the unstable, unpredictable and shifting character of social and political life (Derrida, 1982: 8; 1988: 18). It works on the assumption that signifiers and objects – feminist discourse and political activism included – have no stable, fundamental essence. This is because no signifier or object can be entirely 'self-present' (Derrida, 1982: 9) but is, rather, always contaminated both by its context and by other definitions/identities that are excluded in the process of its constitution (Staten, 1985; Derrida, 1982: 24).

However, beyond these very general philosophical claims, Laclau – along with Chantal Mouffe – has, through the development of his understanding of discourse, provided a more substantial contribution to the question of how one might carry out empirical research informed by post-structuralism. Here, the notion of 'discourse' seeks to provide a means of moving beyond a rigid opposition between the linguistic and extra-linguistic (Torfing, 2005). As David Howarth has pointed out, 'in its most general sense, the concept of discourse in Laclau and Mouffe's theory captures the idea that all objects and actions are meaningful, and that their meaning is conferred by particular systems of significant differences' (2000: 101). Thus, discourse refers to the contingent processes of how we understand and perceive subjects and objects, which is not something that can be taken as self-evident.[21] But what then is the added value of using discourse theory for political analysis – in this case for the analysis of contemporary feminist politics in the UK? In opposition to a 'subsumptive' conception of political analysis – in which cases are viewed in terms of the extent to which they are apt for *subsumption* under more general laws – a discourse theoretic approach directs attention to the subtle processes of the constitution and contestation of political agendas and practices, and necessitates close analysis of the specificities of the research object. Thus, a key task for discourse theorists is to avoid imposing a false homogeneity on particular cases: instead, cases are seen as sites of contestation and potential instability.

However, to prevent the emphasis on specificity drifting into an excessive particularism, I follow Glynos and Howarth (2007) in drawing on the concept of a logic as a route into providing non-subsumptive accounts of broad social and political phenomena. Throughout this book, I use the term 'logic' as an analytical device to group together sets of discursive practices in a manner that establishes continuities across contexts, but avoids the subsumptive and reductive tendencies of mainstream political science. As David Howarth points out, 'at a most abstract level, a logic refers, first, to the rules governing a practice, institution or system of relations between objects and, secondly, to the kinds of entities (and their relations) presupposed by the operation of such rules' (2005: 323). Thus, to name a logic – such as, for instance, the logic of the market, the logic of apartheid or, in the case of the argument presented here, the logic of feminist re-emergence – entails the grouping together of heterogeneous sets of elements such that we can gain a fuller awareness of continuities across contexts. Indeed, 'logics' in this sense have been likened to the Wittgensteinian notion of rule-following (Wittgenstein, 1958: §§ 84–5; Laclau, 2005a: 117; Glynos and Howarth, 2007: 134–5). Thus, to use the parlance of logics implies not a rigid consistency but a loose level of continuity, always subject to varying degrees of reformulation. Indeed, the notion of a logic steers a course between the 'thick descriptive' particularism of classical hermeneutics, relying heavily on subjective self-interpretations on the one hand, and a subsumptive account (such as those drawn from positivism) which largely eschews subjective interpretations, on the other.

While an engagement with the subjective self-understandings of relevant actors is necessary within the context of my research, it will not be sufficient. What is also necessary is an attempt to situate actors' self-understandings within broader logics which may not always be apparent to the actors themselves. In this sense, logics are always at least partly 'citational' in character, in that the reproduction of a logic requires citational repetition, but whereby, as with Butler's account of gender citationality, the logic will be slightly altered in each instance of its citation (Butler, 1993). Thus, we may say that practices such as high-school proms, heterosexual marriage ceremonies or chatting up members of the opposite sex in a high-street nightclub are all citations of logics of heteronormativity (although will be unlikely to be framed as such by the actors involved!). However, they are *logics* rather than (causal) laws inasmuch as each citation is not performed mechanically, but requires a modicum of agentic negotiation. Thus, we may claim that all social practices have a partly agentic character, and that as a result – and perhaps in opposition to Butler – agency is present in both resistant and non-resistant practices. This line of argument thus shares Saba Mahmood's (2005) antipathy towards the tendency in some feminist theory to conflate agency and resistance. While all social practices are (partially) agentic, I argue that it takes a particular type of agency to instantiate political action. In this regard, discourse theorists typically distinguish between *political logics* which pertain to the constitution and contestation of discursive totalities, and *social logics*, pertaining to the reproduction of historically contingent sedimented discursive totalities (Howarth, 2005: 323, Laclau, 2005a: 117).

In more substantive terms, these theoretical interventions necessitate analysis of the interrelationships between the 'ambient' hegemonic context and the groups' construction of their demands, agendas and political strategies. The case studies will thus operate with the post-structuralist conception of radical politics developed in this chapter to enable a critical stance towards the organisations' practices, while the discourse-theory-based notion of 'logics' described here shall allow for a (non-subsumptive) diagnosis of continuities across contexts.

Conclusion: Rethinking 'radicality'

In Chapter 1 I sought to highlight a diversity of problems with current literatures on the state of feminism, both in the UK and transnationally. I argued that many of these works tend to operate with problematic notions of space and time, and tend to reiterate either melancholic narratives of loss and deradicalisation, on the one hand, or celebratory accounts of widespread feminist remobilisation, on the other. I maintained that to interrogate both of these sets of narratives, we require a theoretical perspective which is sensitive to context, and which is able to maintain a critical perspective towards the practices under investigation. To develop this perspective, I foregrounded the notion of 'radicalism', partly because investments in notions of radicalism are crucial to the self-understanding of different forms of feminist politics, and also because the notion of 'radicalism' links to broader notions of a movement's health, vitality and critical capacities.

In view of this, I sought to trouble the ways in which the meaning of the qualifier 'radical' is often assumed to be self-evident, and how there is little or no reflection on what the term means or what might be at stake in characterising certain practices as radical or non-radical. As we saw at the end of Chapter 1, there is a problematic tendency to assume that the signifier 'radical' – to use Austinian parlance – refers constatively to particular types of political spaces or practices. In opposition to this, I claimed that a (feminist) politics might be accurately construed as radical if it foregrounds the notions of equivalence and imagination as highlighted in this chapter. This entails a foregrounding of the performative dimension of political action, that is, the capacity for political action to contingently and unpredictably bring into existence new ways of seeing, understanding and acting in the world. A political action is therefore radical when it performatively – that is, imaginatively – names and brings into existence, through the construction of chains of equivalence, new political possibilities, new political agendas and new ways of seeing that were previously unavailable.

Recasting radicality in these terms is not an esoteric theoretical exercise, but has quite profound implications for how we might conceptualise the history of feminist politics, and indeed radical politics more generally. In contrast to accounts that typically see feminism's radicality as inhering in autonomous anti-statist mobilisations, I want to propose that what was radical about Anglo-American second-wave feminism was its 'world-building' capacity to bring into existence new ways of understanding and seeing the world. For instance, the signifier 'the personal is political' acted as an empty signifier that performatively established equivalential linkages between various concerns that had previously been conceptualised as private or linked to individual pathologies. Similarly, the casting of domestic violence as a product of gendered power relations, rather than individual pathology, was also radical in that it performatively brought into existence a new way of thinking about gender relations in broad structural terms. And, as Zerilli points out, the sex/gender distinction 'provided a form, generated by radical imagination, for giving new meaning to women's experience and opened space for thinking about how that experience would be created otherwise' (2005a: 63).

Thinking radicality in these terms allows us to reactivate the potentiality of the signifier 'radical' to assume a strong critical and evaluative function, rather than using it primarily as a purely descriptive tool constatively referring to certain types of political spaces and practices. In addition, this rethinking opens us to the possibility of radical practices emerging unpredictably in a diversity of contexts. In more general terms, however, the post-structuralist reading of feminist (radical) politics advanced here helps reclaim feminist politics as something dynamic, vibrant and boundless. It also provides a theoretical basis for a more optimistic approach to both the history of feminism and contemporary feminist politics than narratives of decline or deradicalisation, without lapsing either into complacency or a totalising account of feminist re-emergence.

What is at stake in terms of my empirical cases, therefore, is to assess what new insights come to light if a notion of radicality informed by Laclau's and Zerilli's theoretical works is deployed to assess a number of contemporary feminist activist groups in the UK. Through my analyses of the three cases – The Fawcett Society, Women's Aid and The F-word – I will show that existing accounts often underestimate the radicalism of a range of contemporary feminist practices, but will also argue that this should not occasion an uncritical perspective towards the emergence of new feminist practices.

3
The Fawcett Society:
The End of the Road for
Equality Feminism?

Within the context of a critical examination of contemporary feminism in the UK, The Fawcett Society is of particular interest. Fawcett is an influential campaigning organisation which, in its structure, orientation and political practice, significantly departs from many of the key tenets of early second-wave feminist politics. Its hierarchical structure, close links with the heart of national government, sophisticated, professional self-presentation and media-savviness could scarcely seem more at odds with 'seventies' feminist notions of autonomy, equality and anti-statism. In view of this, we could argue that Fawcett's ability to cast itself, in some respects, as the definitive pro-feminist voice in contemporary Britain could be seen as validating narratives of institutionalisation, professionalisation and deradicalisation. By contrast, the post-2005 period has witnessed an apparent increase in Fawcett's radicalism, as well as a higher public profile and a greater willingness to engage with more grass-roots feminist groups which could be read as symptomatic of a re-energised feminist movement more generally.

However, my main aim will be to navigate a course between these two extremes: I shall argue that there are two main logics at work within the organisation that intermesh to provide an altogether complex and contradictory picture. At one level, the organisation is strongly underwritten by a political logic of claim-making directed at political elites, in which – one may argue – a more radical feminist critique is absent. However, by contrast, the evenness of this logic is undermined by a logic of radicalisation that has become especially apparent since late 2005. This logic of radicalisation entails a number of practices, but it refers in particular to Fawcett's recent efforts to cast their demands within the context of a broader intervention into the public gender debate, situated within a more forthright affirmation of feminism.

This has involved a shift towards an articulation of a broader, more positive, image of feminist politics which has arguably heightened the radicality of Fawcett's political activity, via the construction of explicitly feminist counter-hegemonic chains of equivalence that bring more to the fore the antagonistic character of Fawcett's politics. While these two logics are, to a degree, in opposition to one another, they nonetheless criss-cross in diverse and unpredictable ways.

To illustrate the precise nature of this criss-crossing, I draw on three mini case studies which highlight different aspects and dimensions of Fawcett's campaigning. While in general terms my argument will favour a cautiously optimistic reading of Fawcett's post-2005 'radicalisation', this will not come at the cost of a critical stance towards several dimensions of Fawcett's current practices. Finally, the analysis of Fawcett presented here provides insights into the different ways professionalised, bureaucratised feminist NGOs operate, while also highlighting different modalities of contemporary feminist engagement both in and against the national state.

'A jolly good chat': Fawcett's ethos and historical background

The ambiguous character of the current state of The Fawcett Society is down to a number of factors: for one, Fawcett is one of the few high-profile contemporary women's organisations in the UK which campaigns across a broad range of issues (Lovenduski, 2007: 161; Predelli et al., 2008: 21), such that the forms of discourse and practice it uses vary across its campaigns.[1] In addition, Fawcett is witnessing a set of ongoing contestations about its current relationship to its historical roots. The organisation traces its roots back to the group of women who, in 1866, joined forces with John Stuart Mill to gather signatures in support of his Women's Suffrage Amendment to the reform bill (Grant, 2003). Included in this group of women was Milicent Garrett Fawcett, who campaigned for women's voting rights for 60 years until the Equal Franchise Act gave women the vote in 1928. The London and National Women's Service, as it was then known, became The Fawcett Society in 1953, in honour of Milicent Fawcett. The organisation's roots in the early turn-of-the-century liberal feminism still impact upon its ethos today. Indeed, the invocation of the organisation's historical roots is quite crucial to its general self-understanding. Milicent Fawcett's moderate and persuasive campaigning style is frequently invoked and contrasted with the more violent and radical actions of some of her contemporaries (although, as we shall see, this type of invocation of the figure of Milicent Fawcett is being used less often). To this extent, then, there is perhaps a constitutive repudiation of radicalism within The Fawcett Society. As Rachel Bell points out in an edition of the Fawcett magazine *Stop Gap*, Milicent Fawcett was a 'constitutional suffragist, who took a more moderate line through legal means' (Bell, 2005: 4).

Indeed, this repudiation of radicalism is evident in Fawcett's manufacturing of a number of slogan T-shirts, which are enthusiastically worn by members at their meetings. One of these T-shirts bears the slogan 'I've Got Milicent Tendencies', a play on words invoking the radical Trotskyist Militant Tendency of the 1980s British Labour Party. The slippage from 'Militant' to 'Milicent' implies an ironic repudiation of radicalism: its appeal is predicated on the presumption of the members' knowledge of Milicent Fawcett as a generally non-radical campaigner. It presupposes a degree of knowingness and wry humour that were certainly evident in the ripples of laughter when the T-shirt was unveiled at the 2005 Annual General Meeting (AGM). A further instance of distancing from radicalism emerged when, at the 2005 AGM, a new executive committee member announced that she was 'interested in dismantling the patriarchy'. This bold invocation of Radical Feminist discourse was instantly and instinctively taken by many to be ironic: the spontaneous laughter that erupted among the audience seemed indicative of a presumption that the lexicon of 'patriarchy' is either inappropriate or no longer relevant, or indeed both.

This distancing from radicalism ties in more broadly with an attempt to present Fawcett as safe and unthreatening to society as a whole, reinforced by the strong ethos of professionalism that pervades the organisation. Their AGMs, in their organisation and presentation, are sophisticated, clean and respectable looking, with a general mood and style reminiscent of a corporate company rather than a feminist civil society organisation. These values were reflected in their 2005 executive committee elections. Here, the values of professionalism and knowledge of marketing and public relations seemed to take precedence over commitment to, and knowledge of, feminism and women's rights. The skills and experience 'identified as most useful to Fawcett at this stage of our development' in a letter to the members included strategic planning, human resources, financial planning and accounting, experience of media and communications, PR and marketing, legal matters and IT. Furthermore, a corporate/business background was listed as a criterion which 'may also be important'.[2] Partly as a result of its emphasis on respectability and professionalism, Fawcett is now, according to Joni Lovenduski, an integral component of, and driving force behind, the relative success of 'state feminism' in the UK, being a 'highly effective feminist campaigning organisation' which has 'an admirable record of success and good, close, working relationships with other movement organisations including the single-issue or sectoral organisations' (2007: 160–1).

This began in the 1990s, and has intensified in recent years, as the organisation seeks to increase its public profile and become more effective in terms of publicity and influence within the mainstream political process. As Predelli et al. note,

> Across the 1990s, in an effort to reinvigorate the organisation, the power of the executive board was reduced (and that of the director increased) and specialist permanent sub-committees were replaced by expert groups who were called upon only when needed. The Society got involved with increasingly diverse issues around women's equality and forged alliances with a broad range of interest groups. Consequently, it gained many new members and has become a revitalised and influential force.
>
> (2008: 210)

Clearly, this emphasis on professionalism is radically at odds with the 'traditional' feminist values of autonomy and radical critique. In this respect, there are two key ways in which Fawcett's political activity can be seen as 'institutionalised' in a manner that – one may argue – renders it indicative of a broader loss of the vitality, purity and radicalism of post-1970s feminism. For one, The Fawcett Society itself is deeply institutionalised, with a distinctly hierarchical organisational structure. Fawcett has a director, a board of trustees (that takes ultimate responsibility for the organisation's work) plus a number of paid staff responsible for overseeing activity in specific policy areas (ibid.: 5). To some extent, Fawcett has shifted from being 'by the members for the members' (Fawcett staff member, interview, October 2005) to being very much focussed upon the staff team.

This has, in some instances, led to tensions: at both the 2005 and 2006 AGM, the issue of grass-roots involvement from members very much came to the fore. On both occasions, attendees expressed concerns about the lack of input (other than financial) by members into the policy of the organisation, and felt that members' skills were not sufficiently utilised (although at the 2008 AGM, this appeared to have been offset somewhat through focus groups with members concerning campaigning priorities). During both the 2005 and 2006 AGMs it was possible to detect a degree of resentment arising from some members' perception that they were viewed by staff as simply a source of income and nothing more.[3] Indeed, one had a sense that some members' commitment to a more egalitarian mode of feminist organisation motivated their underlying quibbles towards Fawcett's hierarchical structure.

However, a second, and perhaps more important, dimension of The Fawcett Society's institutionalised character is the centrality that it affords to political engagement with national state institutions. Throughout Fawcett's history, and as alluded to above, the pursuit of legislative change has been absolutely crucial to its political activity. In so doing, it is keen to highlight how it has, perhaps partly through its repudiation of radicalism, built up a reputation as an articulate and respectable campaigning organisation with strong links to a number of established political actors and institutions. This attempt to work with, and influence, established political institutions, is absolutely essential to Fawcett and also appears to be a source of significant organisational pride (Katherine Rake, interview, November 2006). Indeed, several staff members have been keen to stress the organisations' close links with certain key actors within government (Grant, 1999): they have referred to how a key task for Fawcett is to identify people within government who are sympathetic to their cause, and to use this as a means to further their aims. As one staff member pointed out in an interview: 'partly because they see us as credible, in terms of the research that we do, and the policy work we do is evidence based .... that's the reason we have that kind of [reputation]' (Fawcett staff member, interview, October 2005).

Rather than seeing the 1997–2010 Labour administration as hostile to their cause, Fawcett viewed the immediate post-1997 political climate in the UK as brimming with possibilities for pro-feminist reform. On this matter one staff member commented as follows:

> I think the government's agenda has given us much more of a chance to get in there and have them listen to us because with the work I'm doing concerned with improving women's productivity, and the concern with child poverty, ... these are issues we can link in with, and we can use our research to prove the connections between the government's agenda and our agenda, and so I think they're definitely listening. Whether they're actually doing anything is a big question, for example around pensions we've managed to get women pensioners right up there onto the policy and political agenda, to the extent that the current and previous secretary of state for work and

pensions have declared it a 'scandal', that is, the situation with the pensions, but we haven't managed to get action, a commitment yet. I think they're listening, they're saying the right things in my work area, but we're not yet seeing the changes we'd like to see.

(Fawcett staff member, interview, October 2005)

Thus, Fawcett's view of the 1997–2010 Labour government was neither defeatist nor naïvely optimistic: there was clearly a degree of frustration when the government neglected to be as proactive as hoped for on particular issues. However, this should not detract attention from the centrality Fawcett afforded to working *with* rather than against the 1997–2010 Labour administration. Indeed, at the start of the 2005 AGM, the acting director Catherine Hellicar was determined to stress how 'negotiations with MPs and other people in government are making a *real* difference', and that Fawcett are exercising influence 'where it really matters' (Catherine Hellicar, Fawcett AGM, 10/09/05). Furthermore, during an overview of the organisation's achievements for 2006, the then director Katherine Rake[4] was keen to stress the continued centrality of engagement with MPs to the organisation's work: she noted that she was particularly pleased to have had face-to-face meetings and established a good rapport with both David Cameron and Menzies Campbell, the then new leaders of the Conservatives and the Liberal Democrats respectively (Katherine Rake, Fawcett AGM, 09/09/06). Furthermore, she was also delighted by former home secretary Charles Clarke's praise for the organisation, who noted that Fawcett had made 'real change' in terms of women and the criminal justice system and had 'welcomed their continual probing' (ibid.). Similarly, at the 2005 AGM, Kate Bellamy, then the Society's senior policy officer for economic inequality, reported on how, during a meeting with David Blunkett (at the time the British Secretary of State for Work and Pensions), he 'agreed with everything they said' and they ended up having a 'jolly good chat' (Kate Bellamy, AGM, 10/09/05). Therefore, one gets a very strong sense of the centrality of Fawcett's rapport with certain sections of the New Labour administration, which in turn seems to be something of which they are extremely proud.

Fawcett attribute the establishment of this close rapport largely to their strong adherence to the pragmatic use of knowledge and evidence to back up its political claims. One of Fawcett's key strategies is the production of detailed and glossy reports detailing, usually with statistics, current issues of concern to women in the UK. These are then used as platforms for the issuing of press releases demanding particular policy changes. In the majority of cases, Fawcett consider the use of detailed quantitative research to be the most effective means of campaigning. Fawcett president Jenni Murray highlights the significance of this: she draws attention to how 'we continue to use reasoned argument and always combine our passion for equality between women and men with clear facts and figures to back it up' (Murray, 2003: 3). Thus, Fawcett's presentation of itself as respectable and sensible ties in very closely with the importance it attaches to the use of evidence and the production of knowledge, which again refers back to the legacy of Milicent Fawcett. According to Rachel Bell, 'her approach was entirely logical and sensible. Her mind was described as "mathematical" and "unsentimental"' (Bell, 2005: 4). Crucial here, however, is that the production of evidence is tied to the presumed force of an argument supported by strong numerical data.

A number of critical comments need to be made at this stage. For one, Fawcett's overall approach arguably renders it complicit with a number of hegemonic logics, perhaps giving rise to question marks over the organisation's radicalism. For one, the invocation of the legacy of Milicent Fawcett is invariably used to distance the organisation from the more radical and threatening dimensions of Fawcett's political aims, which seems to invoke the figure of the 'threatening' radical feminist forcibly denounced in post-feminist discourse. However, as I shall argue subsequently, the organisation has made moves away from this disidentification with the more radical figure of the feminist.

More significant here, however, is the way in which the general background and ethos of the organisation might be seen as tying in with a reparative mode of doing politics, in line with what – as we saw in Chapter 2 – Hannah Arendt and Linda Zerilli understand as the domestication of the political to the social. The lack of engagement with members, and its very intense focus on legislative change is such that perhaps here feminism is reduced to a process of making appeals on behalf of women to the dominant political apparatus. Furthermore, the emphasis on the use of evidence again seems to drift towards an understanding of evidence-based claims as sufficient for a feminist politics. While what we do have is evidence in favour of the continuing existence of gender inequality, what we at first seem to lack are imaginative articulations of alternative visions of womanhood, or alternative visions of political activity. Instead, feminist politics – in this instance – seems to be narrowed down to a process of interaction between the small number of Fawcett staff and those in positions of power within established political institutions. To some degree, the distancing from radicalism, the emphasis on professionalism, the use of evidence and the willingness to work with the current government all tie into a general complicity with a liberal reparative political logic such that current inequalities are seen as mere aberrations in need of redress.[5] Using Laclauian parlance, one could say that Fawcett primarily operates along what we might call a logic of difference (Laclau and Mouffe, 2001: 130). In this case, what is operative is a set of differential demands – around, for instance, childcare, work-life balance, women's political representation – addressed largely in their particularity such that there is only a weak antagonistic frontier between Fawcett and the establishment. Indeed, in recent years, Fawcett's campaigning has largely been structured around the empty signifier of 'gender equality', a term that arguably inspires less antagonism, less threat and less affective investment than the signifier 'feminism'.

However, I want to argue that while aspects of Fawcett's basic ethos and orientation tie in with a reparative political logic, a more detailed examination of their policy goals reveals a more ambitious and radical agenda peeking through. In the following sections, I interrogate whether the logic of reparation and complicity with – to use Arendtian terminology – the social question, which seem at first glance to be quite dominant, do in fact adequately characterise Fawcett's campaigning *in toto*. I do this by looking at three case studies of aspects of Fawcett's practices. First, I address their work on the representation and participation of women in mainstream political institutions, in which their complicity with a reparative, claim-making logic is most apparent (but by no means absolute). Second, I address their work on childcare and work-life balance, in which an ambiguous picture prevails, such that a complicity with a logic of reparation is periodically broken up by appeals to a much more radical transformative agenda. Finally, I look in greater detail at the organisation's recent attempts to address much more explicitly the question of 'feminism' within the public sphere. Here, I argue that the more radical dimensions of Fawcett's politics come to the fore in ways which retroactively complexify the more 'complicit' aspects of Fawcett's political activity.

The question of women's political participation and representation

The perception of The Fawcett Society as complicit with a number of existing hegemonic logics is in some senses reinforced by its stance concerning the question of women's representation in established

British political institutions. Throughout Fawcett's work on the matter, better political representation for women (especially at national level) is often seen as *the* definitive goal for the organisation – arguably opening them up to the charge of neglecting to offer more substantive visions of gender relations beyond a simple increase in political representation. To begin, let us look at the summer 2005 edition of *Towards Equality* (the organisation's magazine, relaunched in 2006 as *Stop Gap*), which details the background to the publication of a report on black and minority ethnic (BME) women in the UK. The magazine opens with a piece by Sue Tiballs, the then chair of The Fawcett Society, titled 'Representation is the key', which argues strongly for the need for institutional means to allow for greater political representation of BME women. She concludes by drawing attention to how

> Fawcett, of course, has its roots in the campaign for women's right to the vote and our battles to ensure the equal representation of women in Parliament and that MPs listen to women's concerns continue ... Milicent Fawcett may have started her campaign back in 1866, but the work of her society is just as relevant when it comes to meeting the needs of today's women in the UK.
>
> (Tiballs, 2005: 3)

Indeed, the proposed solution to the problems facing BME women in the UK at present is to press for greater representation in political institutions (ibid.: 3). This, one could say, all serves to indicate how Fawcett is in some senses complicit with – following Arendt and Zerilli – the domestication of politics to 'the social'. Rather than offering alternative visions of the political involvement of women from ethnic minorities, or making explicit connections/equivalences between feminist concerns and anti-racism, the issue is reduced to a question of institutional reforms.

Throughout Fawcett's work on this issue, there is an underlying assumption that the British electoral system as it stands is a worthwhile and legitimate means of engaging politically, based upon the further assumption that gender biases and the system's apparent lack of responsiveness to women voters are contingent rather than essential features of the current political system.[6] This point is very much brought to the fore in the autumn 2004 edition of *Towards Equality* which, along with short contributions from Gordon Brown (then Chancellor of the Exchequer), Eleanor Laing (then Shadow Minister for Women) and Charles Kennedy (then leader of the Liberal Democrats), presents a 'Manifesto for Equality' demanding various policies to combat continuing gender inequalities (Fawcett Society, 2004a: 6–10). In this document, the emphasis is very much on ensuring that the electoral system becomes more responsive to women voters' wishes, by encouraging women to question their candidates and vote accordingly, and by making a series of pro-feminist demands directed at parliamentary candidates. Thus, the stress is on the *content* of the demands, implicitly accepting the institutional *form* in which the demands are made. There is no discussion, or indeed acknowledgement of, whether there might be limitations to directing their political demands at the institutions of the national state, as opposed to using either non-institutional or less conventional institutional channels for making political demands. It assumes that if enough force is applied within the system as it stands, then eventually it will give way and become more sensitive to women voters' wishes. This is further reinforced by the cover of the spring 2005 edition of *Towards Equality* which boldly states 'a woman's place is at the ballot box'. My claim is not that pushing for reform in terms of political representation at Westminster is illegitimate, but rather that the foregrounding of women's political participation and representation as central gives the impression at some level that it is seen by Fawcett as sufficient.

Furthermore, the bulk of The Fawcett Society's demands in this area are imbued with what might be described as Schumpeterian assumptions concerning the nature of interactions between voters and politicians. In the editorial to the spring 2005 edition of *Towards Equality*, then Fawcett director Katherine Rake notes that 'as women are responsible for the bulk of child and elder care, it is little wonder that taking all ages and classes of women together, the number one priority is healthcare and also on the agenda is work-life balance' (Rake, 2005: 3), an assertion which seems to implicitly assume that women voters vote rationally in view of their interests, which are implicitly seen as self-evident. The other side of this is that a similar model of political behaviour is assumed to apply to politicians. The editorial of the autumn 2004 edition of *Towards Equality* is titled 'Women's Votes: The Key to Electoral Success' (Rake, 2004), working on the assumption that it is within politicians' interests to modify their policy programmes to make them more attractive to women voters. This perhaps explains why the organisation has such faith in the ability of the existing British electoral system to respond to the demands of women voters. If the process of electoral bargaining is assumed to be a process of interaction between two groups of rational actors whereby politicians 'buy' votes from voters, then, logically, it can be assumed that politicians can and will respond to the wishes of women voters, so long as these wishes are articulated with sufficient clarity. This is further reinforced by the way in which Rake draws attention to the fact that women often tend to be floating voters,[7] and that turnout is low among women, and as such there are many potential votes to be won if politicians were to adopt policies which were more attractive to women (ibid.: 3). A similar argument is made in a report on older women voters, who, as Fawcett point out, constitute a significant percentage of the electorate and also tend to be floating voters (Fawcett Society, 2005d: 4).

Thus, Fawcett's political claims for greater sensitivity to women voters' wishes often seem to be predicated on a somewhat utilitarian account of doing politics. They are based on an argument for women's political representation on the basis of broader social utility, inasmuch as it is focussed on highlighting how it is in the electoral interests of political elites to address these issues. As a result, the spring 2005 edition of *Towards Equality* has a rather lethargic, almost unthreatening appeal to it: we have logical, articulate articles, but framed in a manner which seems somehow safe and unchallenging. At its blandest, Fawcett could be seen as an organisation which is professional, well-presented but, in seeking political reform largely within, rather than against established political institutions, it avoids the necessarily 'troubling' dimensions of a more radical conception of feminist politics.

Overall, the bulk of Fawcett's work on the question of political representation does, to a degree, tie in with a reparative logic in which appeals are made to political elites to instigate legislative/institutional change to enact particular feminist demands. To this extent, Fawcett could be seen as non-radical in both the traditional sense (given its institutionalised and hierarchical structure) and also in the sense delineated in Chapter 2. However, I want to complexify this view: the reparative political logic within The Fawcett Society's work is by no means an even process. At some level, there is a certain blandness to Fawcett's work on this issue, arguably most evident in the professional yet rather cold pages of *Towards Equality*. Despite this, at both the 2005 and 2006 AGMs there was a palpable determination concerning this issue, a real sense of affective commitment to the question of women's political representation. Notable in this regard was the 2005 AGM, at which a keynote speech was delivered by the then Conservative Party chair Theresa May, who argued strongly for the need to use special measures to increase the number of Conservative women MPs. This speech was met with thunderous applause and Sue Tibballs, the then chair of Fawcett, said in no uncertain terms 'we wholeheartedly support you'. And yet, how is one to read this? At one level, the very fact that a representative from a political party with a historically very poor record on women's welfare was asked to speak could be taken as symptomatic of Fawcett's lack of a radical agenda. On another level, however, the fact that the bulk of the Fawcett support appears to have little sympathy with the Conservative Party, and yet still Theresa May was well received, could be seen as indicative of the level of commitment and determination on this issue.

Indeed, on the occasions when Katherine Rake has spoken more in depth about the issue of women's political representation, there is something of a shift away from the rather bland, utilitarian feel of some of their written materials on the subject. Rake's commitment and determination on the issue is instantly noticeable: women's political representation is presented not so much as an end in itself, but as part of a broader agenda for the successful pursuit of women's rights. On the campaign to increase the number of women MPs, Rake has commented, 'it's a very institutional view in a way, but our view for the long term is that ... more women in positions of power matters because it's a fairness issue but also the substantive difference they do make when they're there, and I think that's very much been demonstrated at Westminster over the last few years' (Katherine Rake, interview, November 2006). Here, it seems, there is genuine passion and belief in the efficacy of increasing the number of female MPs as a means of achieving substantive change, something which is lacking, or at best elusive, in much of Fawcett's written material on the issue. Notable also is the organisation's pride for the successes it has effected in this area. In an interview, Rake was keen to point out the pride she felt when David Cameron, within minutes of accepting the leadership of the Conservative Party, mentioned the need to promote more women candidates. This, she argued, was indicative of a shifting discursive terrain in terms of the acceptability of the need to promote women candidates for parliamentary elections.[8]

Similar ambiguities come to the fore in Fawcett's explicit calls for the introduction of positive action measures[9] to increase the number of women MPs. Such moves are necessary, Rake argues, because women still suffer widespread discrimination: 'discrimination against women is to be found across all parties and is institutionalised throughout the selection process' (Rake, 2003a: 1). Furthermore, Lovenduski, Campbell and Childs (2005: 4) point out in *Towards Equality* that women's poor prospects for winning seats may arise from decisions made at constituency level where more conservative views on gender and political participation may be prevalent. While I noted at the outset that The Fawcett Society does not explicitly foreground an overarching analysis of women's oppression at a 'systemic' level, it nonetheless invokes a notion of systemic discrimination within the selection procedures for parliamentary candidates as a justification for 'positive action' measures.

This captures a certain ambiguity that pervades almost all of the Fawcett literature on the question of women and political representation. There is an uneven oscillation between a general acceptance of the basic structure of British political institutions, on the one hand, and a more determined and committed effort to offer a more radical vision of an altogether different mode of thinking about political institutions, on the other. This latter dimension has come to the fore in some radio interviews with Katherine Rake. In a piece on the BBC website, she describes how 'we still have a system of man-made politics', grounded upon the fact that 'differences between men and women are some of the most deeply entrenched in our society', and consequently argues that discrimination against women is deeply entrenched into the British political system in ways which are not always visible (Rake, 2003b). This in turn might suggest that the disjuncture between more radical and more modest visions of political transformation may be reflective of a difference between Fawcett's official literature (which may be presented as politically fairly modest, for pragmatic reasons), and the more radical commitments of individual key players within the organisation. Overall, these contradictory forces mesh together to create a series of intersections in Fawcett's work between reparative, institutionalised forms of political practice, and what we might term a logic of radicalisation in which a more transformative agenda is present, though not always made explicit.

The politics of childcare and work-life balance

In terms of The Fawcett Society's orientation towards the question of childcare and work-life balance, once again there is an oscillation between a fairly modest set of proposals governed by a reparative political logic, on the one hand, and an embryonic vision of a broader, more 'troubling' vision of work-life balance, on the other. Arguably, the centrepiece of The Fawcett Society's discourse on these issues is that relating to their proposals on the relationship between parenting and work. Here, the unifying thread concerns the contestation of what Fawcett sees as the preponderance of an excessively meritocratic, paid work-based discourse that undermines both women and men's scope for autonomy in the spheres of childcare and parenting. Fawcett have made a number of key demands on these issues. The first is the demand for a broadening of the scope for new parents to have the right to work part time. As it stands, new parents have the right to *request* that they work part time in order to spend more time with their children, whereas Fawcett argues that there should be a right for the request to be granted. It notes that 'in particular allowing women to combine paid work with spending time with their children is a good way of encouraging women to continue their attachment to the labour market, whilst allowing fathers the right to work part-time would encourage men to share caring responsibilities' (Fawcett Society, 2001b: 1). Thus, not only would such a proposal have an intrinsic value, in that it would allow new parents to spend more time with their children, but it would also carry an instrumental value of preventing women from becoming too detached from the labour market while challenging the hegemonic conception of the woman as the main carer of children. This latter aspect is crucial, for as its stands women in the UK have some legal means to reduce their working hours via the Sex Discrimination Act, whereas fathers have no legal entitlements in this area, and as such gender role stereotypes are reinforced by these institutional arrangements which characterise the mother as the main carer.

In addition, the adoption of the right to more flexible working hours would, Fawcett argues, have further positive repercussions for the pursuit of gender equality. Part-time jobs are more common in 'feminised' sectors of work, which tend to be seen as less skilled, with lower status and are consequently not as well paid as 'men's work'. In light of this, as Fawcett point out, 'tackling this issue and encouraging flexible working to permeate all occupations and at all levels will be vital if the government is committed to enabling women to combine their work and caring responsibilities' (ibid.: 3). Thus, if flexible work permeated all strata of society, then there would be less of a structural imperative for women to be engaged in flexible, low paid, menial tasks, and would also potentially result in the degendering of care as men would have fewer structural impediments to participation in the care of dependents (see also Fawcett Society, 2001c).

In addition to the issue of flexible working hours, Fawcett is also keen to press the issue of improved state childcare provision, typically cast as a demand for a shift towards a more 'Nordic' model of state childcare. Indeed, it is the invocation of a less aggressively meritocratic Scandinavian-style welfarism that seems to pervade almost all of The Fawcett Society literature:[10] one staff member acknowledged in an interview that the economic models of countries such as Denmark and Sweden provide a template for the type of welfare-state regime Fawcett is seeking to move towards (interview with Fawcett staff member, October 2005).

Certainly, their proposals concerning childcare fit this model. In their 'Manifesto for Equality' published just prior to the 2005 general election, Fawcett assert that their vision is 'of a universal childcare service providing quality, affordable and flexible care'. Here, they call for 'a Children's Centre in every community meeting the needs of all children, providing quality care by well-trained and well-rewarded childcare professionals at an affordable price', as well as the demand mentioned earlier that the childcare tax credit meet 90 per cent of childcare costs for poor families (Fawcett Society, 2004a: 9). The demand for universal childcare is certainly an ambitious one, given the relative lack of success of childcare campaigns in the UK in previous decades (Lovenduski and Randall, 1993: 299) and the fact that it would require quite a profound shift towards a more welfare-state-centred mode of liberal democracy in the UK.

In a 2005 report on the continued existence of economic gender disparities, we find what is perhaps Fawcett's most explicit appeal to a Scandinavian style welfare-state system as a basis for childcare policy. It reads,

> Britain has a liberal welfare state that has traditionally been reluctant to intervene in the private sphere or to favour any one family model over another. It is also a relatively small welfare state, and while more extensive welfare states do not necessarily promote gender equality, lower levels of public spending do mean a reduced scope for redistribution from men to women to compensate for their caring, and insufficient funds to provide substitution for care (as is found, for example, in the generously funded Swedish universal childcare system). The UK government has tended to rely on market led solutions to care, meaning a scarce supply of childcare and other caring services as well as serious issues of affordability.
>
> (Bellamy and Rake, 2005:6)

The invocation of a Scandinavian-style welfare-state model is also very much to the fore in Fawcett's literature on the politics of fatherhood and paternity leave, in which Fawcett argues that changes in policy on, and perception of, fatherhood are essential dimensions of a move towards gender equality. As Fawcett's 'Manifesto for Equality' points out, 'very brief paternity leave, combined with lengthier unpaid maternity leave, reinforces gender stereotypes and means many fathers cannot afford to share the pleasures and burdens of being a new parent' (Fawcett Society, 2004a: 8; see also Burgess, 2002). In light of this, Fawcett demands that paternity leave be extended to six weeks combined with the introduction of earnings-related maternity pay, presumably to provide a financial incentive for fathers to take advantage of paternity leave. The 'facts' box on the same page draws attention to how fathers in Sweden are entitled to 12 weeks' paternity leave, compared to just two in the UK (ibid.: 8). Thus, Fawcett's proposals are relatively modest, in that they suggest relatively small-scale changes. However, this contrasts with the invocation of a rather more large-scale Scandinavian welfare-statist imaginary: although on the issue of paternity leave Fawcett does not propose at this stage bringing UK policy into line with Swedish policy, the latter nonetheless acts as a discursive horizon into which Fawcett's demands are inscribed.

In addition, the foregrounding of a shift in popular perceptions of the role of fathers and fatherhood has been a central tenet of The Fawcett Society's recent literature. Here, the central thrust of their argument is that prevalent social norms and expectations (in which the male breadwinner role still predominates) are detrimental to the family life of *both* mothers and fathers. This comes to the fore in the summer 2004 edition of *Towards Equality*, in which Fawcett announce that they are to join forces with the pressure group Fathers Direct to work together on issues of gender equality within the family. Katherine Rake contends that 'both organisations share a belief that men need to be involved in feminist campaigns' (Fisher and Rake, 2004: 3), on the understanding that 'an equal sharing of the breadwinning and caring roles is essential if we are to eradicate gender inequalities in employment, pay and pensions' (ibid.: 3). In a short piece in the same edition of *Towards Equality*, the director of Fathers Direct, Duncan Fisher, reiterates this need for co-operation on the basis of the restrictive character of social norms and expectations reinforced by policy. He writes that 'when he [the father] protests that he is forced into the traditional breadwinner role, because his partner cannot match his earning power because of her lower pay, gendered employment and other inequalities, we hear fresh voices reinvigorating established grievances'. He continues, 'but this broadening of the gender debate, far from obscuring feminist critiques should only strengthen and illuminate them anew' (ibid.: 3).

In this vein, Fawcett enthusiastically welcomed the UK government's 2005 proposals to offer greater flexibility for maternity and paternity leave, where paid maternity leave was extended to nine months and fathers became entitled to take the last three months off if the mother returned to work (Fawcett Society, 2005b). However, Fawcett claims that this is unlikely to significantly change the existing childcare regime in practice, as employers are generally unsupportive of men's caring and also because financial disparities between men and women are such that it usually makes economic sense for the woman to take the leave (ibid.). Again, on this issue, political engagement is restricted to putting pressure on those in power, without offering a more tangible vision of what a new childcare system may look like. Granted, Fawcett are prolific in their publication of press releases, but their press release on this particular issue, as with others, has a somewhat professional yet dry tone to it. Furthermore, their political discourse emphasises less a systemic critique of gender relations and more a need to overcome existing normative and institutional barriers to the pursuit of liberal freedom. There is therefore something of a teleological dimension to their discourse: it implicitly assumes that if elements *within* liberal democratic discourse are successfully appropriated, then it will be possible to realise gender equality more widely (and thus liberal democracy will be rid of its anachronistic 'perversions').

However, this is offset somewhat by the more radical vision of an altogether different childcare regime which emerges periodically. This comes to the fore in Fawcett's articulation of the four principles which it argues should govern the provision of childcare. These are: first, it must foreground the importance of supporting children and their families; second, it must ensure that women are not penalised for the unpaid caring work they undertake; third, it must recognise that women are still more likely to take on caring responsibilities and acknowledge the issues this raises for them, while encouraging the sharing of responsibilities between partners; and fourth, it must focus on increasing women's access to household income (Fawcett Society, 2001a: 2). These proposals suggest quite a radical approach to the provision of childcare, strongly resistant to the market-driven logics of contemporary hegemonic understandings of childcare. However, the precise content of this seemingly more radical vision is not really made explicit: indeed, these proposals lurks unobtrusively in the middle of a rather dry document about tax credits.[11]

Overall, the issue of childcare and parental leave embodies a number of the ambiguities in The Fawcett Society's political practice. There can be little doubt that, as with other issues, Fawcett's tactics on this matter depart significantly from the classic Anglo-American 'second-wave' values of autonomy and purity described in the opening chapter: the willing and enthusiastic engagement with both state institutions and fathers' rights organisations would, from the perspective of a feminist 'politics of purity', be seen as severely compromising the integrity of the feminist message, due to the potentially contaminatory effects of the non-feminist actors involved. By contrast, I want to claim that the more troubling aspects of Fawcett's practices arise not so much the simple fact that it engages with the state/fathers' rights groups etc., but the manner in which it does so. Fawcett's positioning of itself as an 'expert' organisation in the field of gender equality is such that it clearly does occupy a unique position in terms of the respect it garners from those in positions of political power. However, this renders it somewhat complicit with a model of politics in which specific interest groups appeal to political elites to further their agenda. The bulk of Fawcett's campaigning on the issue of childcare takes the form of press releases and meetings with politicians, civil servants etc. which, for the most part, address specific issues *in their particularity*. This means that there is a danger that one loses sight of the broader, more transformative agenda that perhaps motivates the particular demands. Recall the example in Chapter 2 of the Laclauian moment of radicalisation in which a woman, experiencing sexual harassment at work, establishes equivalential linkages with other grievances. In terms of Fawcett's campaigning on childcare, this moment of radicalisation is, in a sense, lacking: the demands are expressed in their particularity rather than being cast as part of a broader transformative agenda. This might be partly explainable by the absence of a strong empty signifier that binds the demands together. While 'gender equality' does act as something of an empty signifier, it remains rather weak. This is because first, the status of Fawcett's demands as tied to a progressive gender politics is not always foregrounded and, second, in comparison to a signifier such as 'feminism', 'gender equality' is rather dry, and seems to lack the power to foster strong affective identifications among the actors involved (this will become clear in the following section).

However, when taken together, Fawcett's proposals concerning childcare and work-life balance imply a need for a more fundamental shift in the structure of hegemonic understandings of the issues at stake. Their proposals are motivated by a different understanding of childcare entailing a move towards a more Nordic welfare-state model, a greater valuing of taking time off from work to look after children, a degendering of dominant understandings of childcare and, implicitly, a shift towards a less work-centred and less aggressively meritocratic socio-economic structure. To this end, as with Fawcett's campaigning on women's political representation, there is an element of radical political imagination at work. Their proposals do not simply stop at the level of expressing singular demands to political elites, but contain within them elements of an embryonic 'figure of the newly thinkable' which offers us a different vision of various aspects of contemporary gender relations. Thus, rather than characterising Fawcett as an essentially liberal reformist organisation without a radical agenda, I want to propose that there are more disruptive, contestatory elements which come to the fore periodically. In other words, while a reparative political logic prevails, this is punctuated and rendered uneven by an incipient logic of radicalisation which manifests itself from time to time.

Fawcett's rebranding and its aftermath

Thus far I have, for the most part, highlighted the ways in which Fawcett's political discourse and practices render it complicit with a number of hegemonic logics, in particular a reparative political logic in line with what, in the opening chapter, I called the 'domestication of politics to the social'. However, in this section I want to partly undermine this line of argument by drawing attention to what might appear to be a fairly dramatic recent change of tack on the part of the organisation. In 2005, Fawcett underwent a rebranding, involving a change of logo, a significant change in the content and layout of their magazine, and a general change in the overall mood of the organisation. Most significantly, however, the organisation's campaigning strategy has seen something of a shift away from simple negotiation with those in positions of power, to a much more forthright and determined engagement across the public sphere. There are three different dimensions to this engagement which I have singled out as being particularly crucial, and I shall look at each of these in turn. These are, first (and most importantly), a more explicit affirmation of, and engagement with, the signifier 'feminism'; second, a much more concerted effort to co-operate with a range of grass-root feminist organisations; and third, a foregrounding of issues concerning ethnic minority women. While some aspects of these new practices from Fawcett are problematic, I argue that they can nonetheless be read as a radicalising of Fawcett's agenda and as symptomatic of a renewed energy and confidence not only within The Fawcett Society, but perhaps within UK-based feminism as a whole. This is reflected in a recent surge in The Fawcett Society membership, as well as, according to Katherine Rake, achieving a media profile 'like never before' (Rake, 2008b: 3), not least due to Rake receiving an OBE for services to equal opportunities.[12] The organisation's recent successes are, she argues, 'the result of a year's work changing our tone and approach' (ibid.: 3). The rest of the chapter shall be devoted to exploring and explaining the different dimensions of these changes.

(1) The signifier 'feminism'

Perhaps the most obvious dimension of this apparent radicalisation is Fawcett's more overtly affirmative relationship to the signifier 'feminism'. In several instances, Fawcett have highlighted the need for a 'third wave' of feminism, and, to use Laclauian parlance, have persistently used either 'feminism' or sometimes 'third-wave feminism' as empty signifiers through which to link together their various political demands and projects. I want to argue that this does represent a significant moment of radicalisation, in which the radical, contestatory dimensions of Fawcett's practices are now much more central to their *modus operandi*. While dramatic, this is not so much a complete U-turn on the part of Fawcett: instead, it is a case of the radicality of its agenda being made more explicit. It is therefore a change of focus rather than a total change of direction. Crucial here is that this is not a moment of radicalisation in the sense of a return to a feminist politics of purity, but a stronger foregrounding of the creation of imaginative political articulations, and a shift to a bolder and more combative mode of engagement.

Fawcett's recent explicit engagement with the signifier 'feminism' is particularly noteworthy because, prior to 2005, there was a tangible reluctance to use the term. An examination of Fawcett publications produced prior to 2005 reveals that the signifier 'feminism' was almost never used. Instead, their demands were typically framed in terms of an appeal to 'justice', 'fairness' or 'equality'. When I asked about the role of feminism at the 2005 AGM, it was explained that the term 'feminism' was used infrequently because it was perceived negatively in focus groups the organisation had conducted, and was described as 'not the core approach' (Jenny Westaway, AGM, 10/09/05). In interviews with Fawcett staff in 2005, the term was described as being confusing, largely due to its contested meanings. Furthermore, one staff member regarded the term as unhelpful in terms of policy, inasmuch as politicians and civil servants may be unclear about what is meant by a feminist agenda for this or that policy area (interview with Fawcett staff member, October 2005). Here, Fawcett's partial disidentification with feminism ties in with its general tendency to present itself as relatively safe and unthreatening.

However, towards the end of 2005 and into 2006 this sense of safeness and disidentification with feminism withered away and was replaced by a new image and self-presentation. This included a new logo, much more striking than the old one, bearing the slogan 'Fawcett: closing the inequality gap since 1866', and a relaunching of the magazine under the name *Stop Gap*, such that it is now a bolder, and yet more playful, publication than its predecessor. Partly motivating this change of tactic, according to one staff member, was that 'what's coming with this new image is being a little bit more direct, and being a little bit more 'gloves off', and with a stronger tone of voice, a little bit less 'polite' (interview with Fawcett staff member, October 2005). This, I think, is crucial: it is indicative of a reflexive awareness on the part of Fawcett that its self-presentation had hitherto been somewhat 'safe' and unthreatening, so there was a deliberate attempt to refashion itself as a bolder and more determined organisation, in part connected to a desire to link with emergent forms of grass-roots feminist politics (a theme explored later in the chapter).

The adoption of a more 'gloves off' approach is particularly apparent in several articles in *Stop Gap* in the 2008–9 period in which it is possible to detect a less overtly identificatory relation to the figure of Milicent Fawcett. In particular, the spring 2008 issue is dedicated to the question of women and the vote. In the editorial, Rake provides a brief overview of the role of both Milicent Fawcett's National Union of Women's Suffrage Societies and Emmeline Pankhurst's Women's Social and Political Union, the latter of which advocated violent direct action in the struggle for women's suffrage (Rake, 2008a: 3). While prior to 2005 Fawcett had always explicitly aligned itself with the former, in the editorial Rake neglects to explicitly align the contemporary Fawcett Society with either strand and a feature article by Alison Clarke (2008) on the same issue praises the legacy of both strands of activism. This subtle realignment of Fawcett's relationship to the competing strands of 'first-wave' feminism can be read as further indication of Fawcett's attempt to assert its affinity with both activist and legislation-based strands of feminist politics.

All this has occurred alongside a sudden willingness on Fawcett's part to affirm feminism boldly and unashamedly. In her speech at the 2006 AGM, Katherine Rake ran through Fawcett's achievements over the preceding 12 months and spoke with pride of how Fawcett have found a new, clear and bold voice from which to enter into the debate around feminism emphatically and unapologetically – 'with all guns blazing', as she put it (Katherine Rake, AGM, 10/09/06). A year later, such sentiments had grown stronger still: writing in the editorial to the autumn 2007 edition of *Stop Gap*, Rake wrote that 'feminism speaks with a new voice, and so does Fawcett. We are bolder, stronger, and we are calling for action now' (Rake, 2007: 3), while in spring 2009 she writes, 'it is wonderful to witness a renewed interest in activism, and the growing number of voices demanding measures to protect and promote women's rights' (Rake, 2009: 3), This explicitly situates Fawcett's renewed assertiveness within the emergence of what, in the Introduction, I called 'the New Feminist Politics'.

This reassertion began in late 2005 and had fully entered its stride with the publication of the autumn 2006 edition of *Stop Gap*, which is more or less entirely dedicated to feminism. The front cover is a striking reddish pink with 'F*******!' in large bold type at the top, with the subtitle 'Reclaim the f-word with Fawcett'. This forthright style of presentation is radically out of character with Fawcett's earlier, safer and more professional mode of self-presentation. Inside the magazine, we find a profile of Simone de Beauvoir, a copy of an article Katherine Rake wrote for left-of-centre UK daily newspaper *The Guardian* about the need to reclaim feminism (about which more shortly), a page of responses to the article posted on the *Guardian Unlimited* website, an editorial by Katherine Rake about responses to the article, and, unusually for Fawcett, an article about the representation of women in men's magazines. All of this represents a shift into previously uncharted territory for Fawcett: rather than reporting on specific policy updates, these debates about feminism are perhaps indicative of a more general attempt to challenge the hegemonic context in which Fawcett operates.

For the most part, these changes appear to have been personally spearheaded by former director, Katherine Rake, but have nonetheless permeated the organisation as a whole.[13] This was apparent in a change of mood at the 2006 AGM. Both the 2005 and 2006 AGMs took place in the same room, and were both characterised by an air of professionalism. However, the 2005 AGM was distinctly calm and safe: there was general approval among the audience but there was a tangible lack of real commitment and determination. The 2006 AGM, by contrast, saw a much stronger appeal to the members' passion and commitment. For one, all panel members were wearing the organisation's mass-marketed 'this is what a feminist looks like' T-shirts, unlike in 2005 where smart-casual attire predominated. Furthermore, throughout the AGM there were explicit invocations of Radical Feminist appeals to a shared set of values: Katherine Rake used the term 'sisterly solidarity', apparently without irony. Also, a question from the floor referred to our 'sisters' overseas, a term enthusiastically embraced by chair Michelle Mitchell in her response. Throughout, terms such as 'feminist agenda', 'we, as feminists' were used on a number of occasions. The chair then concluded the day by noting that Fawcett is united in 'our commitment as feminists' and that there is 'an exciting and radical agenda which Fawcett will take forward' (Michelle Mitchell, AGM, 9/09/06).

These efforts to rally the troops through strong appeals to the affective qualities of signifiers such as 'sisters' and 'feminism' are in stark contrast to the 2005 AGM which consisted simply of reporting and discussing particular policy issues. Indeed, the word 'feminism' was only brought up once at the 2005 meeting (by this author, enquiring into its role within the organisation's self-understanding). This change of mood was perhaps most evident in the apparent U-turn of one particular member who, during the lunch break of the 2005 AGM, accosted me and told me in no uncertain terms that Fawcett is *not* a feminist organisation but is concerned with the question of 'gender equality': there was a strong repudiation on her part of the signifier 'feminism' and its radical connotations. At the 2006 AGM, however, the very same member asked a question from the floor and highlighted the importance of, in her words, 'going out there, being feminists!'

This is indicative of a logic of radicalisation in which the invocation of the signifier 'feminism' and its use in a forthright manner is able to foster a commitment and determination which was previously lacking. It is a logic of radicalisation to the extent that it is not focussed on particular, punctual claims for this or that legislative change, but rather seeks to alter the very hegemonic conditions under which these political manoeuvres are made. It thus moves beyond a domestication of politics to the social and aims at something more ambitious and threatening. However, to fully understand this, we need to look in more detail at the specific content of Fawcett's articulation of a specifically feminist agenda.

Katherine Rake has individually spearheaded Fawcett's efforts at reclaiming feminism, most notably through the publication of an article in *The Guardian* titled 'Let's Reclaim The F-word'.[14] She argues that the popular perception of feminism as 'dungaree-clad, scary, hairy and humourless' detracts attention from feminism's serious and legitimate concerns, namely, 'that the pay gap still exists, that violence against women is at crisis levels, that women's caring roles are so undervalued, that women are still woefully underrepresented in positions of power' (Rake, 2006a). Fawcett, she says elsewhere, is ready to harness its energies to foster a 'mass lobby of women in all their diversity' and put forward a new and bold vision of feminism (Rake, 2006b). This vision, she says, is motivated by a desire to fundamentally alter the very premises of society as a whole. She writes,

> The broader feminist goals are revolutionary, but also fall into line with other social movements which are searching for new values beyond capitalist consumption. If we could create such a vision it may give us the way to engage in feminist debate without resorting to universalistic portrayals of women as helpless victims and men as demons. It may make feminism fun again, and take away the slight air of moral disapproval of certain lifestyles that has hung around feminist thought in the past. And, it might be a way of ensuring that women and men in all their diversity are included in a feminist vision.
>
> (Rake, 2006c)

Although this is a rather vague sound bite, it nonetheless contains elements of an explicit articulation of a radical vision for a feminist agenda that had previously been lacking. Here, there is explicit resistance to thinking about feminist identity in terms of what Wendy Brown calls 'wounded attachments' (1995: 52–76) and it foregrounds feminism's affinity with resisting capitalist consumption. To this extent, it represents a new, radical and positive vision of feminism with which people can identify and critically engage. Unlike Fawcett's earlier political endeavours, Rake here appears to be deliberately trying to provoke and engage people in debate. This again comes to the fore in her piece in *The Guardian* where she points out that

> feminism is not just about allowing women to lead the same lives that men have for many years; it's about changing the rules of the game, mapping out a possible future direction in which activities that do not directly contribute to further swelling the coffers of UK plc, such as caring for family and others, are valued much more highly. It's about more than tinkering at the edges – and that feels threatening to a lot of people.
>
> (Rake, 2006a: 9)

This element is crucially important and contributes to the sense of 'boldness' in Fawcett's feminist agenda: whereas previously Fawcett seemed to go out of its way to appear *unthreatening*, this element of 'threat' is very much brought to the fore. In the editorial to this edition of *Stop Gap*, Rake writes, 'that's not to say we haven't had an aggressive response from some quarters – we have. But if we are threatening established power and ways of doing things then that's inevitable' (Rake, 2006d: 3). Indeed, the hostility of some responses to Rake's article in *The Guardian* was striking. However, a number of them were published in *Stop Gap* and were briefly discussed, to much hilarity, at the 2006 AGM. Indeed, the enthusiasm with which *negative* responses were highlighted seemed to be a source of enjoyment feeding in quite strongly to the affective dimension of Fawcett members' identification with feminism.

(2) Increasing engagement with grass-roots feminist concerns

Notably, on a number of occasions Rake has used the notion of a 'third wave' to name Fawcett's new feminist agenda. Here, the notion is in large part intended to discursively situate Fawcett's new feminist agenda amidst an apparent resurgence of grass-roots feminist activism in the UK more broadly. The 'third wave', according to Rake, is not intended to denigrate the first or second wave, but instead is deployed 'quite loosely to mark a change in the amount of activism that is emerging at the moment, and the kind of discontent that is emerging, because that's all quite new, I mean I think what's interesting is that, it has elements of both first and second wave in terms of basic rights, so we need to fulfil those basic rights, so I think it moves on to some new territory as well' (Katherine Rake, interview, November 2006). Furthermore, Rake mentioned that the 'third wave' refers to how

> a lot of them [issues being discussed by contemporary feminists] are old issues but they have emerged anew, I think what we're hearing about is, I think a lot of younger women are into issues around personal safety, around body image, around the saturation of pornography in society, which are all actually old issues but I think that they have got a special urgency given what's happening, given the Internet, media and all the rest of that gives it a special push at the moment.
>
> (Ibid.)

Also, crucial to this 'third wave' of feminism, says Rake, is that it 'must include those who feminism has failed to reach in the past, such as men,[15] many ethnic minority women, and young women' (Rake, 2006a: 99).

Thus, Rake's appeal to a notion of 'third-wave feminism' is intended to mark the articulation of Fawcett's established agenda with a range of newer concerns being articulated by other grass-roots feminist groups.

It thus discursively marks something of a departure from Fawcett's traditional methods of campaigning. Rake went so far as to say that she thought that this new feminist agenda was perhaps indicative of a move beyond what she calls 'equality feminism' to a broader and more challenging agenda. This is all the more remarkable given the undoubted centrality of 'equality feminism' to Fawcett's political activity throughout its history. Nevertheless, Rake said in no uncertain terms that

> [w]e've run to the end of the road for equality-based feminism, the rules of the labour market and the rules of power have not changed and in some areas there's actually only so far as we can get within those constrictions and it may be about now to actually re-write the rules of the game, and, y'know, at that level it's about thinking about those big concepts ... the environmental movement, which is about saying do we need to look beyond the economy to the whole society and all that stuff about the balance of care and other activities, so I think that that's a distinguishing feature.
>
> (Katherine Rake, interview, November 2006)

Subsequently, she reiterated that she thought that the 'legislative framework is running out of steam', and that broader issues such as deeply entrenched cultural factors which run counter to the pursuit of gender equality need to be addressed. However, she did mention that 'that's not to forget the legislative element – I think that will continue to be the backbone of what we do, but I think it has to be accompanied by a much broader look at how organisations operate and the kind of policies they're promoting and what that means for women and their companies' (ibid.).

Thus, Fawcett's rebranding has entailed both a discursive reframing of its political activity, and a broadening of its remit so as to take on board feminist concerns being articulated outside of the organisation. There have been a diversity of ways in which Fawcett have engaged with these concerns. For instance, Fawcett were actively involved in the FEM05 and FEM 2008 conferences in Sheffield. These events consist of panel discussions involving groups and individuals covering the full breadth of UK feminism, and Kat Banyard, founder and head organiser of the FEM conferences, is now a Fawcett staff member (overseeing the 'Sexism in the City' campaign).[16] Furthermore, Fawcett helped organise, and Katherine Rake chaired, a panel discussion about the 'third wave' of feminism at a conference organised by left-of-centre pressure group Compass in 2006,[17] and held another discussion at the 2008 Compass conference on legislation concerning lap-dancing establishments.[18] Other instances of Fawcett's involvement with grass-roots feminist activism include staging a seminar on equal pay at the Capitalwoman event in London on the 2008 International Women's Day (hosted by the Greater London Authority), joining a large abortion rights demonstration in 2008; joining the London Reclaim the Night march against domestic violence; and Katherine Rake speaking on the issue of objectification of women at the Million Women Rise march in London in 2008. Furthermore, Fawcett has acknowledged and engaged with a number of forms of web-based activism: a feature article by Jo Middleton, titled 'Feminism 2.0', provided an overview of these new forms of web-based activism, and provided links to a range of feminist websites (including The F-word and the London Feminist Network) (Middleton, 2007), while a feature article in the spring 2009 issue of *Stop Gap* outlines how to start a feminist blog and describes The F-word (the subject of Chapter 5) as a 'fantastic source of inspiration'. Fawcett's senior campaigns and policy officer, Zoohra Moosa, is also now a regular blogger for The F-word.

In addition, Fawcett has mass-produced a T-shirt humorously bearing the slogan 'this is what a feminist looks like', which has proved very popular.[19] Recently, this T-shirt has become something of a centrepiece to Fawcett's overall campaigning strategy. In 2006, it launched what it called the 'Fawcett Feminist Challenge', where celebrities were asked to support feminism and Fawcett by having themselves photographed wearing the T-shirt.[20] In addition, Fawcett set up a Myspace page[21] to which people can send pictures of themselves wearing the T-shirt. This constitutes another bold, if somewhat flippant, attempt at resisting logics post-feminist disidentification, and, in pursuing these not conventionally political engagements within civil society, further represents something of a departure from Fawcett's usual style of campaigning. Furthermore, Fawcett's campaigning on the issue of feminism has not been restricted to activity within civil society but has also entailed a more robust fore-grounding of feminism in its liaisons with politicians. Fawcett conducted a series of seminars for MPs titled 'The Future of Feminism', enabling MPs to address the question of feminism and seek some level of cross-party consensus on issues to do with gender equality.

However, the most significant instance of Fawcett working alongside a grass-roots feminist organisation has perhaps been the campaign concerning the licensing of lap-dance establishments,[22] jointly spearheaded by The Fawcett Society and Object. Object is a UK-based group established in 2003 which campaigns against the 'sexual objectification

of women in the media and popular culture' (Object website, http://
www.object.org.uk/index.php/about-us, accessed 07/04/09), and, at the
time of writing, has three members of paid staff. Since 2008, as part of
Fawcett's 'Sexism and the City' campaign (aimed at tackling sexism in
the workplace), Fawcett and Object have jointly pushed for reform of
a loophole in UK legislation whereby lap-dancing clubs are licensed in
the same way as regular pubs or cafes. In this regard, Fawcett and Object
have been remarkably successful both in terms of levels of investment
in the issue by the feminist community at large, and also (partly) in
terms of legislative outcomes. The Crime and Policing Bill (passing
through parliament at the time of writing in 2009) will license lap-
dancing clubs as sex encounter venues, which would subject them to
tighter regulation and would grant local people a say on whether they
object to such an establishment opening in the vicinity of their homes.
However, Object and Fawcett have expressed grievances about how – as
things stand – the reforms presented in the bill are optional and venues
hosting lap dancing less than once a month are exempt (Object and The
Fawcett Society, 2009).

While Fawcett has worked closely with a number of established
organisations such as Age Concern and Oxfam in the recent past, the
campaign with Object represents the first instance of Fawcett campaigning alongside a new grass-roots feminist group for an extended period
of time, and is arguably reflective of Fawcett's desire to participate in,
and engage with, a resurgent feminist politics in the UK. One may
legitimately be critical of aspects of the campaign. For one, the emphasis is on legislative change and the *effects* of lap-dance establishments
on the local area, such that the voices of the lap-dancers themselves,
and concerns over their working conditions seem to be something of a
secondary concern. Second, the level of investment in the issue hovers
dangerously close to a restaging of the 'feminist sex wars' of the 1980s
(in which feminist responses to the question of pornography proved
particularly divisive, mostly in the US but also in Europe).[23] But despite
these potential problems, the campaign is – one may argue – reflective
of a renewed determination on Fawcett's part to engage with other
concerns articulated by sections of the grass-roots feminist movement,
in contrast to the rather aloof, detached style of the pre-2005 period.

(3) Fawcett's campaigning on ethnic minority women's issues

The third and final dimension of Fawcett's apparent post-2005 radicalisation relates to its increasing foregrounding of issues to do with
ethnic minority women. Since 2005, Fawcett has sought to mainstream

race-related concerns within the organisation as a whole (Predelli et al., 2008: 117), and has made campaigning on issues relevant to ethnic minority women a central part of its policy platform. Recall, in the section on women's political representation above, that Fawcett's engagement with the question of race was primarily concerned with increasing the number of ethnic minority women involved in the representative mechanisms of the national state. However, since the publication in February 2005 of their report 'Black and Ethnic Minority Women in the UK', Fawcett have pursued a much more ambitious agenda entailing an articulation of feminism with anti-racism. This has intensified following the 2007 launch of their three-year campaign 'Seeing Double', which covers the full range of the organisation's concerns, namely, money (focussing on ethnic minority women's poverty), power (focussing on political representation) and justice (focussing on ethnic minority women's experiences of the legal system). In addition, Fawcett has recently embarked upon a separate campaign called 'femocracy', which is more directly concerned with the 'political invisibility' of ethnic minority women within the formal decision-making process, and entails 'working in partnership with ethnic minority voluntary and community groups to deliver events across the UK on politics and democracy for ethnic minority women' (Fawcett Society, 2009: 5).

Consequently, Fawcett's post-2005 engagement with ethnic minority women's issues can be read as an attempt to take seriously what Fawcett's senior policy and campaigns officer Zoohra Moosa has described as a pervasive exclusion of black and ethnic minority women from policymaking (Moosa, 2008a: 3), and also to take on board how 'for many ethnic minority women, race trumps gender', an issue which the mainstream feminist movement has hitherto – she argues – 'not really grasped' (Moosa, 2008b: 74).[24] Fawcett's 'Seeing Double' campaign is thus a historically unusual instance of a sustained attempt by a white-dominated, mainstream women's organisation to fully incorporate race-related concerns into its campaigning in a manner that is thorough and imaginative, rather than merely tokenistic. Predelli et al. (2008), in their comprehensive overview of current feminist campaigning around the intersections of gender and race, draw attention to how, in general terms, the tensions between feminism and anti-racism are now less divisive and anxiety-inducing for the feminist movement as a whole than they were 20 years ago, and here Fawcett is singled out as an exemplar of this trend. They write,

> We would like to suggest that Fawcett's 'Seeing Double' project is a highly significant event, and perhaps even a turning point, both in

symbolic and in real terms. Symbolically, it signals that a mainstream and previously white-dominated feminist women's organisation has taken on board criticism which has been voiced by black feminists and black women's movement actors for more than 25 years. In real terms, it actually changes Fawcett itself as it broadens its focus and gives legitimacy to intersectional approaches to inequality. In addition, Fawcett may also be able to effect political change through its evidence-based advocacy work and lobbying on the persistent inequalities experienced by ethnic minority women.

(Predelli et al., 2008: 118)

This suggests that Fawcett's efforts to draw articulations between feminism and anti-racism in a manner that is not merely superficial and tokenistic add weight to my argument that the organisation has undergone a process of 'radicalisation' since 2005. While, in terms of membership, Fawcett remains predominantly white, the articulation of feminism and anti-racism, and the incorporation of race-related concerns into the organisation's campaigning is, one may argue, reflective of the renewed vitality, energy and confidence certainly pervading The Fawcett Society, and perhaps contemporary UK feminism as a whole.

Theorising Fawcett's rebranding

How, in general terms, can we characterise these recent developments in Fawcett's practices? At one level, these developments are truly remarkable, given that they represent a significant decentring of the legislative dimension of Fawcett's work. Consequently, I want to contend that these new practices constitute a logic of radicalisation in a number of respects. For one, consider the example of the Laclauian moment of radicalisation given in Chapter 2. In some ways, Fawcett's recent embracing of a bold feminist agenda mirrors this process. Their efforts within the context of legislative institutions yielded some successes, but there remained a degree of frustration that the broader cultural context had perhaps not significantly changed. As such, equivalences were drawn between Fawcett's legislative work and established feminist demands to do with changing power relations in the private sphere, and contemporary feminist concerns such as body image, self-harm, rape, domestic violence etc. Furthermore, these various demands have been grouped together under the 'empty signifier' of 'feminism' or sometimes 'third-wave feminism'. Unlike within The F-word (in which, as I shall argue, the signifier 'third wave' constatively refers to a specific group of women), here the signifier 'third-wave feminism' has a strong performative dimension. In naming this emergent feminist agenda as specifically 'third-wave feminist', the agenda is, in effect, brought into existence in the moment of naming. Rake is a little imprecise in terms of the precise content of the term 'third-wave feminism', and in some respects it could be argued that this is necessary if it is to maintain its capacity as an umbrella term for a set of diverse feminist demands. Indeed, in this respect, Fawcett's attempt to articulate its own agenda into a broader chain of equivalence with feminist concerns emanating from more autonomous sites (such as Object and The F-word) is, for Rake, a crucial task for Fawcett. She believes Fawcett can act as a national co-ordinator through which to bring together the concerns of various feminist groups, serving to create a more explicit debate and create a broader 'feminist consciousness' (interview, November 2006). This self-understanding of Fawcett is crucial: it implies an awareness of itself as operating in a position of considerable power and authority in terms of struggles around gender relations in the UK. Consequently, its position as a political entrepreneur, able to do the political work necessary to help create this new feminist agenda, is in some senses predicated upon the fact that it was already constituted as a key player within contemporary British gender politics.

One legitimate objection to the characterisation of Fawcett's recent activities presented here would be to say that this is simply a change in presentation, and that the core of their campaigning – the articulation of demands to political elites – has not substantially changed. This is to a certain extent correct: the bulk of their activity continues to focus on the articulation of specific demands to do with, for example, women's political representation, childcare and women's pensions. However, my argument is that this shift in discourse has 'real' effects not reducible to the level of 'mere representation'. Recall that a key dimension of this shift has been a change in the dominant empty signifier structuring Fawcett's discourse: previously it was 'gender equality', now it is '(third wave) feminism'. As I have argued, this shift has had tangible effects on the organisation's self-understanding, inasmuch as there has been a palpable strengthening of the organisation's affective identification with the issues it is dealing with. This, I believe, is partly explainable through the capacity of the signifier 'feminism' – with all its connotations and history – to inspire stronger affective identifications than that of 'gender equality'. Furthermore, the use of the signifier 'feminism' serves to draw equivalences between Fawcett's political campaigning, and the broader, less conventionally political, issues that are of concern to contemporary feminists (such as beauty, sexuality, pornography).

This affective investment in the signifier feminism thus serves to change the character of Fawcett's core demands: through explicitly linking them to more general issues they become part of an effort to effect broader shifts in the co-ordinates of hegemonic gender relations. Given the construction of these equivalential linkages via the investment in the signifier 'feminism' (with its capacity to polarise opinion), the antagonistic character of Fawcett's campaigning becomes more explicit. Thus, while the core demands of Fawcett remain roughly the same in terms of their content, their linking with a set of 'second order' feminist demands and the explicit investment in 'feminism' serves to strengthen their equivalential links, situating them more explicitly in opposition to dominant post-/anti-feminist hegemonic discourses. These shifts in discourse are presented schematically in the table (Table 3.1) below.

Thus, I want to claim that this shift does represent a genuine moment of 'radicalisation' in a number of key respects. To claim otherwise would require one of the following: a belief that Fawcett is being dishonest, the introduction of a strong distinction between discourse and practice or a belief that any sort of political engagement with the institutions of the national state of necessity renders a feminist practice 'less radical'.

Table 3.1 Shifts in Fawcett Society discourse, before and after 2005 rebranding

	Before	After
Empty signifier	'gender equality'	'(third-wave) feminism'
Strength of affective investment	Weak	Strong
Core demands	Childcare, political representation, pensions, women and criminal justice, equal pay	Same, but with added emphasis on race-related concerns
Character of those demands	Differential/particular	Equivalential
'Second order' demands	None	Concerning body image, sexuality, pornography,
Strength of equivalential links between demands	Weak	Fairly strong
Antagonist	Poorly defined	Post-feminism/'death of feminism' thesis
Use of liberal democratic discourse	Generally regarded as sufficient	Potentially useful but insufficient

However, against this, using the post-structuralist theoretical framework outlined in Chapter 2, we can claim that there is a strong radical and imaginative dimension to Fawcett's current political practice. Its articulation of a new feminist agenda is not an attempt to delineate once and for all what feminism signifies. Instead, the claims made are tentative and anticipatory, rather than presupposing a fully constituted political subject, which, again, leaves room for plurality and critical exchange.

Fawcett's new feminist agenda: Some critical remarks

While I have argued so far that Fawcett's efforts seem bold and ambitious, I want to end by sketching a few more troubling dimensions of Fawcett's recent campaigning. The first relates to its invocation of 'third wave' feminism to describe its new feminist agenda. As we saw in Chapter 1, the invocation of a third wave is a highly contested terrain. At one level, it is helpful inasmuch as it provides a discursive space for a new feminist agenda to emerge. On the other hand, the very invocation of the 'wave' metaphor seems to cast contemporary feminism as a site of intergenerational conflict. This may lead to a very 'subject question' oriented discussion focussed on establishing clear (and potentially exclusionary) boundaries around the collective feminist subject. In Fawcett's case, I think this is largely avoided: the signifier 'third-wave feminism' is left deliberately open and is used as something of an 'empty signifier' through which to group together a diverse set of contemporary feminist demands. Unlike The F-word (see Chapter 5), at no point does the debate cohere around the question of who the third wave is as a feminist subject, and so avoids the more divisive tendencies of thinking of waves in the idiom of the 'subject question'. Nevertheless, the very use of the wave metaphor is itself potentially problematic, given the extent to which the term has become attached to problematic forms of generational disidentification (Henry, 2003; Dean, 2009).

A second way in which Fawcett arguably falls short is in that there remains something of a democratic deficit in the organisation. While recently it has engaged more explicitly within the public sphere, there remains an issue of accountability, inasmuch as its general strategy and policy continues to be run by a small group of staff. There are periodic consultations with the members (for example, at the 2008 AGM), but the general structure remains largely hierarchical, such that the opportunities for critical exchanges pertaining to the organisation's practices remain somewhat constrained.

A further possible undemocratic (or, rather, inegalitarian) consequence of Fawcett's already relatively powerful position within UK gender politics is that its 'engagement' with grass-roots feminist concerns may be seen as bandwagon jumping or co-optation. Indeed, as we shall see in Chapter 5, Rake's championing of a 'third wave' was felt to be intrusive towards those who had been self-identifying as 'third wave' for a number of years. Thus, there can be a fine line between productive articulation and unproductive appropriation of feminist concerns developed elsewhere. While this is undoubtedly a danger, at the present time such a critique seems a little disingenuous, especially when one considers that such processes of negotiation are intrinsic to any form of political articulation.

In addition, we may say that there is something of a transnational deficit in The Fawcett Society, as there is an unremittingly UK focus to its campaigning. So far, there has been no attempt to establish connections or make political articulations across national borders. A note of concern about this was raised at the 2005 AGM, at which Fawcett's exclusive UK focus was justified on the basis of decisions made about how to use limited resources most efficiently. Thus, for the time being, Fawcett's political activity remains firmly within the confines of the UK.

Finally, I want to raise some concerns about the 'Fawcett Feminist Challenge', which consists of challenging celebrities and members of the public to don Fawcett's 'this is what a feminist looks like' T-shirts. Clearly, there is a diversity of ways in which the T-shirt can be read, and it would be disingenuous to speculate about the intentionality of individual T-shirt wearers. However, I want to raise some questions about the political desires motivating the production of the T-shirt. Fawcett's T-shirt campaign, as stated earlier, is inextricably tied up with its wider attempt at articulating a new feminist agenda with broad(er) public support. We may then ask what kind of feminist affirmation the T-shirt seeks to effect. I think, broadly speaking, that there are two possible answers to this. The first is that the T-shirt simply seeks to affirm feminism at a time when feminism is perceived to be an identification which is repudiated *across the board*. This invites a reading of the T-shirt as a radical gesture, defying the patriarchal symbolic by saying 'look! I affirm feminism, despite your presumption of widespread feminist disidentification!'

The second possible modality of feminist affirmation engendered by the T-shirt is arguably more problematic. In some cases, the subversive potential of the T-shirt derives not from the simple affirmation of feminism, but from a (perceived) disjuncture between the identity of feminism and certain characteristics of the wearer. Given that the production of the T-shirt is linked to a broader effort on Fawcett's part to shift public perceptions of feminism away from the mythical figure of the old, ugly feminist, one senses that it is presumed that the T-shirt will be at its most efficacious when it is worn by those kinds of bodies which feminism is not perceived to 'stick' to (Ahmed, 2004a). These are bodies such as those of the non-white, the conventionally attractive, the young and, perhaps, the male. But, one may ask, do these desires to (literally) attach feminism to bodies not popularly associated with it perhaps render abject, or at least marginal, the feminist identifications of those bodies (the ugly, older white woman) which do actually more closely resemble the popular stereotype? Put differently, does the desire to wrestle feminism away from its popular associations with older white and – above all – ugly women not replicate the precise modality of (partly generational) disidentification with feminism that the T-shirt seeks to contest? I do not want to suggest that this latter reading is in any fundamental sense 'truer' than the first, but I do want to raise some critical questions about the wearing of the T-shirt which for many people (this author included) is a source of positive affect.[25]

Conclusion

My starting point for this chapter was that The Fawcett Society's ongoing status as a professional, hierarchical organisation with media-savviness and close links to key government figures might be seen as indicative of a decline in the radicalism, vitality and oppositionality of feminist politics in the UK. In critiquing this position, I carried out three case studies of key dimensions of the organisation's current practices, and their changing character. My case selection perhaps accentuated the differences between Fawcett's complicitous and radical dimensions. But my argument is not so much that Fawcett has shifted from a moderate, accomodationist stance to a radical and contestatory position. Instead, my claim is that even during the periods when a more sedate tone pervaded its discourse and practice, elements of a more radical agenda were perhaps implicit in much of Fawcett's work, without necessarily always being brought to the fore. Thus, the two contradictory logics – an accomodationist, reparative political logic and the 'logic of radicalisation' – are, in some respects, always present within Fawcett's political activity. However, in their recent efforts to highlight the question of feminism and engage with a broader range of concerns, the latter logic has come more to the fore.

Crucially, this latter logic entails an articulation of a new feminist agenda which *cuts across* the state/civil society distinction. As such, when Katherine Rake talks about the 'end of the road for equality feminism', this does not refer to a cessation of, or a giving up on, the process of working with and making demands to politicians, civil servants etc. to further a feminist/gender equality agenda. As she points out, it still remains the 'backbone' of Fawcett's work. Operating alongside this 'backbone' is a more explicit articulation of a feminist chain of equivalence, such that these various feminist agendas, rather than being seen in their particularity, come to be seen as part of a broader attempt to alter existing hegemonic norms. Consequently, the moment of radicalisation inheres not in the abandonment of the legislative dimension, but in its recasting as part of a broader, more transformative agenda: it refers to an acknowledgement of the *insufficiency* rather than the *illegitimacy* or 'uselessness' of engaging with formal state institutions.

In framing my analysis in these terms, I do not wish to suggest that The Fawcett Society are perfect and totally undeserving of criticism: there is still something of a democratic deficit in terms of the relation between staff and members, the relationship between Fawcett and less formal feminist groups could be potentially problematic, the T-shirt campaign has some troubling dimensions and there are problems with the notion of 'waves' as a description of contemporary feminism. Overall, though, while not wishing to overplay the optimistic dimensions of my analysis too strongly, I nonetheless want to affirm that The Fawcett Society's recent radicalisation, combined with its heightened media profile and increasing membership, might be seen as indicative of a resurgence of, and heightened interest in, contemporary feminism in the UK.

4
Women's Aid: Professionalised Radicalism?

My second case study, Women's Aid, the UK's national domestic violence charity, throws up a range of questions in many ways similar to those prompted by the preceding analysis of The Fawcett Society. In their present guises, the two organisations are in many respects similar. Like Fawcett, over the past few decades Women's Aid has moved from a position of relative marginality to one in which it is now a respected, influential and media-friendly organisation playing a central role in the provision of services related to domestic violence. However, unlike Fawcett, Women's Aid's roots are in the autonomous strands of 'second-wave' feminism. It could therefore be read as having shifted from a radical, autonomous stance to a now more mainstream position, and might thus be seen as symptomatic of feminism's increasing professionalisation and declining radicalism. This manifests itself through, for example, the organisation's strong willingness to co-operate with both the local and national state, the casting of itself as an expert actor within the field of domestic violence service provision, its strong ethos of professionalism, its willingness to work with the corporate sector, and the centrality that the organisation affords to 'multiagency' work. Consequently, the history of Women's Aid mirrors recurrent themes in existing literature on the trajectory of post-1970s feminism, in the UK and elsewhere.

And yet, these are ambiguous developments. At one extreme, an optimistic reading might suggest that these modes of increasing influence and professionalisation are a feminist success story, showing how far parts of the movement have come, despite humble beginnings. On the other hand, a more pessimistic account might suggest that these developments are indicative of deradicalisation and a loss of feminism's critical position. Both of these possible angles do point towards key aspects of Women's

Aid's current guise. However, rather than framing these developments as indicative of either 'success' or deradicalisation/institutionalisation, I want instead to argue that Women's Aid's current practices continue to be framed within an essentially radical and contestatory discursive frame, such that the more institutional and professionalised elements of Women's Aid's work are articulated together with more autonomous feminist practices into a discursive totality. This discursive totality is structured around a basic and fundamental investment in a feminist analysis of domestic violence, an analysis which, in Zerilli's terms, can be usefully referred to as a 'figure of the newly thinkable'. I argue that Women's Aid's work is underwritten by a continual (re)investment in the challenging, threatening and radical character of their feminist analysis of domestic violence, which enables a certain critical vibrancy to permeate their political work. This study of Women's Aid, therefore, provides us an example of a radical yet (partially) state-oriented and institutionalised feminist group, whose radicalism inheres not in a politics of purity or separatism, but in the articulation of a feminist discourse on domestic violence that cuts across issues and institutional and autonomous sites.

To flesh this out in more detail, I start by providing a short history of the organisation and some general background information. I then provide a typology of the various different forms of 'success' and professionalisation/institutionalisation which permeate Women's Aid's practices, highlighting the multiple ways in which it has moved away from a 'seventies feminist' ideal of autonomy and political purity. The third section turns its attention to the notion of the feminist analysis of domestic violence as a 'figure of the newly thinkable' which resists narratives of feminist success or deradicalisation. Indeed, one could say that Women's Aid's casting of domestic violence in feminist terms, in a manner that serves to disrupt the existing fabric of hegemonic gender relations, at some level represents an exemplar of the feminist political imagination at work. Having then presented a generally favourable picture, towards the end I shall engage more critically with certain aspects of the organisation's political strategies – focussing on the question of 'interest group pluralism' and the 'new managerialism'.

Women's Aid: Origins and historical background

Women's Aid unambiguously situates itself historically as coming out of the autonomous women's movement of the 1970s. As Dobash and Dobash (1992: 27–9) point out, the 'battered women's movement' was originally concerned exclusively with providing shelter for women who were fleeing violent relationships, a need which was identified through the political mobilisations of women that led to the emergence of 'second-wave' feminism.[1] As pointed out in a brief account of its history on the Women's Aid website,

> In those early years, there were very few options available to women seeking alternatives to living with violent men. Protection under civil or family law was almost impossible to get (except in the context of divorce); domestic violence was not accepted as a reason for homelessness, the police dismissed 'domestics' as a trivial and time-wasting use of their resources, and the response of most agencies was 'go back home and make it up'.
>
> (Women's Aid, 2005a)

In light of the need for the provision of shelter and support for women and children seeking refuge from violent partners, Women's Aid emerged out of voluntary efforts by feminists to set up refuges in which such shelter and support could be provided. The development of refuges served the immediate pragmatic need of providing survivors of domestic violence with shelter, support and advice, and so, in a sense, was not explicitly political. However, refuges also served as key mobilising points for survivors and activists in which tactics and policy goals could be formulated (Dobash and Dobash, 1992: 60). The first Women's Aid refuge was set up in the early 1970s in Chiswick, West London, which was followed by the emergence around the country of a number of other refuges for women and children fleeing violent partners. However, the leadership style of Erin Pizzey, founder of Chiswick Women's Aid, was generally viewed unfavourably by the other Women's Aid groups and, as such, the latter split from Chiswick Women's Aid and formed the National Women's Aid Federation in 1974 – hereafter referred to as Women's Aid (ibid.: 33).[2]

Crucial here is that in the early years, Women's Aid's focus was on the voluntary provision of services to women and children in a manner informed by feminist principles and with a strong emphasis on autonomy, self-help and empowerment. In the words of one active feminist in the 1970s, 'Women's Aid came out very much of that self-help ethos, all the first buildings were squatted. It was very exciting, it was very radical, and the idea was that women would go to the refuges, would get involved in consciousness-raising groups in the refuges, would leave their husbands, and everything would be hunky-dory' (interview with feminist activist, February 2007), while Predelli et al. (2008: 27) say that Women's Aid 'embodied the spirit of the women's liberation movement with its ethos of self-help, autonomy and empowerment'. Similarly, the organisation's current director Nicola Harwin has drawn attention to how Women's Aid has its origins in the general emergence of discourses of empowerment, self-determination and scepticism of authority which took hold in the late 1960s as a result of the influence of civil rights and libertarian movements. She points out how Women's Aid's early endeavours were paradigmatic of the second-wave feminist dictum of 'the personal is political', given that 'as our understanding of the dynamics of domestic violence grew, we acknowledged its origins within the traditional and patriarchal family structures of domination and subordination' (Harwin, 1999: 24–5). As a result, in the early years Women's Aid tended to have a confrontational relationship with statutory agencies, as a consequence of their politicisation of an issue which was viewed by the state – and indeed the public at large – as a private, individual and non-political affair, with hugely threatening implications for the sanctity of 'the family' and male privilege more generally.

Thus, the picture I wish to paint of the early years of Women's Aid is one depicting an organisation firmly rooted in 'seventies' feminist values of autonomy, self-help and equality (see Kantola, 2006: 76). Furthermore, its analysis of domestic violence was radically at odds with hegemonic conceptions of the prevalence of domestic violence and notions of familial relations and male privilege. Thus, to some extent, it combined a politics of purity and autonomy with a radically contestatory relationship to prevailing hegemonic discourses.

The present-day Women's Aid: A brief overview

From these relatively humble beginnings, Women's Aid has now established itself as a modern, professional and high-profile campaigning organisation, such that it is one of the leading feminist organisations in the UK at present. However, it would be incorrect to treat the organisation as a unitary actor. The Women's Aid Federation is an England-wide network of, according to its website, over 300 local projects that provide over 500 refuges. Each local group operates autonomously, and as such local groups are not constrained by decisions made at the organisation's headquarters in Bristol. The bulk of the campaigning and lobbying is co-ordinated from Bristol, whereas the local groups tend to focus more on the provision of services. The Scottish and Welsh Women's Aid Federations are entirely autonomous from their English counterparts but have strong co-operative links.[3]

We can now look more closely at the main aims of the organisation. Unlike Fawcett, Women's Aid is a single-issue group, whose chief aim is to end domestic violence against women and children. It argues that this is a crucial concern given the pervasiveness of domestic violence. The majority of Women's Aid reports draw attention to two key statistics: first, that an average of two women are killed each week in England by a current or former partner and second, that one in four women in the UK experience domestic violence at some point over the course of their lifetime (Women's Aid, 2004b: 2). To work towards the aim of eliminating domestic violence, it advocates for abused women and children and seeks to ensure their safety through working locally and nationally to

1   Empower women who have been affected by domestic violence.
2   Meet the needs of children affected by domestic violence.
3   Provide services run by women which are based on listening to survivors.
4   Challenge the disadvantages which result from domestic violence.
5   Support and reflect diversity and promote equality of opportunity.
6   Promote cohesive interagency responses to domestic violence and develop partnerships.

Thus, Women's Aid's strategy is multifaceted, with a number of different ongoing strands. Its most immediate concern is to provide support, shelter and advice for abused women and children (including the publication of *The Gold Book*, which is a national directory of domestic violence services),[4] but is also engaged in the more explicitly political practices of promoting policies and raising awareness.[5] At the start of a number of policy documents and consultation papers, Women's Aid draw attention to how the demands cited are drawn up through 'comprehensive consultation with our national network of domestic violence services and survivors' (Butler, 2003b: 1; See also Hague et al., 2003: 127). Thus, Women's Aid's demands are formulated by giving voice to survivors of domestic violence who use their services.[6]

In view of this, Women's Aid is keen to emphasise how despite having become a sophisticated and professional organisation, it has nonetheless not lost sight of its core commitments. As one Women's Aid document points out,

Over the years Women's Aid has changed and adapted to meet the needs of the women who use our services, our work has received the professional status we have demanded and our services have improved greatly as funding has permitted. What hasn't changed is our ethos and vision of believing women, promoting empowerment and allowing women to determine their own lives.

(Women's Aid, 2005a)

Thus, its autonomous mobilisations within civil society – in the form of consultation in refuges – feed into and inform its more 'institutionalised' modes of engagement such as responding to government consultations. Women's Aid's now seemingly more professionalised and institutionalised character is therefore a broadening of its remit, rather than a replacement of autonomous democratic practices with more professional forms of engagement.

Women's Aid: Success and professionalisation

In this section I want to explore in more detail these logics of institutionalisation and professionalisation, and I also want to begin addressing in greater detail whether these developments might be read as indicative of feminist success, or whether Women's Aid's shift from a marginal, autonomous organisation rooted in early 'second-wave' feminism to the glossy, respected and influential organisation it is today could be read as indicative of a loss of the radicalism and critical edge of post 'second-wave' feminism in the UK. I shall outline five different modalities of Women's Aid's professionalisation.

(1) Engagement and co-operation with formal state institutions

The first, and perhaps most significant, mode of departure from a feminist politics of purity and autonomy is through Women's Aid's now well-established tradition of working alongside formal state institutions in order to further its aims. Indeed, this early in the life of the organisation. As Harwin and Barron point out, 'from the early 1970s, Women's Aid has had a key role as a campaigning organisation working to end domestic violence by lobbying for legislative and social policy change' (Harwin and Barron, 2000: 209; see also Kantola, 2006: 77). Only a matter of months after its inception, Women's Aid contributed to the 1974 Parliamentary Select Committee Hearings on Violence in Marriage (Dobash and Dobash, 1992: 122–8). This set a precedent for Women's Aid's political strategies to be pragmatic and not necessarily confrontational *vis-à-vis* the state. Indeed, Dobash and Dobash point to how Women's Aid has always been aware of the necessity of using the law and the criminal justice system as a means of improving the plight of victims of domestic violence, while maintaining a critical distance from such institutions. They point out that 'the movement has not sought to abolish criminal justice, but to try to use it in order to enable women to eliminate the violence used against them and as a tool to help them establish their own autonomy' (ibid.: 211). In an interview, Nicola Harwin described how, as a refuge worker in the 1970s, 'one would be lucky to get a toe in the door' in terms of setting up meetings with local housing departments and state officials (Nicola Harwin, interview, November 2007). Continuing this analogy, one could say that now Women's Aid has not only got its toe in the door, but has entered the room and is listened to by those inside.

Following on from these initial successes, Women's Aid is now routinely consulted by government on issues related to domestic violence. That is not to say that all Women's Aid's recommendations are necessarily taken on board, but it has nonetheless succeeded in casting itself as an integral actor within the context of the drafting of policy relevant to domestic violence. Thus, the publication of consultation responses constitutes a major element of Women's Aid's campaigning. One of the most important of these in recent years has been its response to *Safety and Justice*, the government's 2003 consultation paper on domestic violence. Here the various demands cohere around a foregrounding of the need for domestic violence to be accepted as a central issue within the dominant legal and political apparatus. These demands include the adoption of a comprehensive legal definition of domestic violence, which would allow for accurate data collection, and it also calls for 'routine questioning/screening for domestic violence to be introduced across all organisations (not only in health), accompanied by mandatory training across all organisations and their partner agencies, which is informed by Women's Aid and other specialist domestic violence services' (Butler, 2003b: 4). In addition, the document outlines the dimensions of Women's Aid's demand for a comprehensive national strategy for combating violence against women, grounded upon the claim that all agencies should implement minimum standards and good practice guidelines, based on human rights principles (ibid.: 4).[7] The appropriation of a human rights-based discourse is crucial: Women's Aid's demands are persistently made through an appeal to the UK government's human rights obligations which it uses to hold the government to account over domestic violence issues. Thus, much like Fawcett, Women's Aid seeks to further its demands directed at those in government through a process of immanent critique via the appropriation of discourses of liberal individualism and universal human rights to contest inaction on the issue of violence against women.

The demands presented in the response to *Safety and Justice* take the form of appeals to government for reforms to a number of state institutions (welfare services, courts, the police, government departments), so as to enhance or expand the range of services related to domestic violence. The demands are articulated in a context in which Women's Aid has become able to position itself as an expert actor within the field. As pointed out in a document marking its 30th anniversary, 'we now work closely with the government and with many different local and national agencies and are recognised as the experts on domestic violence' (Women's Aid, 2004a: 15). It would therefore appear that Women's Aid's position in the context of campaigning on the issue of domestic violence has become institutional-ised to an extent where the lines of antagonism between Women's Aid and the dominant state apparatus have become somewhat blurred. Indeed, Women's Aid's 30th birthday reception was held at 11 Downing Street (the residence of the British Chancellor of the Exchequer) with a large celebrity entourage (Women's Aid, 2004c). In addition, Nicola Harwin has drawn attention to how the organisation has succeeded in formalising its links with a number of government departments since the 1990s and, like Fawcett, has also used the strategy of singling out sympathetic par-liamentarians to further their cause within the national decision-making process (Nicola Harwin, interview, February 2007).[8] This certainly appears to represent a significant shift in the basic thrust of Women's Aid's work since its inception: the picture we are presented with is very much one of a modern, professional organisation with a deeply institutionalised role as an expert voice on issues of domestic violence that the British government is willing to listen to and work with.

(2) Increased 'multiagency' work

In addition to working alongside and co-operating with formal state insti-tutions, logics of professionalisation have also taken the form of increased 'multiagency' co-operation, whereby Women's Aid has worked with a variety of private, state and voluntary sector bodies to improve service provision related to domestic violence. This is seen as necessary given that service provision for survivors of domestic violence encompasses a range of issues and policy domains including health, housing and legal con-cerns. This type of work takes a variety of forms, and is often carried out at local level. Although it is wide-ranging, the various facets of 'multiagency' work are of central concern for Women's Aid (see Hague, 1999). The move towards increasing multiagency work has, to a degree, seen Women's Aid move from a critical, defensive position to one in which it has a more complex, at times fairly amicable, relationship with statutory agencies.

Highlighting the dilemmas of negotiating the consequences of partial success, while still maintaining a critical position, Harwin writes,

> Making the transition from a critical and defensive position, which less powerful individuals and organisations within any community are often forced to adopt, to one of developing new forms of joint working while still maintaining a challenging and feminist perspective on the issues has been a difficult process for many activists, but for many it has been an empowering and worthwhile enterprise undertaken as part of a core aim of ending violence against women and children and of improving their options and choices.
>
> (Harwin, 1999: 29)

Such transitions pose practical as well as strategic and theoretical concerns: increased engagement with agencies may lead to a lack of focus and a consequent decline in the quality of service to residents of refuges (Harwin and Barron, 2000: 222).[9] Thus, it is undoubtedly difficult to generalise about 'multiagency' work, itself a somewhat amorphous term. Indeed, while multiagency work often consists of working with other agencies in order to enhance the provision of services, it can also take the form of more radical campaigning. For instance, Women's Aid has recently worked alongside a number of voluntary sector bodies such as Amnesty International and the National Society for the Prevention of Cruelty to Children (NSPCC) (Women's Aid, 2003d) in the creation of the End Violence Against Women Coalition, which has thus far campaigned to try to encourage the UK government to adopt a more integrated and streamlined approach to tackling violence against women (EVAW, 2006). While this instance of interagency co-operation is focussed on campaigning, it is nonetheless rather state-oriented: thus far, it has produced a set of reports evaluating all government departments in terms of their performance on tackling violence against women, as well as a series of guidelines for improving performance. Women's Aid's multiagency work is thus an ambiguous terrain. At one level, the fact that Women's Aid has positioned itself as a key actor in negotiations over the provision of multiple forms of service provision is arguably indicative of feminist success. However, the vagaries of multiagency work arguably pose limitations on the types of feminist discourse and practices that are possible, particularly in light of recent public sector restructuring: these dilemmas will be addressed in more detail towards the end of the chapter.

(3) Co-operation with the corporate sector

A further set of practices, which could be read as indicative of a lack of feminist radicalism on Women's Aid's part, is its willingness to work with the corporate sector to further its aims. Put simply, this is because, historically, feminist values of autonomy and empowerment, in their ideal type, gave rise to an antipathy towards co-operation with the sorts of male-dominated institutions one finds throughout the private sector. Furthermore, in the British context, the close connections between feminism and radical class politics were such that a principled anti-capitalism was prevalent throughout much early 'second-wave' feminism (Lovenduski, 1995: 128; Bouchier, 1983: 61).

In contrast to this ideal-type of autonomous, socialist-inflected feminist politics central to much of the early 'second-wave' feminism, Women's Aid have pursued a number of forms of engagement with the private sector. For instance, Women's Aid have argued for compulsory domestic violence strategies to be drawn up in workplaces, and to this end collaborated with Opportunity Now (the organisation within Business in the Community[10] working towards gender equality) to produce a good practice guide for employers on domestic violence and the workplace. The good practice guide highlights the benefits to businesses of engaging with domestic violence issues: Women's Aid argues that 'developing a workplace response and protecting the health and safety of all employees makes good business sense. It reduces abuse-related costs and enhances employee well-being and productivity' (Women's Aid, 2003e). Here, the demands are inscribed within a discourse that is palatable to business, emphasising a convergence of interests between businesses and the campaign against domestic violence.

In addition to this, a strategy widely used by Women's Aid which very much comes to the fore when reading their press releases archive is that of liaising with private companies in order to raise money and public awareness. Women's Aid has a particularly close relationship with The Body Shop, a cosmetics franchise which historically has gained a reputation for ethical business practice. Due primarily to the influence of former Body Shop owner Anita Roddick, The Body Shop has launched campaigns against domestic violence in collaboration with Women's Aid. The Body Shop initiatives include a scheme whereby £1.50 from every 'Body Shop Mint Lip Care Stick' is donated to Women's Aid. It has also co-operated in a scheme encouraging people to donate old mobile phones to enable handsets to be converted into personal alarms for those at risk of domestic violence (Women's Aid, 2005c). This scheme was also supported by Transport for London, which provided details of the Body Shop's scheme on London taxicab receipts (Women's Aid, 2005d).[11]

These engagements with the corporate sector present a number of interesting quandaries. What is indisputable is the fact that this particular type of campaigning departs significantly from second-wave feminist conceptions of authentic and radical politics. Such political engagements with the private sector arguably go some way towards reinforcing the hegemonic force of the market, as it implies that even charitable enterprises must be pitched alongside, or in relation to, market logics. Thus, the process of liaising with large companies, in itself, would seem to support narratives of feminist deradicalisation. And yet, such practices are justified on the grounds that Women's Aid is implicated in a terrain in which the accumulation of funds is necessary for campaigning activity to be ongoing. In view of this, the organisation is radically unapologetic in terms of the question of engagement with the corporate sector. One senior Women's Aid staff member outlined how engagement with the corporate sector represents a significant opportunity for the organisation to raise awareness and accumulate funds. She pointed out how:

> Because there are issues there around corporations as employers, and that's accessing an awful lot of people, the employees may experience domestic violence; so it's not just about raising awareness, but it's also what our fundraising team are doing with corporate business, is also about getting them to provide some of the resources. For example, if some corporate businesses have a domestic violence policy and procedures for supporting their employees *or* possibly responding to perpetrators.... it's another way, and we go for all that's possible.
>   (interview with Women's Aid staff member, June 2006)

There is some invocation of an 'inevitability' thesis, taking as given the prevalence of the corporate sector. While this is perhaps indicative of a shift away from traditional feminist radicalism, in terms of critical evaluation the crucial question is whether these engagements have led to a diluting of the more radical dimensions of Women's Aid's work. In the following sections, I shall argue that, for the most part, this has not taken place.

(4) Celebrity endorsement as an awareness-raising strategy

A similar set of difficulties arise when one considers the centrality afforded by the organisation to public endorsement by celebrities. This is not to suggest that celebrity endorsement is of necessity a negative or politically deradicalising force. Whether or not a given celebrity endorsement is troubling will depend in large part on factors such as the nature of the endorsement and the intentionality of the celebrity involved. However, the *centrality* of celebrity endorsement as a key strategy for the contemporary Women's Aid could potentially be seen as troubling, given the extent to which contemporary celebrity culture, and the efficacy that celebrity endorsement is presumed to yield, is tied up with a range of problematically gendered, raced and classed discourses (McRobbie, 2009: 42; Marshall, 1997).

Despite this, the emphasis Women's Aid place on celebrity endorsement is especially apparent in the document produced to mark their 30th anniversary in 2004. It contains a series of celebrity endorsements in which various public figures with varying degrees of fame are pictured along with words of praise for the organisation (Women's Aid, 2004a). Two celebrities have particularly close associations with the organisation: Jenni Murray, presenter of the celebrated BBC Radio 4 programme *Woman's Hour*, is a Women's Aid Patron (it is noteworthy that she is also president of Fawcett) and Will Young, winner of the first UK *Pop Idol* and now a well-established pop performer, is a Women's Aid Ambassador, and has participated in a number of fundraising and awareness-raising activities. Other public figures that feature in the document include singer Beverley Knight, journalist John Humphreys, actor Tony Robinson, comedian Rhona Cameron, actress Fay Ripley, politician David Blunkett, rugby player Lawrence Dallaglio, comedy writer Richard Curtis, author Nick Hornby, comedian and actress Meera Syal and TV presenter Lorraine Kelly.

Celebrity endorsement is an area the organisation is keen to develop: as Nicola Harwin, the organisation's director, points out in the 2002–3 annual review, Women's Aid underwent a rebranding exercise (like Fawcett in 2005) in order to broaden the organisation's appeal, with a move towards producing glossier, more impressive-looking material and placing greater emphasis on celebrity endorsement. As Harwin argues, 'our new brand will help communicate that ... Women's Aid is a modern, female, challenging charity which aims to help vulnerable women and children to rebuild their lives' (Harwin in Women's Aid, 2004b: 4). Furthermore, in 2007 Women's Aid launched a high-profile campaign titled 'Act Until Women And Children Are Safe', which features a number of celebrities – TV presenters Fiona Bruce, Miquita Oliver and Kate Thornton, and actresses Anne-Marie Duff, Anna Friel, Fay Ripley and Honor Blackman – with their faces made up to look as if they have been physically assaulted (Women's Aid, 2007). This, in some respects, goes beyond a simple celebrity 'endorsement'. Rather, the emphasis is on the shock value which is in some senses enhanced by the fact that the faces depicted are (reasonably) well-known public figures. A similar strategy was used in 2009 when Women's Aid launched a new domestic violence awareness campaign centred around a two-minute short film, *Cut*, featuring A-list actress Keira Knightley, which was shown in cinemas and on television, and encouraged viewers to donate £2 a month to the organisation.

The emphasis on celebrity endorsement has been justified pragmatically on the grounds that Women's Aid is always constrained financially and cannot afford to be excessively choosy, or indeed purist, in terms of political strategy. One staff member remarked that 'it is really just about using any means that seem appropriate to raise public awareness' (interview with Women's Aid staff member, June 2006). This again points to how Women's Aid, to some degree, situates itself within a variation of the 'inevitability' thesis concerning the financing of voluntary sector bodies. While at some level this arguably lends weight to narratives of deradicalisation, one might just as easily say that a mass-produced short film in aid of a feminist organisation featuring an A-list actress is surely indicative of feminist success.

(5) The discursive mainstreaming of domestic violence

However, all of these various forms of political engagement need to be contextualised within the shifts in hegemonic discourse in the UK concerning domestic violence that have been effected since the 1970s, due in part to Women's Aid's campaigning. The apparent 'mainstreaming' of domestic violence as a legitimate concern across mainstream culture, law and politics is a source of immense pride for the organisation. As they point out,

> 30 years ago there was a resounding silence on the issue of domestic violence across most criminal justice and social welfare agencies. Today the issue of domestic violence has become increasingly prominent. It is no longer of concern only to women's groups and voluntary organisations, but, largely as a result of our activism, it is also discussed by politicians and legislators, and in the media.
>
> (Women's Aid, 2004a: 1)

Indeed, the majority of the organisation's strategies and demands are situated within a narrative of domestic violence as having previously been a minority issue which was poorly understood and not taken seriously, but is now moving into the mainstream.[12] Women's Aid sees the process of 'mainstreaming' domestic violence concerns as fundamental to raising public and institutional awareness of the issue so as to work towards its elimination (Dobash and Dobash, 1992: 288–90; Hitzin, 2000: 366).

Therefore, we have an overall picture of an organisation which has shifted from an autonomous, critical and defensive position, to one of widespread mainstream recognition. However, to fully assess whether Women's Aid should be read as indicative of feminist success, on the one hand, and/or declining feminist radicalism and vitality, on the other, it will be necessary to look in greater detail at the discursive framing of Women's Aid's political practices.

Domestic violence, immigration and anti-racism

Before exploring Women's Aid's characterisation of domestic violence in greater detail, I want to suggest that its work on issues concerning race and immigration is undercut by both a degree of professionalisation and institutionalisation, and a more radical set of practices. As with The Fawcett Society, Women's Aid has mainstreamed race-related concerns into its practices in a manner which is sustained and not merely tokenistic (Predelli et al., 2008). Women's Aid, frequently in liaison with other women's organisations, has persistently emphasised how the experiences of black and ethnic minority women who experience domestic violence can be particularly unfavourable, partly because, as Women's Aid puts it, racism 'is pervasive in the UK' (Barron, 2005). In addition, Women's Aid points out that there may be additional pressures within one's own community to avoid seeking help on issues related to domestic violence – and, indeed, Women's Aid describes forced marriage as a form of domestic abuse (Women's Aid, 2005c). Women's Aid persistently emphasises the ways in which statutory agencies may be insufficiently aware of, or sensitive to, specific needs of black and minority ethnic women experiencing domestic violence, and as such calls for the needs of such women to be incorporated into mandatory domestic violence training for officials working in statutory agencies.[13] Furthermore, Women's Aid itself provides information on domestic violence support services in a variety of minority languages in the UK (Women's Aid, 2004b: 12).

In addition, Women's Aid has been actively involved in campaigns relating to the government's treatment of domestic violence survivors subject to immigration controls. It contends that 'some laws and regulations effectively prevent groups of women experiencing domestic violence from seeking protection and safety, and can be said to be operating in gross violation of civil liberties and human rights' (Butler, 2002). There are particular problems related to the 'one year' rule, which stipulates that those entering the UK as a spouse or unmarried partner of a person settled in the UK must complete a probationary period of one year (soon to be two years) during which the marriage must subsist before an application for indefinite leave to remain can be considered. This places women and children with this status in a very vulnerable position, as people subject to immigration control have 'no recourse to public funds' and so cannot access state support and services. This, Women's Aid argues, 'forces them into total dependence on the settled spouse or partner and their family. Many women are unable to seek work because of the violence they experience and many women do not speak, or are not allowed to learn, English' (ibid.). Furthermore, this is compounded by the attitudes of statutory agencies whereby 'women experiencing domestic violence are often denied knowledge of their rights and of their immigration position and are kept isolated and subject to continual surveillance' (ibid.). Women's Aid acknowledges that some legislative progress has been made: in 1999 an exemption to these rules was introduced whereby women experiencing domestic violence may be given indefinite leave to remain in the UK irrespective of the relationship with their spouse. However, they argue that this has been ineffective for a number of reasons: women may not know about agencies that offer advice and support, the burden of proof for domestic violence is high (and lack of knowledge or fear of racism may prevent women from engaging with agencies who may be able to help provide such proof) and, as Women's Aid puts it, 'being able to go to a place of safety while criminal or civil proceedings are initiated or while medical attention or other help and support is sought is crucial, but these women have no recourse to public funds and therefore have no access to benefits or safe housing' (ibid., see also Butler, 2003a).

As a result, women subject to immigration controls who are experiencing domestic violence remain vulnerable, and, to highlight this, Women's Aid emphasises how existing legislation may be in breach of the government's human rights obligations. It draws attention to the Human Rights Convention which states that everyone has a right to life. Consequently, the state has a duty to protect life, and so 'women subject to immigration control who also experience domestic violence must have the same right to access and receive services, support and protection from statutory agencies as other abused humans' (ibid). Furthermore, Women's Aid endorses a campaign letter drafted by Southall Black Sisters which similarly calls the government to account on this issue by invoking its human rights obligations. It reads,

> The Government has acknowledged that benefits and support are 'life-saving and critical' if victims of domestic violence are to leave

abuse. Why do these women and their children not have the same right to protection and life as other victims in the UK? The Government says that they cannot help these women as this would undermine the integrity of the immigration and benefit rules. The reality is that a small but extremely vulnerable minority of women are being denied protection available to all other victims. This is discriminatory and a breach of the UK Government's human rights obligations.

(Southall Black Sisters, 2004)

In order for the exclusion and lack of awareness of the issue to be challenged, Women's Aid again proposes 'mainstreaming' domestic violence issues into agencies dealing with immigration via the provision of information to criminal justice agencies, the public, family and immigration lawyers on domestic violence and its impacts on women and immigration. It also highlights the need for greater publicity to increase awareness for all women concerning their rights on domestic violence and immigration, including access to translated information at the point of entry into the country. And, perhaps most importantly, Women's Aid, along with a number of other women's groups, argues for an exemption to the 'no recourse to public funds' rule for women experiencing domestic violence (ibid.) so as to enhance safety and support.[14] As we saw in the introduction, campaigns around the 'no recourse to public funds' rule spearheaded by Southall Black Sisters, represent, according to Predelli et al. (2008), an instance of successful and sustained political agitation by a coalition of predominantly white women's groups and ethnic minority women's groups. Thus, Women's Aid's campaigning on race and immigration issues could be read as symptomatic of the partial reconciliation between white-dominated feminism and feminist anti-racism identified by Predelli et al. While such a reading might be a little overcelebratory, it is clear that some established predominantly white women's groups such as Fawcett and Women's Aid are beginning to more systematically explore possibilities for productive political articulations across the divide between majority white and ethnic minority feminist groups.

Domestic violence as a 'figure of the newly thinkable'

In this section, I want to explore the ways in which, despite the modes of professionalisation and institutionalisation described above, Women's Aid has managed to maintain a political radicalism and commitment to a resolutely counter-hegemonic politics. This is partly as a result of their articulations of feminist and anti-racist demands described above, but is also a consequence of their continued fidelity to the bold and threatening dimensions of their understanding of domestic violence. In this vein, I argue that their characterisation of domestic violence could be conceptualised as a 'figure of the newly thinkable' in Zerilli's terms – that is, a new, imaginative vision through which to conceptualise domestic violence. There is, I argue, a conscious effort by the organisation to continuously reiterate, revisit and reactivate the excitement and sense of newness produced by the 'discovery' of domestic violence. This (re)investment takes place *across* the various different spaces and contexts in which Women's Aid engages politically. Thus, the radicality of Women's Aid inheres not so much in the fact that it maintains an autonomous strand, but in the articulation of the organisation's various practices into a feminist analysis of domestic violence – which could be usefully conceptualised as *both* a 'figure of the newly thinkable' (in Zerilli's terms) or an 'empty signifier' (in Laclau's terms).

It is crucial to point out that its characterisation of domestic violence in feminist terms permeates all of Women's Aid's work, and thus it is pertinent to look in some detail at this characterisation. In response to the question 'what is domestic violence?', Women's Aid defines domestic violence as

> Physical, sexual, psychological or financial violence that takes place within an intimate or family-type relationship and that forms a pattern of coercive or controlling behaviour. This can include forced marriage and so-called 'honour crimes'. Domestic violence may, and often does, involve a range of abusive behaviours, not all of which are, in themselves, inherently 'violent'.
>
> (Women's Aid, 2005c)

Here, a number of aspects come to the fore. Crucially, domestic violence is not conceived in terms of a series of isolated incidents of physical violence, but is thought more in terms of a structure of domination in which a multitude of tactics are used persistently over time. Also, an equivalence is drawn between 'conventional' domestic violence and other forms of family-based coercion of women, which further highlights the structural character of women's oppression in that it implies that these various forms of coercion are rooted in structural understandings of gender relations, rather than existing in isolation from one another. Furthermore, the final sentence reinforces this by drawing attention to how domestic violence is typically embedded in a system of coercive measures, rather than entailing singular acts of physical violence.

Subsequently in the same paragraph, Women's Aid draws attention to how domestic violence is gender specific (that is, it is typically enacted by men and experienced by women) and that all women can experience domestic violence irrespective of their demographic characteristics (ibid.).[15] This implicitly rests on an understanding of domestic violence as being primarily an issue of *gender* relations rather than necessarily being endemic to a specific class, ethnic or other demographic group. Domestic violence is presented as first and foremost rooted in sedimented structures of gender relations: gender is thus the privileged dimension and is implicitly afforded a systemic character. Johanna Kantola (2006: 75) refers to this as a *universal* domestic violence discourse. It is 'universal' to the extent that it emphasises how any woman can potentially experience domestic violence, and that this can only be adequately addressed by improving 'the general position of women in society' (ibid.: 75). This point was keenly reiterated by Nicola Harwin in an interview. She said,

> I will try and explain it [domestic violence] in terms of power and control, in terms of institutionalised power and control historically, and the fact that it may seem that it's just the individual man who is being unreasonable and wants to control his partner, but you have to locate that in the fact that 150 years ago he would legally have the right to hit her. What I often say is, we have new models of equality and respect and what we think relationships should be about now, but [concerning] patriarchy: 150 years ago women were legally the property of men and some people still have that view in their heads and culture is a lot slower to change. And so we will locate it, explanation is in inequality, I'll say in countries where women have the lowest status, there is the highest level of domestic abuse.[16]
>
> (Nicola Harwin, interview, February 2007)

Crucial here is that the understanding of domestic violence in systemic terms rooted in long-term structural inequalities is fundamentally a *feminist* analysis, inasmuch as it foregrounds its gendered character and resists explaining it in terms of the pathologies of individual men. On the question of feminism, Women's Aid explicitly self-identifies as a feminist organisation. However, although some documents begin by stating unambiguously that Women's Aid is a feminist organisation, its feminist identity is not usually highlighted to any significant extent. In spite of this, a feminist ethos runs through the entire organisation. As a senior staff member commented,

Feminism is not a main goal of Women's Aid but it underpins Women's Aid's approach to stopping violence against women. So that's never gone away ... even though Women's Aid is no longer a collective nationally, it still is very clear about gender relations and that domestic violence is based on women's inequality in a historical context, and that you will find is also the approach to how local service providers support women, because it comes from what we call a survivor-centred approach which is based on an 'empowerment-model' which enables women to take control of their lives, so it's never gone away really, because it's embedded in our practices.

(interview with Women's Aid staff member, June 2006)

The centrality afforded to a specifically feminist understanding of domestic violence comes to the fore in, for instance, its work on perpetrator responsibility and its critique of restorative justice. Here, there is a strong emphasis on holding the abuser, as an autonomous individual, responsible for his actions.[17] Despite this emphasis on the systemic characteristics of violence against women, in the account of the need for abusers to take responsibility for their actions one finds a strong emphasis on classical liberal notions of choice and responsibility. There is therefore perhaps something of a tension between the systemic analysis of domestic violence, on the one hand, and their uncompromising account of perpetrator responsibility on the other. Indeed these discourses, as with the rest of Women's Aid's work, cohere around an attempt to maximise scope for autonomy and self-determination of women. The emphasis on structural inequality points towards the conditions of possibility for domestic violence to be tolerated, accepted, indeed almost condoned, as opposed to it entirely determining the actions of the perpetrator (Women's Aid, date not specified, (a)).

A related point is that in talking about domestic violence, Women's Aid is conscious of the fact that this runs the risk of sedimenting patriarchal conceptions of women as weak and helpless and liable to be subsumed under the category of 'victim'. However, Women's Aid's discourse seeks to counteract such a view by putting forth an understanding of women who have been subjected to domestic violence as strong, resilient and proactive (see Bacchi, 1999: 172). A Women's Aid document quotes approvingly from a study of victims of domestic violence which asserts that

The women in this study were also found to be actively engaged in trying to deal with violence and seeking outside assistance with these efforts. These women were neither helpless or hopeless [*sic*]. While they did speak of the negative effects of living with violence,

most had considerable strengths and held many positive views about
themselves despite the harm and denigration they had suffered.
(Dobash and Dobash, in Women's Aid, 2005c)

In this respect, Women's Aid's discourse is very much inflected with individualistic notions of empowerment and taking control of one's own life:
indeed, these dimensions are given precedence and there is no reference
to 'sisterhood' or any notion of feminist and/or female collective identity. This emphasis on individual strength and empowerment is further
brought to light in Women's Aid's insistence that the term 'survivor' be
used as opposed to 'victim', given the former signifier's connotations of
strength, resourcefulness and resilience (Barron, 2005). More theoretically,
we might say that the interplay between radical feminist notions such as
autonomy, 'taking control' and a structural analysis of gendered violence,
combined with a more classical liberal invocation of choice and human
rights are such that Women's Aid could perhaps best be characterised as
'radical liberal feminist'. The discursive framing of Women's Aid's practices thus prompts a scepticism of the tendency identified in the opening
chapter to treat liberalism and radicalism as constitutive opposites.

In more general terms, I want to contend that this 'radical liberal
feminist' analysis of domestic violence functions – to use Laclauian
parlance – as something of a nodal point which ties together the various
strands of Women's Aid's campaigning. Its specifically feminist account
is reiterated at the outset in almost every report, document and policy
consultation which the organisation produces. Using the criteria for
feminist radicalism advanced in Chapter 2, a strong case can be made
that one of the most radical elements of the early days of second-wave
feminism was the 'discovery' of domestic violence or, rather, the emergence of an account of domestic violence situated within an analysis of
the historical legacy of gender inequality. While a feminist analysis of
domestic violence is, to some degree, taken as given and therefore sedimented within the organisation, this does not lead to a bland consensus.
I want to argue instead that there has been a constant revisiting on the
part of the organisation of this radical moment of 'discovery', and that
this gives the organisation's work a certain energy and vibrancy. To this
extent, we can say that the 'discovery' of domestic violence constitutes
a quintessential moment of political imagination, via the articulation of
a 'figure of the newly thinkable', in Zerilli's terms. Recall that a figure of
the newly thinkable is a means through which a person's understanding
or perception of something is altered not through providing knowledge
or empirical examples, but through imaginatively offering a new way

to make sense of a particular object or phenomenon. In this case, the object is domestic violence, but with broader implications for how one conceptualises gender relations and the institution of the family. With this in mind, a case could be made that the ongoing politicisation of domestic violence by Women's Aid represents the clearest exemplar of the feminist political imagination among the instances of feminist politics analysed in this book.[18] This is inasmuch as it renders visible that which was previously invisible, radically disrupts the fabric of existing hegemonic gender relations, and entails the construction of links between elements that have no necessary relation: in this case, between domestic violence and broader gendered power inequalities.

This investment in the radicality of the 'discovery' of domestic violence is something that the organisation as a whole seems very keen to reiterate. To this extent, the organisation often emphasises how despite the increasing engagement with formal institutions and its emergence as a sophisticated, professional organisation, it has nonetheless kept the same basic values and principles. When I put it to Nicola Harwin that one could say there is a strong contrast between its current incarnation as sophisticated and professional and its origins as an autonomous second-wave organisation, she responded emphatically by stating, 'I don't think it is a contrast because the values base is still the same …. That's the key thing, the values base and the principles are still the same … which is about empowering survivors and their voices to be heard in the development of service provision and the development of policy, government policy, I think that's absolutely stayed the same throughout' (Nicola Harwin, interview, February 2007). She drew attention to how, at the outset

> the whole point was to bring women together so that their individual experience began to be, in a sense, partly transcended, or they had an opportunity to reflect on, in the way that women's consciousness-raising groups in the early 70s did exactly the same, which was about reflecting on your own experience to actually feel that there are threads and strands and social forces which are stronger and which are affecting you, which aren't just about your individual, personal experience – they're broader than that and I think that that was a very important thing about the refuge movement.
>
> (Ibid.)

Rather than characterising this in terms of a bland continuity with older aspects of Women's Aid's work, it is more pertinent to characterise it as a process of revisiting, of reinvesting in the radicality and newness of the initial 'discovery' of domestic violence. Even though it was originally formulated in 1974, Women's Aid's feminist analysis of domestic violence remains a figure of the *newly* thinkable by virtue of the continued prevalence of anti-feminist hegemonic understandings of domestic violence (Hague and Malos, 2005: 51–9). Indeed, Nicola Harwin was keen to stress how their arguments remain extremely threatening to dominant notions of familial relations and intimate relationships. She also pointed out that that tackling gender-related issues more generally remains very challenging and threatening for the public at large. Consequently, although the extent to which Women's Aid has engaged with formal institutions has undoubtedly varied over recent years, it has – for the most part – resisted undergoing a process of deradicalisation by virtue of its commitment to 'commemorating' and revisiting that contingent moment of political freedom in which the feminist analysis of domestic violence was first articulated.

Critical assessments: A drift towards the 'new managerialism'?

Until this point I have presented a generally favourable picture of the organisation, looking at the various ways in which Women's Aid has continued to engage in relatively radical feminist practices despite becoming increasingly professionalised. Despite this, I want to qualify what I have said thus far: in particular, I want to raise the question of whether the organisation's enthusiasm for multiagency work, coupled with its position as an 'expert' voice, renders them partially complicit with the logics of what we might call 'interest group pluralism', in a manner that may curtail the organisation's vitality and radicalism. For the purposes of this discussion, interest group pluralism refers to a mode of governance in which various actors are engaged in processes of making political claims which are then adjudicated by the governmental apparatus, and is thus symptomatic of what Zerilli and Arendt refer to as the domestication of politics to 'the social'. A further dimension of interest group pluralism, as Iris Marion Young has pointed out, is that it tends to reduce politics to a process of rule by experts who are delegated responsibility for particular issues (Young, 1990: 70–4). I want to contend that there is a sense in which Women's Aid's largely successful casting of itself as an expert voice within the field of domestic violence can, and at times possibly does, render it complicit with this particular mode of governance.

These concerns are particularly pressing when one considers the
centrality afforded to multiagency work in Women's Aid. As Hague and
Malos point out, 'Women's Aid and the network of local domestic violence
services as a whole have welcomed interagency work, applaud its inten-
tions and the improved services it can engender and have become more
and more involved in it over the years' (2005: 175). Within the literature
produced by the organisation, there is a surprising lack of sustained critical
engagement with the potential drawbacks of multiagency work. This perhaps highlights the concerns raised by Pragna Patel (1999: 62) of Southall
Black Sisters, who argues that a sustained feminist debate on the vicissitudes
of multiagency work has thus far not been forthcoming in the UK context.
She draws attention to a number of potential problems with multiagency
work, focussing on how they often give the impression of enabling inclusive discussion between statutory and voluntary bodies, but in a manner
that deflects attention from the power inequalities inherent in such relations. She argues that the terminology used in the context of multia-gency
work reflects what she calls the 'new realism' or 'new corporatism' in local
authority governance, overlooking power inequalities by, for example,
describing the police as a 'service provider' rather than a 'force' (ibid,: 66).[19]
This points to how the use of inclusive forms of discourse (as in terms
such as co-operation, inclusion and consensus) might risk deflecting critical attention from the power inequalities within multiagency fora (Kelly,
1999; Hague and Malos, 2005: 40–1; and Newman, 2002: 90). A similar
point is made by Hague et al. (2003: 28), who argue that consultations with
users of domestic violence services may have counter-productive effects.
For instance, the presence of representatives from the domestic violence
sector on decision-making bodies may add legitimacy to decisions that are
made, even though the views of the representatives may not be accurately
reflected in those decisions. Other tactics used to minimise the more challenging dimensions of having service users on board include 'delaying
tactics, diverting users into alternative agendas ... and inviting tokenistic
individuals rather than representative groups of users' (ibid.: 28).

The increasing burden of consultative and multiagency work certainly
has implications for the internal workings of the organisation. Hague,
Mullender and Aris also draw attention to how refuge workers – whose
time and resources are already constrained – are frequently forced to
balance refuge work (the actual provision of assistance to women) with
consultative and multiagency work, which may have deleterious effects
on both. Indeed, in some respects it is in this sense that modes of
deradicalisation can be most clearly felt in respect to Women's Aid, such
that the early emphasis on autonomy and collectivity has given way to

a more managerialist ethos, which has implications for the experience
of women in refuges, as these quotes from domestic violence survivors
illustrate (Hague et al., 2003: 159):

> The old policy of trying to offer jobs to suitable ex-residents in
> Women's Aid was great. Women's Aid don't do that so much now.
> Now you need qualifications and to be good on computers. It's not
> so hands on any more.
>   Now it's all policies and management and protocols and not much
> time for the women. Refuges tend to have a full-time manager who
> never works with the women, so it's not much of a collective any
> more. They've forgotten about empowerment a bit.

In raising these issues, my claim is not that Women's Aid should avoid
multiagency work. Instead, I simply wish to draw attention to a relative
absence of a *critical* purchase on these trends: in Women's Aid publicly
available material, there is no clear statement or engagement with the
potential shortcomings of interagency work, especially in relation to
new forms of governance within the public sector and local authorities.
In particular, there is a danger that the original radical feminist 'nodal
points' of autonomy and self-empowerment run the risk of being reart-
iculated into a discourse in line with the new corporatism/new public
management described by Patel above.

And, indeed, to a degree one can claim that such a process has already
been set in motion. In 2006, Women's Aid published a set of national
standards for service providers of domestic violence, seeking to create
uniform baseline standards for domestic violence service providers.
Noteworthy in this document is that, while it is certainly imbued with
a feminist analysis of domestic violence, it generally lacks the more
challenging, uncompromising tone which permeates much of Women's
Aid's published material. In particular, the terminology and framing of
the concerns appear very much in line with the 'new public management' alluded to above. In terms of delivering services to survivors of
domestic violence, the document claims that a desired outcome is that

> Services ensure that survivors are able to identify and express their
> needs and make decisions in a supportive and non-judgemental
> environment; that survivors are treated with dignity, respect and
> sensitivity; and that they promote service-user involvement in the
> development and delivery of services.
>
> (Women's Aid, 2006: 15)

This forms the basis of a 'survivor-centred approach', emphasising 'self-help, empowerment and inclusion, to enable survivors to take control of their own lives' (ibid.: 15). Such sentiments clearly have their roots in the autonomous strands of the women's movement; however, within the context of a somewhat dry document which frames survivors as 'service users', they take on a meaning which seems more in tune with the focus on 'customer service' and individualism characteristic of the 'new public management' and the general encroachment of private sector discourse into the provision of public services.[20] That is not to say that the publication of such a document is counter-productive, but rather to highlight that an organisation such as Women's Aid perhaps risks weakening its more critical dimensions if there is an absence of an explicit engagement with the potential limitations of multiagency work and 'new corporatist' modes of governance.

In raising these issues, I do not intend to suggest that Women's Aid is heading in the wrong direction in terms of its political strategy, or to be in any way prescriptive. Rather, having thus far outlined how Women's Aid continued to enact a range of radical practices (despite forms of professionalisation and institutionalisation), what I want to do is suggest some ways in which these more challenging aspects could be seen as being under threat. I want to propose that the casting of itself as an expert voice on the issue of domestic violence runs the risk of the issue being addressed *in its particularity*. That is, it potentially ties in with interest group pluralism inasmuch as the more threatening elements of the campaign against domestic violence – the profound critique of gender relations for example – potentially become marginalised. For the most part, I think this has been avoided. However, the critical points raised here about multiagency work feed into a more general concern, namely, that the apparent professionalisation of groups like Fawcett and Women's Aid is such that they are now part of an established community of 'insider' feminist groups, with the possible unintended consequence that less professionalised groups become marginalised. As Predelli et al. put it,

We have suggested that organisations such as Southall Black Sisters, Imkaan, Fawcett Society, Women's Resource Centre, Women's Aid, Refuge, and EVAW are part of a relatively stable policy community of 'insiders' with access to state-level policy circles. These organisations are regularly drawn on by government to provide either formal or informal input to decision-making processes concerning gender equality issues, including violence against women issues. These organisations have achieved their insider status as a result of their own hard work and in conjunction with the government's policy to engage with community groups and its need to receive policy input in order to achieve legitimacy for policies. Representatives from women's organisations themselves, however, do not label or present their own organisations as insiders, but rather as outsiders to government, thus emphasising their independence from, rather than possible co-optation by, the state.

(2008: 183)

This alludes to the potentially somewhat schizophrenic consequences of feminist 'success'. While being listened to by government is desirable for many feminist organisations, it is acknowledged – albeit often implicitly – that this may then lead to co-optation, compromise and the marginalisation of other critical voices. I have argued that, for the most part, groups like Fawcett and Women's Aid tend not to experience compromise or deradicalisation as a necessary consequence of feminist success, but nonetheless this is a tension which continues to be negotiated by both organisations.

Conclusion

I framed this chapter by setting up an apparent contrast between the early Women's Aid, with its classic 'second-wave' values of autonomy and empowerment, and its present day incarnation as a professionalised and sophisticated campaigning organisation. While such a framing, of course, highlights significant discontinuities between the 1970s and the present, I sought to trouble such a reading by highlighting how the persistent recourse to what Kantola (2006: 75) calls a universal domestic violence discourse disrupts an emphasis on discontinuity. This in turn illustrates another of my key claims: while forms of compromise and a move towards a less critical position *may* occur as a result of professionalisation and increasing engagement by feminist groups with state institutions (such as local and national government, courts and police), it is by no means inevitable that such an outcome will occur – and indeed the precise character of such an outcome will of course vary. In this respect, I have argued, for the most part, that Women's Aid has avoided losing its critical force, partly through the exploration of imaginative articulations between feminism and anti-racism, but primarily through an ongoing process of reinvestment in the radicality of the original 'discovery' of domestic violence. In this sense, through a feminist and thus *gendered* analysis of domestic violence, Women's Aid has been able to retain an investment in a feminist approach to the issue which, I argue, can be characterised as a 'figure of the newly thinkable'.

Crucially, the radicalism of this ongoing re-investment also derives in large part from its imaginative articulation of 'seventies' feminist radicalism with a more liberal set of discursive tenets. Women's Aid's analysis shares with 'traditional' radical feminism an emphasis on gendered violence as systemic, and thus irreducible to characteristics of individual perpetrators and/or victims/survivors. However, it also shares with liberalism an emphasis on notions such as autonomy and individual empowerment. As we have seen, these elements of liberalism can be articulated within politically inegalitarian chains of equivalence, used to justify the encroachment of private sector modes of management into the public sector. And yet, when articulated within feminist chains of equivalence that incorporate a systemic and gendered account of domestic violence, they can be integral to a progressive feminist politics that cuts across different types of (non) institutional space. This in turn reinforces the simple yet fundamental and often overlooked point that liberalism and radicalism are not constitutive opposites. Rather, key elements of liberal political discourse are not irredeemably confined to reformism or incipient conservatism, but are 'up for grabs' within feminist struggle. Consequently, the divergent appropriations of liberalism present in Women's Aid's feminist radicalism, on the one hand, and the conservatism of neoliberal 'new public management discourse', on the other, are both instances of ongoing contestations over the terms of liberal discourse.

These complex ongoing negotiations of radicalism and liberalism in a diversity of practices and types of space certainly call into question the validity of narratives of feminist decline, and feminist re-emergence, both of which are predicated on a paradigm break between the feminist seventies and the feminist present. They also demonstrate the need for an assessment of contemporary feminism which avoids familiar dichotomies (such as liberal/radical, inside/outside) and refuses to overplay the incommensurability of elements of distinct analytical frameworks. As with Fawcett, this calls for cautious yet critical optimism alert to the potential radicalism of various forms of feminist appropriations of liberal discourse and engagements with state institutions.

5
The F-Word: Cultural Politics and Third-Wave Feminism

My third case study, The F-word website and its activist offshoot, the London Thirdwave Feminists (hereafter London Thirdwave), is qualitatively distinct from the previous two inasmuch as it takes the form of an autonomous online space. Perhaps more importantly, The F-word sits at the epicentre of what appears to be a resurgence of feminist mobilisation in the UK, and thus an analysis of it is integral to an exploration of contemporary feminist practices in the British context. The F-word is not an 'active' group in any meaningful sense, but rather, acts as a forum for discussion between, and noticeboard for, the diverse voices within contemporary feminist politics in the UK. As we shall see, this diversity is integral to The F-word's self-understanding. However, despite this diversity, I argue that there are two key elements to The F-word, which I explore throughout this chapter. These are, first, the centrality of debate and political activity related to the negotiation of feminism 'in and against' popular culture, and, second, the negotiation of generational dynamics within contemporary feminism, linked to The F-word's self-understanding as a specifically 'young' feminist space.

The bulk of the chapter is geared towards a critical analysis of these two key elements. I argue that both dimensions of The F-word throw up a range of conflicting concerns. As I shall make clear, the focus on the politics of popular culture can at times lead to a depoliticised and individualised reading of contemporary feminist subjectivity, while the emphasis on generational subjectivity at times re-instantiates problematic conceptions of feminist generational temporality. In these respects, The F-word could be read as symptomatic of logics of political disengagement and feminist deradicalisation, as feminism comes to be practiced as a form of consumption or individualised self-identification, rather than as a mode of political action. However, to characterise The F-word in these terms would not do justice to the vibrancy of the site, coupled with the strong affective investments in a feminist community on the part of the site's users. Furthermore, from the critical perspective advanced in Chapter 2 I shall argue that The F-word's articulation of a new feminist agenda linked to a notion of a 'third wave' could be seen as a radical, transformative move in two respects. First, the emphasis on openness and inclusiveness within this agenda creates, to some degree, a space for an open critical exchange about current issues relevant to feminism in a manner which – following Zerilli's lexicon – presupposes plurality and avoids the temptation of the 'subject question'. Secondly, the articulation of The F-word as a specifically 'third-wave' space is such that, as with Fawcett, 'third-wave feminism' assumes the character of – again in Zerilli's terms – a 'figure of the newly thinkable' allowing young women to be brought into a feminist agenda in a manner resistant to hegemonic post-feminist logics.

However, while there is much to applaud on The F-word, I shall contend that these radical, freedom-centred practices are to some extent undone, in two ways. First, the delineation of The F-word as a specifically *third-wave* space perhaps inadvertently creates a range of problematic exclusions, and is structured around a preoccupation with constructing the basis of a collective political subject in advance of an actual political engagement. Second, while there is a conscious and determined attempt to resist the hegemonic logics of post-feminism, this is undermined somewhat by the construction of a generational subjectivity complicit with logics of post-feminist *dis*identification with second-wave feminism. I shall flesh out these points by first providing some background information about the emergence and general orientation of The F-word, before looking at modes of negotiation of the relation between feminism and popular culture. I will finish with a detailed account of the discourses and practices involved in articulating a 'third-wave' feminist agenda within The F-word.

My normative aim, in some senses, is to steer a course between, on the one hand, a dismissive account of The F-word/London Thirdwave as irredeemably apolitical and deradicalised, and, on the other, an overly celebratory account of the 'return of feminism' – the latter of which seems to crop up fairly frequently in the liberal left broadsheet press (see, for example, Rachel Bell, 2007; Bennett, 2007). Instead, what we are witnessing is a diversity of practices, some of which have radical and imaginative dimensions, and others in which scope for feminist radicalism is narrowed or closed. Thus, the picture we are presented with is in some ways irretrievably complex and not apt to be subsumed under either a totalising or unitary narrative of feminist depoliticisation or a more celebratory account.

Feminism and the Internet

Research for this chapter consisted primarily of analysis of feature articles on The F-word website, alongside email correspondence with a number of regular contributors and some participation in the London Thirdwave Yahoo discussion group. The primarily web-based nature of the analysis throws up a host of questions relating to the character of feminism on the web and its comparability with non web-based political activism. Key here are debates concerning 'cyberfeminism' – that is, a feminism that utilises a range of new media technologies. While varied, the cyberfeminism literature is characterised by a number of common assumptions. For instance, it tends to strongly invoke a notion of radical break or paradigm shift from 'old' forms of politics to a 'new' feminism utterly imbricated in the throes of new media technologies. In addition, accounts are often distinctly utopian, emphasising the radical possibilities that new technology opens up for feminism (Haraway, 1991; Pollock and Sutton, 1999; Hawthorne and Klein, 1999; Richards and Schnall, 2003).[1] Exceptions include Wilding's (date not specified) emphasis on the oppressive and regulatory character of new media technologies, and Braidotti's (date not specified) articulation of a position that sits somewhere between these twin extremes.

However, I do not think any of these perspectives accurately get to grips with the character of The F-word and London Thirdwave in its current guise. The debates around cyberfeminism seem rather prone to exaggeration, either in terms of emphasising the 'newness' of the phenomena described or being excessively optimistic/pessimistic in terms of the analysis. Rather than seeing The F-word, or indeed web-based feminism in general, as something radically 'new', I think it is pertinent to emphasise a strong level of continuity with earlier forms of feminist activism. The Internet certainly opens up a range of new possibilities inasmuch as the exchange of information becomes much easier, and this is illustrated by the recent proliferation of feminist websites and blogs (Cochrane, 2006). Indeed, the Internet's central role in facilitating increased exchange of ideas and information among feminists in the UK and transnationally can hardly be overstated (see Ferree and Pudrovska, 2006). However, while the Internet certainly facilitates feminist activity, I want to caution against seeing this as indicative of a profound and radical break. Indeed, F-word founder Catherine

Redfern is keen to draw an analogy between The F-word and *Spare Rib* (the key publication from the height of 'second-wave' feminism in the UK that to some extent acted as a noticeboard for the feminist movement). Thus, avoiding cyberfeminist accounts of radical break, I do not think that a fundamentally different analytical frame is required when analysing web-based feminist activism. However, one must remain alert to the possibilities that are opened up – and indeed sometimes closed down – by web-based political activity.

The F-word: Diversity, inclusiveness and reasserting feminism

We are now ready for a more detailed outline of the aims, structure and content of the site. The F-word was set up by London-based archivist Catherine Redfern[2] in 2001 'to help encourage a new sense of community among UK feminists' (Redfern, date not specified (a)). She writes,

> I tried to find newsgroups, mailing lists, magazines, but nothing really seemed to be out there, and believe me, I really tried. Everything that had once existed, like *Spare Rib*, seemed to have gone defunct. I knew that feminists existed, but they seemed invisible, like they had gone underground or something, and you had to be 'in the know' to find out what was going on.
>
> (Redfern, date not specified (b))

In particular, Redfern was concerned that there seemed to be a perception that feminism had ceased to be relevant to younger women, allowing scope for the fostering of a new, updated version of feminism. As she puts it, 'I was keen to embrace a feminism that was relevant to my life and the life of my peers: modern British women in their teens, 20s and 30s. I wanted to be involved in an exchange of ideas, views and opinions' (ibid.). In particular, there are two interrelated assumptions which The F-word, despite its diversity, seeks to contest. The first is the widespread assumption that feminism is dead, outmoded and no longer relevant. Related to this is the view that where feminism does exist, it is the preserve of ageing 'second-wavers' and therefore no longer relevant to young women and girls. Redfern set up the site to 'show the doubters that feminism still exists here, today, now – and is as relevant to the lives of the younger generation as it was to those in the 60s and 70s' (Redfern, date not specified (a)).

In terms of its format, The F-word consists of feature articles addressing a wide variety of issues relevant to contemporary feminists,[3] as well as a blog (which is updated regularly), reviews of books/films etc., a comments section and an extensive list of links to other feminist resources on the Internet. It is specifically aimed at young women and girls in their teens, 20s and 30s, although it does welcome contributions from men as well. Its key declared aims are as follows (Redfern, 2001b):

- To give young women a space where they can express their views
- To enable young feminists to share ideas together – when this opportunity is usually so rare
- To enable young women to find their voice, to encourage them to express themselves and develop if they have not had this chance before
- To find out more about young women who are producing zines, who are involved with the riot grrrl movement, what's known as 'girlie' feminism, or 'third-wave' feminists
- To find out what other people my age are thinking and doing about feminism
- To say to the world – we are young and feminist and we *exist*! In other words, to contradict the viewpoint that young women do not care about feminism!

In view of this, The F-word is absolutely central to British feminist activity at the present time. On announcing her stepping down from the editorship at The F-word, Redfern (2007) wrote, 'Six years on, the site has grown to include 315 articles and reviews written by 115 contributors, a regularly updated blog, we have tens of thousands of readers, we have been publicised in the national press and the site is archived by the British Library'.. Its significance is such that The F-word serves a similar function to that served by *Spare Rib* in the 1970s and 1980s, or by the US-based site Feministing,[4] which currently has half a million readers a month.

In addition to analysis of The F-word, this chapter shall also make reference to its affiliated activist group, the London Thirdwave Feminists. London Thirdwave has a Yahoo email discussion group, which is generally lively, but has become quieter in recent years after having peaked in summer 2003, perhaps due to migration to the now much livelier London Feminist Network mailing list.[5] London Thirdwave also used to hold regular meetings, although these also have been less frequent of late; indeed several members of London Thirdwave mentioned in email correspondence that they are saddened that due to time constraints they have not been able to keep up the level of sustained political activism that they would have liked. The group was formed as a result of a group of people on The F-word mailing list meeting up in person and deciding to create an official 'real' group in addition to The F-word. Redfern also founded the UK Feminist Action Yahoo mailing list, partly as a result of a general sense that London Thirdwave should 'do more activism' (email from F-word contributor). The UK Feminist Action group is gearing towards announcements about forthcoming feminist activist events, rather than being discussion-based.[6]

To a significant degree, The F-word has succeeded in radically rein-vigorating a feminist agenda within the public sphere. It has proved to be hugely popular, and has emphatically achieved its aim of drawing together voices of young UK feminists, and has received recognition in the media. Redfern was included in a feature in UK broadsheet news-paper *The Guardian* in 2003 about influential young women in the UK today, which stated that 'Redfern is responsible for reinvigorating the debate around feminism in the UK, bringing young politicised women together and giving them a voice' (Brooks, 2003). In addition, in a feature in *The Guardian* in 2005 about interesting magazines aimed at women, Mira Katbamna (2005) wrote the following about The F-word:

> Set up by Catherine Redfern in 2001 as a forum for young feminists, The F-word has grown into the community hub for activists from across the spectrum, and will quickly reassure you that feminism is alive, well and definitely kicking. The perfect antidote to ranting at dinner parties, if you're gutted that you missed the revolution the first time around, take a look at thefword's [*sic*] resources and news sections, sign up for the newsletter and start campaigning.

This alludes to the way in which the site has a perceptible liveliness and vibrancy, reflected in its seemingly strong interpellative capacity: that is, its capacity to prompt readers to identify anew, and with vig-our, with a feminist agenda (a theme explored in greater detail later).[7] This renders The F-word particularly important as a site through which young women are able to come together and identify with a feminist agenda: Redfern (2003b) has been particularly keen to emphasise the site's appeal to young women. During a talk on the subject of third-wave feminism at a conference organised by left-wing pressure group Compass in London in June 2006, Redfern described how she had received numerous emails expressing 'I thought I was alone' type sentiments from younger feminists, while, on stepping down from the editorship, she wrote, 'I have been told that feminists have felt inspired by what they have read and have gone on to form other groups, campaigns, organisations and websites of their own. The feminist community in the UK is now incredibly vibrant and increasingly visible and active. It is pleasing to see that young women are at the forefront of this and I hope that this site has contributed in some small way to the resurgence of feminism in recent years. I am incredibly proud to have been part of that' (Redfern, 2007). In a not dissimilar vein, emphasising the centrality of The F-word to contemporary British feminism, one regular contributor to The F-word pointed out, 'The F-word is great because it brings together a range of opinions on feminism and opens up the floor to normal people to write about the things they believe in. It's totally grassroots, but the standards are really high. Also, I think it's a great repository for information and contacts – I know that other message boards I belong to get a stream of new members by linking through from there' (email from F-word contributor).

In this respect, the main purpose of The F-word is not to advance a particular political agenda (like Women's Aid or The Fawcett Society). Instead, its prime function is its capacity to act as a means of reasserting feminism counter to the dominant assumption that feminism is outmoded, unfashionable and no longer necessary. To this extent, many of the articles posted on the site have a somewhat defiant tone: many implicitly accept (although in non-academic terms) the central claims of those works that characterise the contemporary conjuncture as specifically 'post-feminist'. Indeed, if one were to extract one key element from the various contributions to The F-word, it would be that it seeks to reaffirm feminism within the context of what McRobbie has called the 'post-feminist gender settlement'. As one F-word contributor argued, 'I would say that a major success of The F-word is that it has served to draw attention to feminism and to its continued existence (despite postfeminist claims)' (email from F-word contributor; see also Cosh, 2006).

Of course, the very name 'The F-word' is clearly indicative of a reflexive awareness of the disavowed nature of feminism within the current conjuncture. This is borne out by Catherine Redfern's explanation of how she came to use the term. She writes,

> I saw this on the cover of the magazine Bust: it was their 'feminism' issue and Gloria Steinem was wearing a t-shirt with the phrase 'The F Word' on it. I thought it was a brilliant name for the site as it encapsulated everything I wanted to say about the site: the fact that feminism is supposed to be a taboo for young British women, and the fact that the website was to feature writing by young feminists.
>
> (Redfern, year not specified (b))

In providing an online space for the reassertion and negotiation of contemporary feminism, The F-word attributes considerable importance to keeping open the question of what feminism 'is' or should be. In response to the question of 'what is contemporary UK feminism?' (the site's subtitle), Redfern responds,

> It is impossible to define: it can appear in many different people's lives in many different ways. The F-word does not define what contemporary UK feminism is but instead allows a place for different people to share their different opinions and views. The contributors to the site may have opposing views on certain issues, and that's fine; it simply demonstrates that feminism is a diverse, living and healthy ideology which is confident enough to question itself. There is no 'party line' in feminism, there is no 'feminist rule-book'. Feminism in the UK today is whatever we make it.
>
> (Ibid.)

Thus, there are efforts to make the site as inclusive as possible: there is a sense that young women often feel alienated from feminism because of its associations with a strict, puritanical approach to issues such as fashion and sexuality (see, for example, Walter, 1998: 106–7). Consequently, the diverse and often conflictual nature of feminism is emphasised in order to bring as many young women into the fold as possible, and to divorce feminism from any doctrinal or puritanical associations (Redfern, 2001a; 2001c). Indeed, several people have praised The F-word and London Thirdwave for the way in which they have provided space for the articulation of a diverse range of perspectives on feminism, while remaining amicable and vibrant. One contributor, for instance, mentioned,

> It has widened my perception of feminism. There are people of widely differing viewpoints on L3W. At the beginning, the three third-wavers who I hung out with socially were a great comfort, but they had quite different attitudes within feminism. One, for example, takes a pro-sex work stance that I disagree strongly with, identifying as I do with a radical feminist position on sex work as violence. Yet somehow we were able to unite as young feminists and get on despite our differences. I'm not sure that would have happened thirty years ago.
>
> (Email from F-word contributor)

This foregrounding of diversity and inclusiveness, with its emphasis on a plurality of *opinions* rather than a diversity of identities, can be seen to tie in with Zerilli's account of a freedom-centred feminism based on openness and critical exchange.[8] In contrast to a politics of purity, there is an affirmation of plurality and there is no attempt to think through a feminist agenda in terms of the construction of 'woman' or 'feminism' as a unified or coherent category. Furthermore, one could say that in providing a forum for comment and discussion it creates space for inter-action and practices of critical judgement between feminists. A gener-ous, though not altogether inaccurate, reading of The F-word would thus be to say that in some respects it represents a quintessential example of a freedom-centred democratic space.[9] In this vein, The F-word could be taken as a site that ties in with the types of critical agonistic spaces championed by Chantal Mouffe in her account of 'agonistic pluralism'. For Mouffe, such spaces are constituted around a mediation between a minimal consensus over its constituent bases – in this case a subjective identification with feminism – and a fidelity to dissensus and debate within that space (Mouffe, 2000: 80–105).

In some respects, this emphasis on diversity and openness, coupled with the attempt on the part of The F-word and London Thirdwave to carve out a space for a new feminist agenda, represents a radical move in view of the prevalence of post-feminist hegemonic discourses which incite young women to disavow any identification with feminism. To some degree, in carving out a space for feminism, we are witnessing an important instance of the feminist political imagination. Through an avoidance of the ascrip-tion of too rigid a meaning to this new feminist agenda, spaces for feminist political freedom are opened up, thus clearing the way for the formulation of a diversity of claims that resist the pervasive logics of post-feminism. It is in this capacity that The F-word is at its most radical, at times taking the form of an assertive denunciation of the logics of post-feminism in a manner which does not close down discussion or debate.

Cultural politics and feminist individualism

Having established the basic terrain, I now turn to the analysis of the substantive aspects of The F-word. In the following sections, I want to explore the consequences of the attempt by the editorship at The F-word to encourage contributors to write articles pertaining to feminist attitudes towards the popular cultural domain. I want to suggest that, in some instances, the focus on popular culture and media serves to bracket out more engaged political concerns in favour of a more playful feminist sen-sibility, tying in with logics of feminist individualisation and depoliticisa-tion. As we shall see, a number of articles are more overtly politicised, but nonetheless, feminism is, in many instances, presented less as a mode of critical engagement with broader socio-political phenomena and more as an affirmative yet individualised form of subjective self-identification. In an early F-word article by Catherine Redfern consisting of a typology of different types of feminism, this mode of feminism is described as 'pop-feminism' or 'feminism 'lite'. In this piece, in which she comes across as ambivalent towards this type of feminism, Redfern writes,

> This is spice-girls feminism: girl power! Feminism as a fleeting fashion trend. Buffy the Vampire Slayer as a feminist icon. Madonna as the women we all aspire to be. This is the feminism that has filtered down to the girls who read Sugar and Just 17. Girls are so much better than boys, and wearing a wonderbra is a statement of empowerment.
>
> (Redfern, 2001a)

This closely parallels Angela McRobbie's reading of the emergence of what she calls 'popular feminism'. This refers to the emergence of new forms of sexual, social and economic assertiveness among young women but whereby this is not in any way constructed as political (McRobbie, 1999: 124; see also Walter, 1998: 32–54). Traces of this individualistic, 'go-getting' feminism are pervasive in much of the material on The F-word website. Indeed, even articles which are not explicitly in this vein often include traces of a depoliticised 'girl power' feminism. For instance, one of the most explicitly 'pop' feminist contributions was an entertaining article titled 'Feminine Feminism', with an introductory blurb that is truly paradigmatic of 'pop feminism'. It reads, 'Laura Wadsworth [the author] loves lipstick, fashion, boys, and the colour pink. Does that mean she's not a feminist? No way! Girly girls can be just as feminist as anyone else, she argues' (Wadsworth, 2004; see also Redfern, 2002a). Wadsworth goes on to define 'modern feminism' as 'being proud of our gender and not taking any stick from males, without hating men', rhetoric reminiscent of the Spice Girls' espousals of 'girl power' in the late 1990s (note also that the 'without hating men' qualification carries the traces of a disavowal of the generationally specific figure of the 'man hating' feminism).[10] Not entirely dissimilar sentiments come to the fore in an article titled 'Ball Breaking? Coming Out of the Feminist Closet' by Lorraine Smith. In discussing how it might be feasible to promote feminism to the public at large, she suggests,

> Get a top advertising agency on the case, rope some intelligent and attractive female celebrities to front the campaign and feminism

would be back on its feet before you could say 'girl power'. But who would fund all this nonsense? Perhaps a better idea would be for us all, across the globe to put one pound/dollar/euro in to hire Kylie [Minogue] for a photo session and interview. Once the Antipodean temptress had reassured our doubting sisters and frightened men-folk that feminism is really nothing to be scared of, we'd all be ready to come out of the closet in no time.

(Smith, 2003a; see also Thurgood, 2003)

Such a line of argument is clearly imbued with more than a little sarcasm, but it nonetheless presupposes a close link between popular celebrity culture and feminist (dis)identifications. This arguably reflects a more general tendency for some types of feminism on The F-word (particularly in its early stages) to tie in with hegemonic discourses of competitive individualism and empowerment. This came to light in an email exchange with a regular contributor to The F-word blog, who noted how the drift towards individualism in contemporary feminism might risk leading to an unintended complicity with patriarchal norms. In debating whether contemporary feminism might be seen as 'less radical' than in the past, she mused,

The whole 'I'm doing it for me' mantra is terribly difficult to get around – that age-old feminist issue of body hair, even. It's totally unacceptable for anyone but the most alternative of feminists to go around sporting hairy legs and armpits in this generation of feminists. Ask most of them and they'll tell you they just feel 'more comfortable' or 'more sexy' that way – they're not doing it for male approval but to make them feel better about themselves, and that's a right-on, feminist objective. But where is this standard against which they're benchmarking their opinion about themselves from? I kind of wish my generation (and myself included) had the guts to just say 'do you know what? Women have hair on their bodies – get over it'. And we don't have the guts, where the previous generation did, and I think that's kind of a shame. It smacks of paying lip-service to liberation even whilst we bow to patriarchal norms.

(Email from F-word contributor)

The melancholic sentiments expressed here belie a despondency with the way in which certain modes of feminism promulgated by young women, while encouraging a feminist sensibility, nonetheless engender a somewhat uncritical stance towards aspects of normative femininity. This in turn might be seen as reflective of a more general tendency in Anglo-American feminism to seek to foster feminist identifications among young women by smoothing over presumed tensions between feminism and femininity (Baumgardner and Richards, 2004; Levinson, 2009). Frequently, as the above quote suggests, this process of 'smoothing over' in practices often entails the withholding of a critique of normative femininity.

In a similar vein, several other contributors have expressed concerns that the (perceived) preoccupation with feminist individualism on the F-word has led to a bracketing out of a range of key feminist concerns. Finn Mackay, a self-identified 'Radical Lesbian Feminist' who contributes to The F-word and founded the London Feminist Network, has argued for the reassertion of 'traditional' second-wave demands in place of the more superficial concerns which she implicitly sees as being prevalent on The F-word. She writes,

> Making demands such as equal pay, free childcare, an end to violence against women; all demands made in the 1970s which we still have not achieved. Our big sisters in the 70s had some good points, let's not throw away a whole movement for the sake of being able to do pole-dancing classes, gawp at male models in women's magazines or take up a career in prostitution – these things are not our liberation, and they are not worth all those lives that are lost, wasted and taken by this unequal world.
>
> (Mackay, 2004)

A similar set of concerns are expressed by JoJo Kirtley, who argues for a re-engagement with issues around male violence. Here, there appears to be a subtext that contemporary concerns have become excessively flippant, and that a return to the 'second-wave' concern with male violence is something which should be encouraged. She writes,

> Don't get me wrong, I do get pissed off at men's magazines projecting the 'perfect' image of women, I cringe when I hear a sexist joke, I'm not too happy with page three, I hate being whistled at in the street, I can't stand the thought of dieting to 'please my man', and I hate the fact that lesbianism is still frowned upon. But compared to a battered wife, a woman who has been raped, or a young girl who has just been forced to have her clitoris chopped off – is it hardly significant in comparison? It astounds me that we as British women have forgotten about these extremely important issues, and if we haven't then why are we ignoring them?
>
> (Kirtley, 2002)

Clearly implicit here is a frustration with what she perceives as a neglect of traditional, 'serious' second-wave concerns relating to male violence. Her argument describes a frustration with a perceived shift from a serious, politically engaged feminism in the 1970s to a less serious and more frivolous mode of feminism in the present. Her argument thus suggests an uneasiness with the tendency, in the context of an articulation of a new feminist agenda, to overemphasise the division between new and old (leading on to the problems of feminist generations that shall be dealt with shortly).

In some senses, certain articulations of feminism on The F-word could be seen as indicative of a shift from a politically engaged and critical feminism, to one characterised by affirmations of individualism at the expense of politics. Here, we might say that some forms of affect circulating on The F-word are centred upon an articulation of feminism as an individualised mode of self-identification, whereby that self-identification is linked to an affirmation of assertiveness rather than a mode of political subjectivity. While that identification arguably arises from an irritation or disaffection with certain hegemonic perceptions of feminism, one might reasonably argue that this irritation jars with the shared, collective sense of 'rage' which was a crucial sustaining element of certain strands of UK second-wave feminism. On The F-word, rather than a sense of rage or anger, one finds a pervasive sense of irritation coupled with an ethos of mild frivolity and playfulness.

However, we can qualify this line of argument in several ways. For one, the critiques of feminist frivolity and individualism described above, while often positioning themselves as marginal, critical voices, are of course constitutive, rather than external, to the F-word's discourse. Furthermore, the apparent oppositional contrasts between individualism and collectivity, irritation and rage, femininity and feminism need to be qualified. After all, it is very easy, from a critical theoretical perspective, to dismiss these rather 'pop feminist' concerns as indicative of deradicalisation and a complicity with prevailing hegemonic logics. As I have indicated, this is clearly justified to some degree. However one must be careful not to dismiss them too quickly. As we saw in the section on post-feminism in Chapter 1, there is an array of contradictory forms of regulation of post-feminist female subjectivity presently at work, and, as such, it is not altogether surprising that concerns such as 'can you be feminine and feminist?' emerge as topics of discussion. A more optimistic, and less dismissive, reading might be to suggest that such seemingly apolitical affirmations of feminism are nonetheless *latently* political, open to the possibility of incorporation into a more critical and transformative chain of equivalence. Let's take Laura Wadsworth's article as an example. While at one level, it could simply be written off as depoliticised 'girlie' feminism, a more sympathetic reading would be to argue that it draws equivalences between feminism and conventional femininity in a manner which could provide a springboard for a progressive counter-hegemonic articulation. Indeed, her article was certainly well received by some readers who were keen to endorse her equivalence between feminism and femininity. One comment posted on the website read,

> I just had to give kudos for the article by Laura Wadsworth ... about being girly and feminist [Feminine Feminism]. I'm a Women's Studies major in college and it really bothered me how too many feminists (and non-feminists, too) think that being feminist requires ditching femininity. I ended up making tees that say 'feminine feminist' to boycott the idea and just recently started offering them again. Yea for girly girls that believe in equality!
>
> (Teresa Coates, comment posted
> on The F-word, June 2006)

Thus, clearly the 'girlie feminist' concerns expressed on The F-word do have the potential to be taken up and used in a more radical fashion. Thus, my claim is not that there is anything inherently 'non-radical' or 'apolitical' in seeking to articulate concerns relating to popular culture, or in seeking to draw an equivalence between feminism and conventional femininity. After all, femininity is, of course, not static but always open to creative and progressive reworkings and reinstantiations, and there may be a progressive political mileage in revalorising those dimensions of femininity which have historically been belittled. As argued in a further enthusiastic endorsement of Laura Wadsworth's article:

> I find it incredibly annoying, patronising and reductive when people argue or assume that you cannot possibly be a feminist if you wear tiny skirts, the colour pink or take the slightest bit of pride in your appearance. Simone de Beauvoir was honest about her desire to look good and wear lipstick. Does this make her less of a feminist icon? I think it's dangerous for feminists to be prescriptive and say that 'girlies' are bad for feminism. Girliness is great!
>
> (Comment posted on The F-word by
> 'microchipette', August 2005)

Indeed, a properly hegemonic political engagement (that is, one that is aware of the mechanics of hegemony) must, as Gramsci (1971), Laclau (1990) and Hall (1988) have all pointed out, relate its concerns to those of 'ordinary people' if it is to have any interpellative capacity. A similar point was made forcefully by one F-word contributor who stated, 'I had made the point that feminism will become esoteric and elitist if seemingly shallow and everyday issues in popular culture that interest a large number of people are not addressed from a feminist perspective' (email from F-word contributor).

Thus, while we can affirm that an apolitical, individualised identification with 'pop feminism' might nonetheless be characterised as latently political, in these instances what is perhaps lacking is a discursive framework – a 'figure of the newly thinkable' – through which to think through these concerns in more political terms. Instead, what we have is a set of singular concerns relating to feminism and femininity which are then met with a positive response – of the 'you go girl!' mould – but in a manner where feminism remains an individualistic pursuit. Furthermore, some of the above attempts to instantiate a reconciliation between feminism and femininity might suggest a certain logic of feminist depoliticisation. Of course, as we saw, femininity can be imaginatively reworked, but, in the majority of the above examples, the affirmation of a feminine feminism seems less geared towards the adoption of a critical stance towards hegemonic discourses on feminism and femininity, and more towards fostering a depoliticised 'sigh of relief' that one no longer has to worry about advancing a critique of normative femininity. As with Baumgardner and Richards' (2004) articulation of a 'third-wave' reconciliation of feminism and femininity – titled 'How We Learned to Stop Worrying and Love the Thong' – such a view risks repositioning a problematic feminist temporality in which the second-wave feminist critique of mainstream femininity is positioned as excessive and abject. We shall return to the question of feminist generational temporalities at the end of the chapter.

Anger, affect and resistance: Contesting feminist depoliticisation

While I have noted that at times there emerge on the F-word forms of complicity with logics of feminist individualism and depoliticisation, one must be careful not to overplay this. In this section, I shall draw attention to how various forms of articulation centred around the feminist politics of popular culture constitute serious points of resistance to a number of hegemonic discourses. Let us consider for a moment some of the implications of the feminist individualisation narrative advanced above (and also of the accounts of 'post-feminism(s)' presented in Chapter 1). Such narratives suggest that there has been a shift to a less politically engaged mode of feminism, with the implication that the strength of the affective identification with feminism is perhaps not as strong as in the past. In comparison to notions such as 'rage' and 'anger', which – one may argue – were important forces in sustaining the collective dimensions of some strands of second-wave feminism, there is an assumption that contemporary identifications with feminism are based more on a looser sense of individualism and lifestyle. In addition, the narratives suggest that feminist individualisation entails a disidentification with the more radical strands of feminism: it is assumed that contemporary feminism is underwritten by a standpoint largely unthreatening to dominant patriarchal logics.

However, as one might expect, things are not that simple. I want to argue that, at a basic empirical level, there are a number of ways in which such accounts – as articulated thus far – do not adequately grasp a number of crucial aspects of The F-word and London Thirdwave's activity. In this section, I shall draw attention to four key ways in which framing The F-word in terms of feminist individualisation and depoliticisation might be rendered problematic.

(1) The interpellative moment

As I have indicated already, The F-word at times exhibits a strong interpellative capacity, such that it is able to bring young women into a feminist agenda, or is able to reignite and re-engage a residual identification with feminism which may have been buried or forgotten. As one contributor told me in an email, The F-word 'reaffirmed rather than changed my view of contemporary feminism and brought me back in touch with a group of thinking, active women from whom I've forged some close friendships and productive working relationships'. In this sense, The F-word's capacity to instil not only an identification as feminist, but also a bold, determined and vigorous identification with feminism jars with the above account of feminist frivolity and a lack of a strong affective investment. The force of the identifications with feminism is, I think, detectable in the following assertions from F-word contributors which, unless states, are all drawn from emails sent to me (see also Redfern, 2003a):

> I've no idea what my life would be like if I hadn't found The F-word .... Finding it was really a pivotal point in my life .... Writing for free in a space that would be accessed by the people I wanted

to communicate my ideas to gave me that freedom immediately. Without The F-word, I wouldn't have gained that sense of direction I have now.

I think that because younger women are very cut off from each other, they have a lot of trouble finding each other, and The F-word is a central focus. And again it was the initiative of one woman, which is great.

It comforted me in making me realise I wasn't alone .... This was the first time I met a large group of young women I felt I could identify with who call themselves feminist.

London Thirdwave is a way of re-energising one's feminism through discussion and action .... I'm grateful that its meetings are informal .... and I like the creativity of the meetings.

Until I found your site I was beginning to think that not only was I alone but also that any hope of a communal third wave was long gone.

(Comment posted on The F-word, July 2003)

In this sense, The F-word's capacity to bring about what Wittgenstein (1958: 194) called an 'aspect change', that is, a change in the manner of one's perception of a given object or phenomenon, as well as a strong affective investment in feminism, is indicative of a level of commitment and *collective* identification which is not grasped by narratives of depoliticisation or deradicalisation. While the identifications with 'girl power' described earlier clearly imply some modicum of collective identification with a female solidarity, they do so in a manner where the emphasis is on individual empowerment and self-esteem. What the above quotes indicate, by contrast, is not a simple subjective identification with feminism – 'I am a feminist' – but rather a strong, affective investment in a membership of a feminist *community* in which the sense of collectivity takes precedence over individual subjective identification.

Thus, rather than characterising The F-word in terms of individualisation and depoliticisation, a more generous – and, I think, more accurate – reading of The F-word would be to claim that under conditions of intense individualisation, the construction of communal quasi-political spaces for young women becomes ever more important.

McRobbie argues that under present conditions, young women are 'three times over subjects of melancholic self-beratement' (McRobbie, 2007b) through a combination of the loss of the same-sex love object, the process of oedipalisation and the loss of the ideal of feminism. Implicit in McRobbie's current work is that a key political task for young women is the development of practices that provide outlets for a return to female communality, and what she calls a 'detachment from the [melancholic] self-berating ego' (ibid.). Recall from the Chapter 1 that McRobbie argues that 'the cultural practices of subculture and group rather than self, can be said to have offered this possibility to young people .... [and] it is possible to read activities like Riot grrrl, the website The F-word ... and organisations like Ladyfest in exactly these terms' (ibid.).[11] Despite some serious ambiguities in McRobbie's account (outlined in Chapter 1), her analysis of post-feminist individualisation sheds important light on the role that autonomous subcultural practices such as The F-word might play under present conditions. From this perspective, the radicality of The F-word could be seen to inhere in the ways in which it acts as an imaginative 'figure of the newly thinkable', in that it provides a space for female communality that provides refuge from, and resistance to, logics of post-feminist individualisation and the hegemonic injunction to disidentify with the figure of the feminist.

(2) A subjective identification with 'radicalism'

This sense of a collective identification with feminism is in some cases enhanced by the ways in which a number of people involved in The F-word explicitly identify with the qualifier 'radical' in relation to their feminism. Here, the invocation of 'radicalism' in relation to one's feminism reflects a conscious effort on the part of a number of participants to affirm the strength of their subjective commitment to feminism. For one, Finn MacKay, an F-word contributor and founder of the London Feminist Network, mentioned the importance of her continued investment in Radical Feminism. She said, 'I think Radical Feminism offers a useful view of why society is the way it is. I believe struggle starts at the standpoint of those most oppressed so I believe women's equality is the way to full equality for all' (Finn MacKay, email, 08/02/07). In addition, one F-word contributor described how she came to hear of The F-word from an email sent to members of a group called 'Womenspeakout', an email discussion group for 'radical, anti-capitalist women' (email from F-word contributor).[12] Also, one contributor was keen to affirm her identification with a radical feminist perspective on sex work (email from F-word contributor).

However, notable here is that the subjective identification with a radical agenda is not necessarily indicative of a simple identification with the body of thought known as 'Radical Feminism'. Indeed, several F-word contributors have been fairly critical of Radical Feminism, but nonetheless have sought to identify with 'radicalism' by rearticulating the term in a manner that divorces it from its strict association with Radical Feminism, and its connotations of a reductive account of patriarchy and female sexuality. One F-word contributor, for instance, commented, 'I just know that, despite not being a 'radical' feminist on paper (that is, accordingly to the typically understood definition, I *do* want things to *radically change*' (email from F-word contributor). To this extent, articles by Natasha Forrest (Forrest, 2002a) and myself (Dean, 2006) both sought to move beyond the structuring of feminist discourse by a rigid radical/liberal dichotomy. Indeed, it appeared that these efforts were well received (by some, at least) to the extent that they provide discursive space for an identification with feminist 'radicalism' which remains critical of certain aspects of Radical Feminism.

(3) 'Raunch culture' and resistance to hegemonic gender norms

While, as I have made clear, there is evidence of a strong affective investment in the identification with feminism on the part of a number of contributors, in this section I shall draw attention to how certain issues within contemporary feminist cultural politics seem particularly strong in their capacity to generate affective identifications. In particular, I argue that forms of affective hostility to the reinforcement of rigid binary gender norms within the public domain – and particularly in relation to female sexuality – is especially strong in binding F-word contributors together in terms of a shared feminist agenda. In this respect, The F-word is particularly important as a site for the articulation of critiques of discourses of gendered subjectivity within the popular cultural domain. Indeed, the paradigmatic F-word article takes as its object of enquiry a magazine, a piece of advertising, a TV show or other popular cultural artefact, and explores the ways in which certain views of femininity and masculinity are perpetuated by these media. Let me provide a few examples. One of the most insightful contributions is that made by Jo Knowles (2004) analysing media treatment of Maxine Carr.[13] Here, she draws attention to the ways in which problematic oppositional constructions of womanhood were prevalent throughout media treatment of the issue, which appeared to shore up certain hegemonic understandings of 'proper' femininity. She describes how, even though Carr's misdemeanours were of far less seriousness than those of Ian Huntley, Carr was demonised to the same degree given that, as a woman, she was measured against a higher ethical standard than Huntley. Thus, Knowles seeks to decisively call into question received norms concerning our understandings of 'proper' feminine behaviour. Indeed, the ethical double standards applied to women are a recurrent theme in the efforts of various F-word contributors to highlight injustices and inconsistencies in the cultural policing of gender norms. There is frequently a concern with the ways in which certain anti-social behaviours are tolerated, even condoned, if committed by men, but perceived to be a serious problem if women are involved. Another article asserts that

> I intensely dislike this attitude that seems to exist within modern society whereby if young men are going out and getting drunk, having sex and getting into fights, it's seen as 'boys will be boys', whereas if young women are doing it, it's suddenly a big social problem.
>
> (Ellery, 2006)

This, and other articles on the cultural policing of masculinity and femininity by Plant (2006), Bowden (2003) and Thurgood (2003) all serve to highlight the centrality of The F-word as a space for the pro-feminist negotiation of contemporary gendered subjectivity, with particularly strong emphasis on the negotiation of the paradox whereby female freedom and independence is espoused, but at the same time strong normative constraints are imposed upon what counts as an authentic, intelligible female subjectivity. Throughout the site, there are numerous articles outlining the injustices and pressures resulting from the promotion of idealised notions of female beauty. This comes across as a pertinent and pressing issue for many of the contributors, for whom the representation of gender within the realm of popular culture is a key object of critique. Both women's and men's magazines are criticised for promoting an unattainable idealised version of female beauty, which, a number of contributors argue, leads to social and sexual anxiety and disappointment for both men and women.[14]

These elements come to the fore even more in the contributions that highlight a pervasive frustration with the ways in which normative perceptions of female sexuality are regulated and maintained. For example, Kristin Aune (a regular contributor) draws attention to how 'the feminist call for women's right to choose their sexuality has, in this postfeminist era, been transformed into an emphasis on compulsory sex, a state in which women are no longer free to choose not to have sex, not to be part of a couple' (Aune, 2002; see also O'Reilly, 2006). Similarly, an extensive article by Jennifer Drew highlights the constraints placed on female sexuality via the invocation of the myth of female sexual dysfunction, concluding that 'when women try to restrain or limit their sexual desires within male-defined boundaries, I am not surprised many women experience low or non-existent sexual desire' (Drew, 2003b). Here, there is a drive to contest a number of hegemonic assumptions about female sexuality. For one, there is resistance to the assumption that women are now fully sexually liberated. In addition, Drew refutes the belief that heteronormative sexual configurations arise naturally, along with the popular view that there are natural masculine and feminine sexual predispositions. By contrast, she claims that such views are in fact products of quite specific hegemonic power relations, which are reinstated through a constant policing of women's sexuality.[15]

All these contributions are arguably indicative of a shared collective anger and frustration – if perhaps not quite 'rage' – with the ways in which certain hegemonic norms surrounding masculinity and femininity (particularly in relation to sexuality) are articulated across the public domain. If anything, it is a shared hostility towards the *cultural policing of female sexuality* that acts as a key 'identificatory glue' enabling a collective hostility towards the status quo. This is not to claim that other issues are unimportant to F-word contributors. Rather, my claim is that it is a hostility towards hegemonic gender norms, particularly in relation to sexuality, that has become perhaps *the* key force sustaining a shared, collective agenda. This is made visible by the way in which issues such as the proliferation of pornography in the public domain, the fetishisation of women's bodies, and the abundance of damagingly exploitative representations of femininity and female sexuality were all cited by F-word contributors – in the course of email correspondence – as key issues in contemporary feminism. The significance of these topics again came to light as a result of the heated, yet energising, debates surrounding the notion of 'raunch culture' ignited by the publication of Ariel Levy's *Female Chauvinist Pigs: Women and the Rise of Raunch Culture* in 2006.

Levy's main target of attack is contemporary American women's apparently widespread consent to a male-centred and deeply commercialised construction of female sexuality that privileges commodifiability over the pursuit of sexual pleasure. As Levy puts it, 'suddenly we were getting implants and wearing a bunny logo as supposed symbols of liberation' (Levy, 2005: 3). Consequently, 'a tawdry, tarty, cartoon-like version of female sexuality has become so ubiquitous, it no longer seems particular. What was once regarded as a *kind* of sexual expression we now view *as* sexuality' (ibid.: 5; emphasis in original). In this context, 'raunch culture' refers to the way in which this particular, commodified view of sexuality is becoming increasingly prevalent throughout popular culture and media, rather than being confined to the sex industry. Essentially, the key thesis of the book is that 'because we have determined that all empowered women must be overtly and publicly sexual, and because the only sign of sexuality we seem to be able to recognize is a direct allusion to red-light entertainment, we have laced the sleazy energy and aesthetic of a topless club or a *Penthouse* shoot throughout our entire culture' (ibid.: 26). The notion of 'raunch' seemed to strike a chord within the public domain and prompted lively debate both on the London Thirdwave Yahoo group and also on The F-word (see Bateman et al., 2007). Overall, the power of these issues to mobilise debate and foster a certain passion and determination among young feminists is indicative of a level of affectivity and investment in contemporary feminism which one must remain alert to.

(4) Modes of substantive feminist activism

Thus far, the analysis has been primarily 'textual', and has tended to overlook the ways in which The F-word and London Thirdwave (as well as the UK Feminist Action Yahoo group, also founded by Redfern) are not merely 'virtual' but also act as sounding boards for instances of feminist activism. While The F-word doesn't act politically in any substantive way, it nonetheless provides information about a range of instances of feminist activism, and is thus a key focal point facilitating the emergence of what in Chapter 1 I called the 'New Feminist Politics'. Indeed, when Redfern made a presentation at a large London conference organised by left-wing pressure group Compass in June 2006, she simply read out a long list of the different types of feminist activism which she was aware of. Notably, the relentlessness of the list had a palpable effect on the audience (which included women from a broad span of age groups), who seemed genuinely impressed/surprised/relieved by the extent of the feminist activity Redfern described. Let us look for a moment at some of these instances of recent feminist activism. As indicated, one of the most significant has been the Reclaim the Night marches in London – organised primarily by the London Feminist Network (LFN) but supported and promoted by The F-word and London Thirdwave (as well as a range of other London-based feminist groups). These events, which protest against the continued prevalence of male violence against women, have risen in size and popularity over recent years (Bell, 2006). On the role of Reclaim the Night and the LFN, Finn MacKay commented,

> I think LFN is a very active group of women who are angry and who are not apologetic about feminism. It takes a lot of energy to justify oneself all the time, to explain that women organising politically together is not anti-men etc. So the LFN is a space where women can use their energy instead to focus on organising and some wonderful things come out of the meeting of these women and I'm very proud of having put that space together.
>
> (Finn MacKay, email, 8/02/07)

In addition to the emergence of LFN and Reclaim the Night, Ladyfest events have also recently increased in size and popularity. These are decentralised, locally organised cultural and political events that seek to provide positive images of creativity and collective action by women. Other instances of feminist activism mentioned by Redfern at the Compass Conference included Object (referred to in the Fawcett chapter); a number of new feminist magazines, websites and blogs; Justice for Women – which campaigns on behalf of women who have been imprisoned for killing violent husbands; the UK anti-street harassment website; the London Radical Cheerleaders (whose performances resemble conventional cheerleading but with chants denouncing capitalism and patriarchy); Mind the Gap – who campaign around highlighting quantitatively identifiable gender inequalities; and Frock On – a Glasgow-based feminist event.[16]

A point made – I think correctly – by Redfern was that these different types of feminist activity are demonstrative of a renewed appetite for feminist efforts in a variety of domains, which clearly runs counter to hegemonic discourses claiming the 'end of feminism'. Indeed, these instances of substantive feminist activism, as well as the recent proliferation of blogs, websites and the ever-increasing popularity of The F-word, could be read as indicative of a renewed identification with feminism on the part of moderately large numbers of young women.

Notably, there seems to have been, in the period 2006–9, a shift away from articles focussing on, for example, constructions of femininity or female sexuality within the popular cultural domain, and towards announcements of, or reports from, more substantive instances of feminist activism, such as those described above. For instance, during 2008 and early 2009, The F-word carried feature articles on activism around pornography, the struggle for reproductive rights in Ireland, the Million

Women Rise march against sexual violence, Object's campaign around lap-dancing licensing laws, the widely-publicised protests against the 'Miss London University' beauty contests, and Reclaim the Night marches in various UK towns and cities. This is in addition to the numerous announcements about feminist events and new feminist groups across the country on The F-word blog. One possible interpretation of this apparent shift might be that the earlier articles on representations of female sexuality and related issues were part of a mobilisation and articulation process, which, subsequent to this initial process of feminist (re)identification, is now beginning to translate into emergent feminist activism. The fact that a significant number of individuals involved in The F-word since its arrival on the scene are also involved in several of the activities mentioned above might support this claim, as would the fact that issues such as beauty, sexuality and 'objectification' are key areas around which feminists are currently mobilising. Furthermore, the F-word is no longer unambiguously the focal point for UK-based feminism, even though the amount of activity on the site remains undiminished. Whereas previously The F-word was *the* key autonomous voice within UK feminism, during the late 2000s, numerous other groups, blogs and websites have emerged, decentring The F-word somewhat. Ironically, one could thus say that The F-word has become a victim of its own success, inasmuch as its initial role as a point of contact between disparate feminists has now led to the formation of other groups and modes of feminist activity.

Negotiating the third wave

Despite the above, I want to resist the temptation to drift too quickly into an overly celebratory account of the 'return of feminism'. To explore the character of this apparent resurgence of feminist politics in the UK, partly centred around The F-word, it will be necessary to explore in more detail its generational dynamics, specifically with regard to the question of the 'third wave'. As indicated in Chapter 1, 'third-wave feminism' is a diverse and contested discursive terrain. However, it requires further exploration given the importance of the 'third wave' to the F-word's self-understanding. Indeed, Catherine Redfern began a talk on a panel discussion at a conference in London organised by left-wing pressure group Compass in June 2006 called 'Is this the third wave of feminism?' by stating that 'we [at The F-word] are the third wave, [there is] no more discussion about it'. But this of course gives rise to the question of what precisely is understood by the term 'third-wave feminism' within the context of The F-word and London Thirdwave.

At one level, therefore, and as with the work of some American third-wavers such as Baumgardner and Richards (2000), the term appears to refer solely to a generational shift without specifying any particular content to the concerns of the new generation of feminists. However, there is a sense that these generational divisions yield certain key cultural and political differences. Indeed, in the present British context, we can identify two key substantive dimensions of third-wave feminism (see Redfern, 2001a, 2002b). First, the notion of a 'third wave' has come to have strong associations with a specific form of youth subculture (sometimes called the 'riot grrrl' movement) with its roots in a pro-feminist punk ethos, and associated with particular styles of music and clothing (Blase, 2004a, 2004b, 2005a, 2005b). It has also come to be associated with specific viewpoints that may differ from established 'second-wave' perspectives. For instance, third-wavers seem more likely to engage with issues related to popular culture, are less likely to be 'anti-porn' and are (generally) more open to bringing men into a pro-feminist agenda (see, for example, Forrest, 2002a, 2002b; Smith, 2003c; Bateman, 2007).

More broadly, my claim is that within the context of The F-word and London Thirdwave there are two different modes of the usage of the signifier 'third wave', which are somewhat in tension with one another. On the one hand, as with The Fawcett Society, the term is not so much tied to any particular signified but is instead a discursive tool – an 'empty signifier' almost – through which a discursive *space* is carved out for young feminists to occupy and use. One the other, there is a certain possessiveness over the term, such that 'third wave' is assumed to constatively refer to a particular subjective disposition, at times even a particular empirical group of women, in a manner that to some extent undoes its more radical dimensions. These two divergent uses of the signifier 'third wave' merit closer examination. As indicated in Chapter 1, most existing material on the third wave addresses the question of what the third wave *means*, often taking the form of a teleological drive towards a decisive fixing of the meaning of the term. By contrast, here I want to shift the focus to how the signifier 'third wave' is *used* by contemporary feminists, casting it as a discursive resource that can be appropriated in a multitude of different ways by feminist actors.

At some level, the signifier 'third wave' has come to operate as an 'empty signifier' that performatively brings into existence a collective feminist subjectivity for young women who have had different experiences and thus may hold different priorities to those who were active during the second-wave. In this sense, the use of the term 'third-wave feminism' could be seen as quite radical to the extent that it consists of a new articulation of feminism open to young women grounded in interaction and exchange among young feminists. However, this articulation does seem to be predicated on a consensus surrounding the character of second-wave feminism. The latter is (often implicitly) presented as somewhat narrow, constraining and prescriptive, in contrast to third-wave feminism which is presented as open, welcoming, diverse and inclusive. In so doing, the 'third wave' seeks to carve out a feminist discursive space with which young women can identify and engage. Witness these accounts, drawn from email correspondence, of what is understood by 'third-wave feminism' by users of The F-word:

> I think it's a very useful rallying point for young women and a way to stress feminism's relevance for their own lives. It recognises that younger women's lives are different from those of their foremothers.

> Basically, it must define a generation of women who have grown up under the gains made by those 2nd wavers in the 60s/70s. This isn't to say all the work has been done, it isn't to deny the existence of a backlash, and it isn't to say that 3rdwavers have it all right but nevertheless, we grew up in a different world to that of our mothers – with different expectations, entitlements and oppressions, and I think this term acknowledges that.

> Second-wave theories never sat comfortably with my own brand of radical, leftist, feminist, queer activism. Third Wave is much more open to the challenge of overlapping and interlinking concerns.

> While the Thirdwave is built upon the radical blocks of the second it also involves greater attention to diversity, deconstruction and overlapping positions.

Thus, the picture we are presented with here is one in which the third wave signifies a generational shift, and also refers to the emergence of a new and *inclusive* feminist agenda, with the implication that the 'old' feminism was perhaps less inclusive. As one regular contributor to London Thirdwave and The F-word has pointed out (in a quote referred to above) 'somehow we [at London Thirdwave] were able to unite as young feminists and get on despite our differences. *I'm not sure that would have happened thirty years ago*' (email from F-word contributor; my emphasis). This latter comment is clearly imbued with a disidentification with the 'less inclusive' elements of second-wave feminism. Indeed, a palpable dissaffection with certain aspects of second-wave feminism is evident in an F-word contributor's assertion that 'there has been an increasing dissonance between the concerns and interests of younger feminists and of 2nd Wave feminists. I have had experiences of being patronised because of my age .... I think there was a sense of young feminists having to 'serve their time' in exactly the same way that patriarchal structures use that apprenticeship model which felt uncomfortable and denied a voice to me (and others)' (email from F-word contributor).

Consequently, there is an attempt to create a new feminist agenda autonomous from second-wave feminism: in this context, the appeal to a specifically 'third-wave' agenda again does not refer to any necessary content. Rather, it is used to open up a discursive *space* for young feminists, without specifying in advance the precise content of that space. In this context, the specifically performative character of the signifier 'third wave' is very much brought to the fore. To some extent, it makes sense to claim that the signifier 'third wave' is invoked here to bring into existence a feminist space that was previously only tenuously existent, if at all. And yet, despite this, the way in which the third-wave agenda is characterised does, to some degree, present a number of problems.

One potential problem is that this attempt to cast The F-word's third-wave feminist agenda as something new and relevant to young women entails a distancing from, and perhaps a repudiation of, second-wave feminism. This is such that, while the term 'third wave' has been a dominant paradigm through which The F-word's feminism is framed, it nonetheless has been met with a measure of uneasiness – at times even hostility – from a number of participants. As with the critiques of feminist individualism alluded to earlier, these expressions of uneasiness are articulated *within* The F-word – and are thus constitutive of it – but are positioned as in opposition to the (presumed) dominant, pro-third-wave position. These critiques of the 'third wave' can take a number of forms. For one, several participants are unhappy with the way in which the 'wave' metaphor characterises feminist history. One contributor, in an email exchange, made the following comment:

> To be honest I don't really understand the term '3rd Wave'! For one, I don't think that there have been clearly defined feminist movements that can be labelled as waves. Yes, there have been upsurges, but the real business of feminism and women's liberation has been going on throughout time, in individual women's lives, and when women

gather together and take collective action. The upsurges that look like waves are probably only points in history when women's liberation has received more attention from mainstream society.

(Email from F-word contributor)

In a similar vein, one F-word reader who has been active in UK feminism since the 1970s expressed grave concerns about the appropriateness of using the 'wave' metaphor to characterise feminist history. She stated,

It seems to me that the political differences lie vertically [that is, they run in parallel], so I think that's one problem. Another problem is that it is actually an American import, and, like a lot of American imports, they get adopted rather uncritically. The other thing is I do feel quite critical, it's a rather academic construct, and I'm a bit opposed to academic constructs that don't have much relationship to real life.

(Interview with F-word reader, February 2007)

Furthermore, the term 'third wave' has been criticised for implying that second-wave feminism is no longer necessary or relevant. Indeed, Finn MacKay has strongly argued for a reaffirmation of second-wave values and priorities. In an email exchange, she commented,

I have always had a personal problem with the term third wave, because I don't think the second-wave is over yet. We are still living in a defensive time of strong backlash against the gains made by the second-wave women's liberation movement. What we are doing is still defending those gains and trying to advance the very same goals spelt out then, the seven demands, which we still have not achieved. The extent of the backlash and the force of it is an indication of the threat posed by second-wave feminism so I think we should carry on and finish the job.

(Finn MacKay, email, 09/02/07)

Red Chidgey, another prominent feminist activist, expressed a similar set of concerns about the notion of a 'third wave' and the 'wave' metaphor more generally. She commented,

Our feminist heritage is far more complicated than this – to talk of waves, not only ignores the continuous stream of women's activism and antagonism across the ages, it also places a conceptual/discursive gag on inter-generational politics. Are older women, by default, excluded from the workings and actions of the 'third wave'? Do we, as feminists, have an expiry date? It not only ignores the continuous stream of women's activism and antagonism across the ages, and indeed across the globe (it's quite telling that 'waves' more readily refers to contemporary Western feminisms), it also places a conceptual/discursive gag on inter-generational politics

> (Red Chidgey, comment posted on
> The F-word, date not specified)

Overall, within The F-word and London Thirdwave, the preoccupation with 'waves' appears to be symptomatic of a concern with establishing exactly whom the groups are for, and which feminist demographics they intend to address. This is rendered palpable by a heated debate that ensued over the relationship between the website and older feminists.

When the site was initially set up in 2001, it was subtitled 'young UK feminism'. However, in 2003 this was – after considerable debate – changed to 'contemporary UK feminism'. The name change was prompted by a complaint from an older reader that the focus on younger women was discriminatory against older feminists. The term 'contemporary' was chosen in order to maintain its links with youth but also in order to make it seem less off-putting to older readers. In describing the reasons for the name change, Redfern writes, 'I feared that whatever I chose to do would disappoint somebody, and yet there was a risk that if I tried to please everybody the site could lose whatever precious identity it had gained. How could I reconcile what I felt was two totally valid but seemingly conflicting points?' (Redfern, 2003b). Thus, even though Redfern wishes to make visible the open and contested character of feminism, there is nonetheless ongoing concern as to which generational demographic the site is intended to speak to. At some level, the actual process of discussion opened up space for critical practices of judging, although this came to be undermined somewhat by the grounding of the discussion within the 'subject question'. Rather than seeing the critical exchanges – which brought about a sharp increase in the liveliness of the site – as something with an inherent value, they were cast as part of a teleological move towards a final discursive closure concerning the generational cohort that the site wishes to speak to (or for).

This issue resurfaced somewhat during the summer of 2006 when Katherine Rake – then director of The Fawcett Society – published a piece in *The Guardian* calling for a third wave of feminism. This provoked a somewhat defensive response in some quarters, on the grounds that Rake was perceived to have ignored the fact that a 'third wave' already existed. Furthermore, one anonymous contributor wrote, in response to Rake, 'I find the idea that young women need older women to spearhead the third wave decidedly suspect.' Jess McCabe (2006), the current editor of The F-word, commented, 'While this is a laudable attempt to swell the ranks, Rake is calling for a third wave of feminism. If anything, she should be calling for a fourth wave. I hate to sound pernickety .... but seriously, do we really need to re-invent the wheel yet again?' (McCabe, 2006). This seems to cast contemporary feminism as fundamentally and only a site of intergenerational conflict, almost to the point where the 'third wave' is presented as the preserve of a specific, generationally defined empirical group of women. However, from a perspective closer to my own, one comment read, 'I feel a bit nervous that some of the posts declaiming Rake's article as ignoring the 3rd wave are veering towards driving a wedge between feminists .... The vision that Rake outlined in her article was clear and I think it is one we can all sign up to' (email to London Thirdwave Yahoo group).

Indeed, this debate may also be indicative of certain differences between the understandings of 'third-wave feminism' articulated by The Fawcett Society and The F-word. While those on London Thirdwave are undoubtedly correct to criticise Rake for having an insufficient awareness of the recent history of contemporary feminism in the UK, the level of defensiveness seems to imply a sense of ownership of the term 'third wave'. In contrast, Rake's use of the term (described in detail in the Fawcett chapter) sees it more as a discursive tool through which a new feminist politics can be articulated. However, it could be argued that any use of the lexicon of 'waves' under present discursive conditions carries at least some trace of the overdetermination of feminism by intergenerational conflict.

These debates would seem to be indicative of a level of anxiety and a possible lack of clarity concerning the identity of the feminist subject. However, in resolving this by seeking to sediment the group's identity as young and third wave, there is a troubling sense in which this closes down scope for debate and limits space for feminist practices of freedom, thus somewhat contradicting the strong emphasis on openness and plurality. Furthermore, there is a significant tension between the bold and indeed commendable attempt to keep alive feminism's character as a 'floating signifier' – that is, a term whose meaning is visibly flexible and not apt to a final and decisive closure – and the closure brought about in stating that its status as third wave is no longer under discussion.

Let me clarify my point, which is at core fairly simple. I have described two different modalities of the use of the signifier 'third-wave feminism' operative within the discourse of contemporary feminist activists in the UK. On the one hand, it can be used as an 'empty signifier', a discursive device capable of performatively creating new feminist discursive spaces with which people can identify and critically engage with. It is in this sense that it is used by The Fawcett Society and by some contributions to The F-word. Here, the aim is not so much to arrive at a decisive closure but to bring into existence a new feminist agenda while maintaining a level of openness. In this context there is a clear aspiration to challenge the basic co-ordinates of hegemonic discourses on feminism and gender relations. In contrast to thinking of 'third-wave feminism' as an empty signifier, its formulation in the idiom of the subject question reduces scope for openness and contestation. Here, the aspiration appears to be less concerned with challenging existing hegemonic discourses concerning gender relations, but is more to do with establishing exactly who or what the feminist subject is prior to any political engagement. This is because, in terms of some contributions to The F-word, the appellation 'third wave' is seen as having a necessary relation to a specific group of young women who claim ownership of the term. Simplifying to the extreme, under the first instance the signifier 'third wave' is used in the context of the claim that 'this is the third wave', whereas in the second the claim is that 'we are the third wave'. The former implies a modicum of openness and engagement, whereas the latter suggests closure and defensiveness. Another way of putting it, to use J. L. Austin's (1975) theoretical lexicon, would be to say that the former uses the 'third wave' performatively (in that it brings new feminist possibilities into existence) whereas the latter uses it constatively (in that the 'third wave' describes a feminist subject that is already assumed to exist). In the final section, I shall argue that the sedimentation of the 'third wave' as signifying a 'young' feminism leads it into further, perhaps even more fundamental, problems.

Generational disidentifications, or, who's afraid of third-wave feminism?

The above critiques of third-wave feminism point towards the danger of closing down debate, discussion and possibilities for feminist politics by invoking a notion of a historical shift from a second to a third wave that perpetuates divisive distinctions between groups of feminists.

The charge that the 'third wave' has caused unnecessary generational divisiveness is well established within feminist theory (Henry, 2003; McRobbie, 2009: 156–9). However, the consequences of this generational division often remain unexplored. Here, I want to argue that the tendency to think the third wave as specifically referring to young women, indeed sometimes even a particular group of young women, is such that it may have further detrimental consequences relating to the relationship between feminism and hegemonic gender discourses.

This arises from the fact that, within the generational paradigm of third-wave feminism, there is, of course, some sort of an identification with second-wave feminism, whereas on another level the very identity of the 'third wave' is predicated on its distancing from second-wave feminism. As mentioned in Chapter 1, Astrid Henry points out that third-wave feminists' 'simultaneous identification with and rejection of second-wave feminism is what grants them an identity to call their own' (2003: 215). She writes, 'paradoxically, many of these third-wave writers attempt to recreate the exhilaration and freedom of the feminist past by breaking away from feminism' (ibid.: 220). Henry argues that third-wave feminists cast themselves in a relation of 'disidentification' with second-wave feminism. Henry's use of the term is drawn from Judith Butler's work on processes of repudiation in the formation of gendered subjectivities, and is used to describe a process whereby subjects distance themselves from an identification which one fears to make *'only because one has already made it'* (Butler, 1993: 112, my italics; see also Fuss, 1995: 1–7). Logics of disidentification occur when one's behaviour, social situation, self-presentation or other salient category entails, at some level, an identification which, for context-specific reasons, is perceived as threatening or subversive, either by the subject or by others. A logic of disidentification thus occurs when a deeper, more fundamental identification is perceived as potentially undermining the stability and coherence of one's identity. In particular, I want to suggest that this deeper identification may often be disavowed because it takes the form of a bodily incorporation that is perceived as threatening. It is thus often characterised by strong affective investments in the 'othering' of an identity that is seen to potentially destabilise the subject's stability and coherence. While one can reasonably claim that affective investments produce the boundaries that are constitutive of social reality itself (Ahmed, 2004b; Laclau, 2005a: 110–17), a specifically disidentificatory affective investment arises when, at some level, an identification with that which is 'othered' has already been made, thus necessitating its repeated and hyperbolic denunciation.

My contention is that this logic of disidentification is at work in the third-wave feminist (non) identity with second-wave feminism, in which there is of course some identification with the figure of the 'second-waver', but whereby that identification threatens to undermine the subjective integrity of the younger, third-wave feminist. Perhaps more significantly, however, I want to contend that a similar logic of disidentitication with second-wave feminism is prevalent within hegemonic discourses on contemporary feminine subjectivity.

Recall that, in McRobbie's (2009) account of post-feminism, she casts contemporary young women as standing not in a relation of simple non-identity with feminism but, rather, in a relation of *dis*identification with the figure of the (implicitly second-wave) feminist. The forceful denunciations of feminism that McRobbie describes implicitly come about because the (depoliticised) promotion and incorporation of female social, sexual and economic freedom risks invoking the spectre of the feminist. As such, in post-feminist discourse, the fear of the feminist arises from the fact that, at some level, an identification *with* the feminist has in fact already been made. One may argue that some articulations of third-wave subjectivity on The F-word (and some popular texts such as Levinson, 2009) seem to tie in with a logic of disidentification with second-wave feminism which is in fact partly complicit with dominant post-/anti-feminist discourses. This is because the characterisation of second-wave feminism as domineering, prescriptive and constraining invokes traces of the very same mythical figure of the (hairy, dungaree-clad) feminist invoked in post-/anti-feminist discourse.

This logic of disidentification with second-wave feminism is tied to the continuous framing of feminism in terms of a mother/daughter trope that seems to reproduce a certain heterosexual/oedipal/intergenerational conflict among women which poses little threat to hegemonic discourses of masculine privilege. McRobbie eloquently expresses the concerns related to generational logics within feminism in asserting that 'these feminist concerns with generation remain locked into normative temporalities and spatialities which have been dictated by the reproductive dynamics associated with the norms of heterosexual family life' (McRobbie, 2007b). Indeed, it is now well established that the mainstream media relishes a 'catfight' between different generations of feminists, which, in a British context, typically takes the form of Germaine Greer lambasting a younger feminist (see Greer, 1999). The emphasis on drawing clear boundaries between these different generational cohorts has, Astrid Henry argues, caused contemporary feminism to become overdetermined by the mother/daughter trope in a manner which is unhelpful and at times destructive. Using such a trope, Henry (2003: 215–22) argues, accentuates intergenerational conflict between feminists and heightens the attraction for third-wave feminists of breaking away from their (symbolic, second-wave) mothers (Henry, 2003: 215–20). Thus, what I have sought to demonstrate in this section is that there are a number of paradoxes involved in The F-word's efforts to articulate a 'third-wave' feminist agenda. This should not be read as an all-encompassing assault on the term: its performative force evidently has significant potential to bring about new feminist agendas and identities. However, my sense is that this is at least partly undone by the tendency to think the 'third wave' in terms of the subject question, coupled with the persistence of notions of intergenerational conflict and disidentification. Overall, my claim is that the attachment to a third-wave subjectivity risks undermining the threatening and radical dimensions of feminism by casting it in terms that resemble hegemonic heteronormative models of conflict between women. This potentially renders feminism unthreatening, indeed perhaps even comical, from the point of view of an anti-feminist onlooker.

Concluding reflections and critical comments

This chapter has dealt with two main themes: cultural politics and individualisation, and the question of the 'third wave' and feminist generational temporalities. On the first issue, I argued that in some cases the emphasis on popular culture, coupled with the at times overtly apolitical, almost frivolous tone of some of the articles might lead us to suggest that The F-word could be read as symptomatic of feminist disengagement and depoliticisation. This was in some ways exacerbated by the fact that, for many contributors, the affirmation of feminism was framed more in terms of individualisation and self-identity, and less as a political commitment. However, while these characterisations hold merit, I cautioned against an excessive focus on these characteristics of The F-word by drawing attention to how the articulation of a new feminist agenda on The F-word exhibits a strong interpellative capacity and enables young women to identify anew and with vigour with a fantasmatic feminist community, in a manner resistant to the individualising forces at work in the logics of post-feminism.

When we turned our attention to the question of the 'third wave' and generational dynamics, a similar set of ambiguities arose. While the construction of The F-word as a specifically 'third wave' space undoubtedly creatively produces new discursive spaces for feminist articulations, these articulations are, for the most part, grounded within what Linda Zerilli calls a 'subject question' mode of political practice – that is, a process of seeking to establish precisely who 'we' at The F-word are. In so doing, the preoccupation with the subject question, and the over-determination of feminism by the wave metaphor, potentially limits the radicalism of certain dimensions of the F-word.

I have presented a more sustained analysis of the British 'third wave' in the international context elsewhere (Dean, 2009), but it suffices to say here that the invocation of the 'third wave' is undoubtedly hugely problematic in terms of the creation of feminist articulations across spatial and temporal boundaries. The invocation of the 'third wave' arguably serves to establish Anglo-American transatlantic articulations, but perhaps restricts scope for more 'transnational' forms of feminist discourse. Indeed, the American influence can be felt in The F-word's similarity to Feministing, and the emphasis on popular culture and individualism arguably betrays an American inheritance.[17]

If we were to take this to the extreme, we could say that The F-word represents a specifically Anglo-American feminism, characterised by modes of discourse and practices that tend to reflect privileged, white, middle-class, predominantly heterosexual women. This would of course be an exaggeration, but it would be less of an exaggeration to claim that there are relatively few instances of articulations between feminism and anti-racism and/or socialism. Some recent articles have sought to address these issues: a piece by Terese Jonsson (2009) tackles the question of feminism and racial privilege, while Anna Spalding (2008) describes an anxiety about several recent high-profile feminist events having been dominated by white, middle-class women. Further back, articles by Collins (2002) and Whittle (2005) addressed questions of feminism, class and leftist politics, while someone with the pseudonym Missmogga (2002) wrote a biting critique of mainstream feminism's lack of concern for non-white and working-class women. Thus, while articles tackling points of convergence and divergence between feminism and leftist and anti-racist politics do crop up, the general absence of more sustained articulations between feminism and other modes of counter-hegemonic politics might be cause for further critical examination.

However, as with the previous chapters, I shall end on a less critical note. I want to suggest that certain new developments on The F-word could be read as indicative of an increasing vibrancy and radicalism of feminist politics more generally, by virtue of the ways in which logics of feminist individualisation – entailing the affirmation of feminism as a mode of self-identity and little more – are in some cases being translated into substantive political action. This is perhaps a problematically teleological way of framing things, inasmuch as at any given time there will always be people who self-identify as feminist in a manner which may or may not lead to a more politically action-oriented subjectivity. Nevertheless, my key point here is that the initial processes of affirming feminist self-identification are now being replaced with accounts of more overt forms of feminist activism. Clearly, in some cases, the self-identity as feminist is symptomatic of modes of apolitical feminist individualisation, that is, a feminism that ties in with the 'individualisation' thesis advanced by social theorists such as Beck (Beck and Beck-Gernsheim, 2002), Bauman (2000, 2001) and Giddens (1991) (who emphasise the ways in which a breakdown of traditional social structures is such that there are now stronger imperatives towards reflexive self-monitoring and management). However, in other instances, the self-identity as feminist need not occasion a drift into apolitical complicity with logics of individualisation but, rather, translates into a more engaged political awareness, feeding into the increasing radicalism of groups such as The F-word (a similar logic is also at work in The Fawcett Society).

Furthermore, while certain forms of feminist articulation have not been forthcoming, at the time of writing in 2010 the notion of a 'third wave' seems to be invoked and discussed rather less than in the mid-2000s, suggesting that perhaps the notion of a 'third wave' has run its course. Indeed, the most recent piece on The F-word that tackles the question of third-wave feminism is a biting critique of the wave metaphor by Red Chidgey (2008), calling for an abandonment of the notion of a 'third wave' to allow space for greater acknowledgement of the diversity of feminist histories. It is not yet clear where this apparent decentring of a 'third wave' might lead, but it is notable that this has also coincided with shifts away from analyses of popular culture and forms of feminist individualisation, and towards a more overtly action-oriented framework.[18] Consequently, The F-word both reflects and has facilitated the growing emergence of forms of activism such as Reclaim the Night, Million Women Rise, Ladyfest, Feminist Fightback, Feminist Activist Forum, Object and several others. While the full potential of The F-word as a site for the articulation of equivalences between feminism and progressive politics around class, race and sexuality (and indeed between feminisms transnationally) may not have been realised quite yet, there is nonetheless a sense that the present conjuncture is characterised by a range of new forms of feminist mobilisation.

Conclusion: The Consequences of Optimism

The preceding chapters presented a broadly favourable account of current developments in feminist politics. I suggested that, despite having undergone a number of potentially troubling post-1970s transformations, feminism in the UK has maintained a certain vibrancy and radicalism which is underplayed by accounts framed by notions such as deradicalisation, depoliticisation, fragmentation and institutionalisation. I acknowledge that the account of the 'New Feminist Politics' presented in the preceding chapters might strike some as naively optimistic and/or celebratory, but in this concluding section I want to explore in more detail the theoretical underpinnings and consequences of the cautious political optimism I am advancing. In more general terms, I want to suggest that the account of the 'New Feminist Politics' presented here occasions not a naïve political optimism, but a scepticism towards the diverse forms of what Wendy Brown – after Walter Benjamin – has termed left melancholia that one often finds in contemporary theoretical accounts of oppositional politics. Therefore, in this concluding section, I want to explore how aspects of contemporary feminist politics analysed in this book might impact upon a theorisation of political optimism or, rather, how to weave an engaged and not complacent optimism into our political theorising. I do this, first, by briefly reiterating some of the empirical dimensions of the 'resurgent' feminist politics described in earlier chapters. I use this as an occasion for a critical reflection on certain strands of post-structuralist and post-Marxist political theory and their relation to notions of political optimism and/or pessimism.

In so doing, I examine several different theoretical perspectives that have explicitly sought to counter the dangers of left melancholic political defeatism or cynicism. These include the 'heroism' of Lacanian influenced authors such as Žižek and Badiou, new strands of Deleuzian theory which stand in opposition to the alleged anthropocentrism and overemphasis on negativity present in Lacanian perspectives, and Hardt and Negri's Deleuzian Marxism. I do not provide a comprehensive overview of these perspectives but, instead, explore the different ways in which they seek to resist a political pessimism and/or defeatism. However, I argue that all these perspectives – and the Deleuzians in particular – rest on problematic assumptions about the nature of contemporary political struggle. As such, drawing on the preceding analysis of contemporary feminism, I suggest that some of these problems could be fruitfully addressed via a re-foregrounding of the 'Gramscian moment'. In so doing, I provide not a detailed analysis of the influence of Gramsci, but, rather, I argue for a reinvigoration of the Gramscian *ethos* of cautious (as opposed to naïve or complacent) optimism. My aim is to suggest ways in which the analysis of contemporary feminism presented here might occasion a reclamation of the terrain of cautious and responsible political optimism from its current Deleuzian monopoly, and to reaffirm an antipathy towards political defeatism which was integral to the 'turn to Gramsci' (Bennett, 1986) in both cultural studies and political theory.

Contemporary feminism and political optimism

Although I have sought to avoid framing contemporary feminist politics in the UK in terms of a totalising narrative of feminist resurgence, I have nonetheless provided a generally optimistic account of the emergence of new forms of feminist politics. Recall, in Chapter 1, I drew attention to how, at present (writing in 2010), one no longer has to search particularly hard to locate instances of feminist politics in the UK. This is in contrast to the late 1990s, when to critique the 'death of feminism' thesis typically meant having to impute feminist values to objects and discourses which were not avowedly feminist, for instance by looking for feminist sentiment in women-only book groups or cultural productions such as American TV show *Buffy the Vampire Slayer*. More substantively, amidst this changing terrain, I have presented a generally positive account of a an increasing vibrancy and radicalism across much UK-based feminism, evident in, for example, the emergence of productive articulations between established, formal feminist groups and newer, more informal groups; a continued and renewed investment in a feminist radicalism by established, institutionalised organisations; more sustained modes of resistance to 'post-feminist' discourse; an increasingly critical perspective on problematic generational framings of feminist politics; the emergence of collective rather than individualised feminist critiques of hegemonic representations of female sexuality; the articulation of a progressive feminist anti-racist politics within established feminist organisations; and new forms of coalitional politics around domestic violence.

The overall picture might point to a new twist to a (UK-based) feminist temporality, whereby we might retroactively argue that Paul Byrne's 1996 assessment of feminism as a social movement in 'abeyance' was in many respects correct (whereby, for Byrne, 'abeyance' meant not death but, rather, a mode of political retreat that nonetheless yielded to the potential to re-emerge). In comparison to the 1990s, the present UK context is undoubtedly characterised by the (re)emergence of various forms of feminist politics, as well as, for instance, an increasing amount of discoursing on the current state of feminism in quality newspapers such as *The Guardian* (see Dean, forthcoming 2010). At the time of writing, the current global economic crisis has also given rise to re-emergent forms of political protest, and, to some extent, the articulation of critiques of dominant modes of economic production and consumption.[1] Thus, while I do not want to go so far as to portray the current conjuncture as one characterised by widespread political re-engagement, I nonetheless want to suggest that the logics of feminist re-emergence outlined here might be situated within broader logics of re-emergent political protest.

I realise that in framing the analysis in these terms, one might legitimately say that I am simply reproducing a problematically optimistic narrative of feminist re-emergence similar to those that I have critiqued throughout the book. For instance, one might want to qualify this optimism if one takes into account the ways in which the 'New Feminist Politics' remains grounded within a largely Anglo-American discursive spatial frame: all of Fawcett's campaigning, the vast majority of Women's Aid's campaigning, and the majority of articles on The F-word, presuppose the British nation state as the spatial unit in which the campaigning and discussions take place. While instances of transnational exchange can and do take place between feminists based in the UK and overseas,[2] we may want to qualify the optimism advanced here in acknowledging that the new (British) feminist politics has not yet mushroomed into anything resembling (in Mohanty's terms) a 'Feminism Without Borders'.[3]

Thus, although my analysis is certainly optimistic in some respects, it is intended to be a cautious optimism, alert to how spaces for new political possibilities are always in danger of being constrained or squeezed out altogether, and alert to the spatial and temporal specificities of any sort of optimistic or pessimistic account of the emergence of progressive political practices in different contexts. As indicated, this political optimism is partly driven by the empirical emergence of a range of contemporary feminist practices. However, there is also a mode of political optimism woven into the theoretical dimensions of the argument presented in this book. I argued that the theoretical underpinnings of notions of radicalism in much feminist literature and many strands of contemporary political theory restrict authentic 'radical (feminist) politics' to too narrow a range of practices. The appropriation of Laclau and Zerilli presented in Chapter 2 was, fundamentally, an attempt to contest notions of feminist depoliticisation and/or deradicalisation by formulating a theoretical lens which affirms the radical character of certain forms of politics which existing perspectives might regard as non-radical and insufficiently critical. Such practices include, for example, specific modes of 'state feminism' and forms of feminist contestation in and against popular culture. Crucially, this affirmation of the radicalism of much contemporary feminism does not entail a relinquishing of one's critical capacities. To the contrary, it is grounded on a rethinking of what it means to engage in critical political practice.

Of course, this book has focussed on a problematisation of specifically *feminist* narratives of depoliticisation, but the arguments presented over the preceding chapters throw up questions which are crucial not only for feminism, but also for accounts of counter-hegemonic politics more generally. Given that, as indicated, both the empirical and theoretical dimensions of my argument are imbued with a certain spirit of optimism, I want, over the following pages, to explore notions of optimism and pessimism and their political consequences. In so doing, I reflect in greater detail on the conception of political optimism engendered by my analysis of empirical and theoretical aspects of contemporary feminism, and signal some ways in which this might impact upon our understandings of feminism and contemporary radical politics more broadly.

Optimism, pessimism and 'post-politics'

In this section, I outline how this cautiously optimistic account of the emergence of new forms of feminist politics might prompt a rethinking of some of the theoretical issues raised in the course of the book (primarily in Chapter 2). I want to suggest that all theoretical accounts of the current political conjuncture are, usually implicitly, informed by some sort of affective investment in either a political optimism or pessimism, often in ways that do not simply or clearly map on to different theoretical positions. As indicated in Chapter 2, I have found several strands of what has been variously referred to as 'post-foundational,' 'post-Marxist' and 'post-structuralist' political theory to be extremely useful for my analysis of contemporary feminist politics. However, as we saw, these theoretical strands encompass a number of different political standpoints, grounded in different forms of investment along the optimism/pessimism continuum. One of the concerns I have is that the theoretical perspectives I have drawn on to analyse contemporary feminism – particularly those articulated by Laclau and those influenced by him – stand in an ambiguous relationship to the optimism/pessimism divide. In some respects, this is no bad thing: after all, one would want to avoid the twin extremes of melancholic defeatism or celebratory naivety. Despite this, I want to argue that a key ethical imperative of a 'Laclauian' conception of politics, drawing as it does on a Gramscian understanding of hegemony, is that it demands an ethos of cautious optimism, and assumes an engaged political responsibility open to the possible (and perhaps unexpected) emergence of different modes of political contestation. However, I am concerned that this 'cautious optimism' integral to Gramscian and post-Gramscian understandings of politics is in danger of slipping away, by virtue of the ways in which some strands of contemporary post-structuralist thought – along with some feminist narratives of decline and depoliticisation – bear what I consider to be an insufficiently sceptical attitude towards narratives of depoliticisation.

The partial demise of this spirit of cautious optimism is, I want to suggest, due to a series of reconfigurations of key debates on the post-structuralist left, which I want to problematise. These reconfigurations result from the fact that arguably the most trenchant critiques of political pessimism/ defeatism articulated in recent years have been advanced by theorists whose main source of inspiration is the work of Giles Deleuze. These new strands of Deleuzian political theory have contested political cynicism and pessimism, by foregrounding an ontology of immanence and abundance, in contrast to perspectives drawing on Gramsci and Lacan that emphasise transcendence and lack. My intention here is not to provide a comprehensive overview of these debates, but, rather, to suggest ways of weakening the Deleuzian monopoly on political optimism. Against the new Deleuzians, and drawing on the preceding analysis of contemporary feminism, I argue that an appropriate theoretical response to the cautious optimism engendered by the emergence of the 'New Feminist Politics' is a re-foregrounding of the Gramscian spirit of cautious optimism in post-structuralist political theory, through revisiting the affinities between Laclau-inspired post-Marxism and Stuart Hall-inspired cultural studies. I thus seek to affirm a specifically Gramscian political optimism linked to notions of responsibility and openness to what Oliver Marchant calls the 'play of political difference', as opposed to an optimism grounded in complacency (by which I mean an insufficiently critical relation to existing forms of oppositional political practice). In many respects, this is not a substantive argument, but rather an argument about the ethos and types of affective investment that motivate our political theorising.

But what, precisely, is the nature of the problem being addressed here? First, it speaks to a particular type of ambivalence which besets contemporary feminist and left political theory. In these bodies of work one often finds that, descriptively, there is an emphasis on the multiple ways in which the current conjuncture is characterised by the emergence of diverse logics of depoliticisation, coupled with a normative desire to avoid being sucked into the temptation of political cynicism and defeatism that these logics of depoliticisation might provoke. Mouffe (2005), for instance, frames the current conjuncture in terms of a 'post-political' displacement of the constitutive antagonisms proper to politics; Stavrakakis (2007) provides a Lacanian analysis of the displacement of politics by designating the present as characterised by a consumerist, post-democratic injunction to 'enjoy' (a *jouissance à venir*); Žižek (2000) laments the emergence of an apolitical 'postmodern politics'; Todd May (2008) begins a monograph on Jacques Rancière by fleshing out the claim that ours is an age of political passivity, while Rancière himself (1999, 2006) frames the present in terms of a post-democratic 'hatred of democracy'. While diverse, these accounts exhibit variations on a similar theme: that is, the displacement of 'politics proper' – characterised by antagonism and public contestation – by forms of consumerism and managerial forms of governance, in which antagonisms are sidelined and decision-making is delegated to experts. Such accounts thus share family resemblances with Iris Marion Young's (1990) analysis of the rise of 'interest group pluralism' and even Hannah Arendt's (1958) account of the 'rise of the social'. Despite the often rather totalising gestures in these accounts, all of these authors are nonetheless – and in very different ways – partly committed to theorising the possible emergence of authentically political forms of antagonism in ways that resist the temptation of political cynicism or defeatism engendered by logics of depoliticisation.

While, of course, acknowledging the diversity of these accounts of the political valence (or otherwise) of the current conjuncture, I want to raise a number of critical points. First, while these interventions are all resolutely concerned with theorising the possibility for resistance, the preceding analysis of feminist politics suggests that such accounts risk exaggerating the extent to which the present is marked by totalising logics of depoliticisation, an approach which arguably lets a certain type of political defeatism in through the back door. For instance, within the feminist practices analysed in the preceding chapters, new forms of political mobilisation have, paradoxically, arisen precisely *in response to discourses of feminist depoliticisation*, whereby those discursive attempts at *undoing* feminism (described by McRobbie, 2009) in fact occasion avowed political resistances to that very undoing/depoliticisation. This in turn provides insights into possible routes through which certain depoliticising discursive gestures, perhaps even 'post-democratic' forms of governance more generally, may in fact engender the very political antagonisms they seek to displace. While the onset of forms of (post) feminist depoliticisation, and indeed post-political, post-democratic or consensus-based forms of governance may provoke cynicism, pessimism and defeatism, these insights suggest that the appropriate response from the perspective of a feminist and critical political theory is to remain open to the possible emergence of breakages and forms of contestation. This seems a banal point in some respects, but it is as pressing as ever at a time when levels of (conventional) political participation in the 'advanced' democracies are generally low and forms of political resistance to pervasive structures of oppression seem relatively infrequent.

Furthermore, as with the narratives of feminist depoliticisiation outlined in Chapter 1, I worry that the above-mentioned accounts of 'post-politics' or 'post-democracy' inadvertently – and in different ways – risk reproducing a particular temporality that constitutes the present as largely apolitical, and risk presuming a politicised 'golden era' located in the relatively recent past (akin to certain narratives of feminist institutionalisation and depoliticsiation critiqued in Chapter 1). This is a reading of recent political temporality which one would want to be sceptical towards, but this is not my main concern here. Rather, my main concern is to explore different theorisations of the appropriate critical response to the prevalence of 'post-political' or 'post-democratic' logics.

Theorising political optimism

One possible – and indeed attractive – response to the apparent prevalence of logics of post-political governance is to use recourse to an unashamedly heroic account of radical political agency. Such a perspective finds its clearest articulation in the works of Slavoj Žižek and Alain Badiou. Despite a complex range of often ambiguous points of divergence between these two authors, both adhere to a particular kind of 'Lacanian heroism', characterised by an investment in a notion of 'proper' politics as tied to the sudden emergence of a militant political subject instigating a *singular* political act which radically contests the terrain of a dominant discursive field. For Žižek, this is linked to the affirmation of the 'disavowed structuring principle' of a given symbolic order (Žižek, 2000: 125; Glynos, 2003), while Badiou, as we saw in Chapter 2, advocates a fidelity to an 'event' – a militant political intervention which remains radically heterogeneous to the situation into which it intervenes. Such accounts are appealing inasmuch as they are grounded on a principled theorisation of resistance amidst widespread 'cynical apathy and/or pessimism' (Stavrakakis, 2007: 114). However, their heroic account of political action has come under fire from several quarters (Stavrakakis, 2007; Laclau, 2004; Critchley, 2000; Coles, 2005). I do not wish to rehash these critiques here. Rather, I want to raise some questions not so much about the substantive elements of their theorising but, rather, about the type of political optimism their interventions seek to engender. Specifically, while at some level their interventions provide a counterpoint to a post-political cynicism, my concern is that they nonetheless provide inadequate theoretical tools for instilling an ethos of cautious political optimism. This is because, as I argued in Chapter 2, a 'heroic' conception of political action is predicated upon sudden rupturing and clearly visible instances of political contest: anything else is implicitly viewed with suspicion and risks being cast as 'inauthentic'. As the majority of instances of feminist politics analysed in this book depart significantly from the heroic notion of radical politics advanced by Žižek and Badiou, my sense is that a 'heroic' approach risks consigning a range of radical practices to the realm of the inauthentic and apolitical. Furthermore, the appeal to notions of 'authenticity' or 'fidelity' in Žižek and Badiou's accounts of radical politics betrays an almost theological – and undoubtedly resolutely masculinist – standpoint, and belies a political purism which strikes me as ill-equipped to grasp the locatedness and inevitable messiness of processes of feminist political articulation.[4] The appeal to the heroic militant political subject also seems to entail a lack of political responsibility, and risks letting in a cynicism in through the back door while the political analyst – quite literally – holds out for a hero to disrupt the post-political consensus.

Moving on from a Lacanian heroism, my worry is that there is also a residual heroism in the work of authors such as Ernesto Laclau and

Jacques Rancière, whose positions are much closer to my own. Laclau's recent work is explicitly pitched in terms of a critique of what we might call a heroic conception of political resistance, highlighting the ways in which the heroism in the accounts of political action offered by for instance Žižek or Alenka Zupančić (2000) rely on a problematic notion of a unified subject (Laclau, 2005a: 228–9). For Laclau, by contrast, the political subject is always internally divided, and the result of a delicate process of political articulation. Not only that, Laclau's recent work makes some extremely optimistic assessments about the potential politicality of the current conjuncture, noting that 'perhaps what is dawning is the arrival of a ... fully political era, because the dissolution of the marks of certainty does not give the political game any aprioristic necessary terrain, but, rather, the possibility of constantly redefining the terrain itself' (ibid.: 222). Despite this clear-cut optimism, there is still, I think, a residual heroism in Laclau's claim that the (oppositional) political moment *par excellence* consists in the emergence of a populist logic, that is, the performative constitution of a 'people' via the condensation of a series of 'anti-system' demands into an equivalential chain (ibid.: 153–4). From this perspective, as Glynos and Howarth (2007: 115) point out, politics entails the *public* contestation of social norms 'in a particular site or space where persons addressed are publicly recognized as taking on official roles', such that 'a demand is political to the extent that it publicly contests the norms of a particular practice or system of practices in the name of a principle or ideal' (ibid.: 115). Similarly, Jacques Rancière (1999) offers a somewhat optimistic account of the possibilities for the emergence of political action, inasmuch as he is absolutely insistent on the unpredictable and untamed character of politics: to predict or master in advance the characteristics of a political action would be to pre-emptively undo its political valence (although his account of 'post-democracy' suffers from a number of the problems alluded to above).

Despite this emphasis on unpredictability and the impossibility of mastery, one can nonetheless detect a residual heroism lurking in these texts. The substantive examples given by the likes of Laclau and Rancière of paradigm cases of oppositional politics all take the form of large-scale, often clearly visible and spectacular, civil society mobilisations against specific sets of institutions, such as the factory, university or national state (Rancière, 1995; Laclau, 2005a; see also Glynos and Howarth, 2007). Thus, while emphasising the unpredictable and erratic character of politics, authors such as Laclau and Rancière nonetheless operate with a notion of the genuine political moment as inhering in quite spatially and temporally specific modes of spectacular, anti-institutional politics (see May, 2008, who situates Rancière's anti-institutionalism within an anarchist genealogy). A possible consequence of this is that – in line with my critique of Lacanian heroism – it might risk characterising less visible, less spectacular and less overtly 'anti-systemic' modes of political organisation as somehow not 'authentically' political, risking a melancholic defeatism and a drift away from the cautious optimism I seek to affirm here. Furthermore, my concern is that – in Rancière's work in particular – such a view is predicated upon a sharp distinction between ongoing post-democratic governance ('police logic' in Rancière's terminology) and periodic moments of political interruption. While Rancière's account of political action is in no sense overtly heroic, his theorisation of oppositional politics nonetheless seems to underplay the kinds of (sub)cultural political practices of subversion and rearticulation which remain crucial to feminist, queer and antiracist politics. Consequently, again, it seems a certain defeatism almost inevitably creeps in: if one argues, as Rancière (1999: 17) does, that authentic politics happens only infrequently, then it seems to absolve the political analyst of responsibility for exploring possible political emergence in the present, thus, again, carrying with it the risk of delegitimising certain forms of political or latently political oppositional practices.

However, I think it would be legitimate to claim that these are contingent rather than necessary problems in Rancière's account, inasmuch as they are merely 'risks' or 'dangers' rather than irrevocable points of contention. By contrast, I think a more fundamental set of problems arise when we turn our attention to recent theoretical interventions that draw inspiration from the work of Giles Deleuze. This is an emergent and diverse field, and as such I cannot possibly do justice to its complexity here. However, I shall map out a few of its common elements, as well as its investments in political optimism and their implications for our analysis of feminist politics. New strands of Deleuzian theory take as their point of departure a critique of several aspects of post-Marxist political theory. These include a problematic preoccupation with the political subject, and a fixation on a Lacanian and/or Derridean conception of the social world as constituted by absence, lack and negativity, inasmuch as no subject or discourse is seen as fully self-present, but as constituted by processes of in/exclusion. Laclau's (2005a) account of populism, for example, is predicated upon the Lacanian notion of the subject-as-lack whose investment in an oppositional political discourse secures a temporary 'suturing' of the constitutive lack. Deleuzians argue that this emphasis on the ontological primacy of lack/absence/negativity reifies the Oedpial subject, and in so doing offers an insufficiently critical account of dominant modes of subject formation (Newman, 2007: 78–80; Deleuze and Guattari, 1972: 116). By contrast, the new Deleuzian political theory is framed in terms of an ontological imaginary of *abundance*, whereby radical political possibilities are opened up by the sheer abundance of life that exceeds any attempt to arrest 'the swarm of differences that exist below actuality', as William Connolly (2005: 240) puts it (see also Patton, 2005; Widder, 2005).

The ontological imaginary of abundance (also often tied to an emphasis on immanence in contrast to the Derridean/Lacanian emphasis on transcendence) is frequently deployed as an antidote to the alleged joylessness and political pessimism of much post-Marxist theorising. In contrast to melancholic accounts of post-democratic governance and depoliticisation, the Deleuzians paint a picture of the world as brimming with political possibilities and unconventional forms of political experimentation outwith the confines of mainstream politics. Thus, Deleuzian theorists of abundance, such as Paul Patton (2005) and Jane Bennett (2001), have tended to be more insistent on the centrality of creativity, imagination and experimentation in democratic politics than those coming from a lack-based Lacanian or post-Gramscian strand.

Similarly, from an overtly feminist perspective, Rosi Braidotti's (1994) affirmative feminism and formulation of a nomadic ethics draws on Deleuze to emphasise the centrality of notions of creativity, non-unitary subjectivity, post-humanism and deterritorialisation. Her 'nomadic' conception of feminist ethics emphasises immanent possibilities for feminist transformation in a variety of unexpected sites outside the purview of mainstream politics. She uses the notion of a 'figuration' to signify the immanent potential for these new feminist possibilities to emerge. She writes,

> A figuration is the expression of one's specific positioning in both space and time. It marks certain territorial or geopolitical co-ordinates, but it also points out one's sense of genealogy or of historical inscription. Figurations deterritorialize and destabilise the certainties of the subject and allow for a proliferation of situated or 'micro' narratives of self and others. As is often the case, artists and activists respond more properly to the call for more creativity than professional academics do.
>
> (Braidotti, 2006: 90, see also p. 170)

This conceptualisation of 'figuration' is attractive in a number of respects. For one, it is sensitive to the situatedness and contextual inscription of feminist actors, and thus perhaps avoids the attachment to quite specific modes of political protest that one arguably finds in Laclau and Rancière. It is also alert to the role of imagination and (artistic) creativity in the construction of a counter-hegemonic politics. The emphasis on immanent political possibilities, 'fugitive energies' and lines of flight is such that, for Braidotti and other Deleuzian theorists, a particular mode of political optimism is woven into the fabric of their theoretical lexicon. Braidotti in particular provides an undeniably seductive account of the ethical possibilities of post-humanism (that is, moving beyond an anthropocentric conception of political agency). However, along with a number of Deleuzians, her account is underwritten by a curious preoccupation with the destabilisation of the subject as an end in itself, without interrogating what might follow politically from that destabilisation, as well as an aprioristic privileging of minoritarian and 'micro' practices over 'macro' or 'majoritarian' modes of politics (Newman, 2007: 79). Also, she inherits from Deleuze the tendency to frame the discussions with an attractive yet thinly operationalised lexicon of flows, assemblages and deterritorialisation (Deleuze and Guattari, 2004: 3–29). Furthermore, for the purposes of the analysis advanced here, Braidotti does not provide insights into the more empirical/sociological questions of the interpellative routes into a radical/nomadic political engagement, or assess the punitive conditions that delimit possible forms of nomadic political identification (McRobbie, 2009: 160).

That said, my framing of this discussion undoubtedly does an injustice to the diversity of the new Deleuzian theories. For one, it is inaccurate to claim that the Deleuzians are in any sense uniformly or simplistically 'optimistic'. William Connolly, for one (who, while drawing on Deleuze, is far from being a full-fledged Deleuzian), emphasises the tragic character of the Nietzschean notion of immanence/abundance, 'belying those fools who equate a philosophy of immanence and abundance with a mood of "optimism"' (Connolly, 2005: 244). But despite this, they tend to share an *affirmative* view of ongoing political possibilities. Consequently, the spirit in which their interventions are conducted is in many ways similar to that which I seek to advance here. Not only that, the new Deleuzians – more so than post-Marxists such as Laclau and Rancière – emphasise the potential political valence of a diversity of cultural practices beyond the purview of conventional (oppositional) politics, and, as we shall see in more detail, are arguably more alert to the possibility for progressive political practices to emerge within the popular cultural realm (Simons, 2005). Thus, from a Deleuzian perspective, one could read new feminist cultural politics such as The F-word and Ladyfest as progressive, deterritorialising modes of experimentation beyond the scope of conventional models of political action.

Furthermore, their trenchant critique of anthropocentrism in political theory advanced by Deleuze-influenced authors such as Braidotti (2006) and Jane Bennett (2001, 2009) ties in with the feminist critique of a specifically masculine heroism and will-to-mastery that recurs in much political theory, as well as (and this is particularly strong in Bennett's work) opening up possibilities for a post-human ecofeminism. In addition, the Deleuzian critique of the foundational status of the subject shares with Zerilli a concern with the politically limiting effects of a recourse to a sovereign conception of political agency.

Consequently, it would seem at first glance that the new theoretical interventions drawing on Deleuze overlap considerably with the arguments advanced in this book. However, while I would affirm the desirability of a cautious optimism in one's political theory, I am concerned about the Deleuzian monopoly on political optimism. In particular, my sense is that Deleuzian political theory does not adequately grasp the *specificity* of politics, as we are given little indication, from a Deleuzian perspective, of what it would mean for something to become *politicised*. Rather, Deleuzian political theory derives its efficacy from affirming the creative political *potentiality* of, for example, an advertisement for GAP jeans (Bennett, 2001: 111–30) or the agentic capacities of non-human actants (Vikki Bell, 2007: 97–120; Braidotti, 2006, Bennett, 2009). However, the Deleuzians are frustratingly imprecise about the distinction between the mere *existence* of political potentiality and the *realisation* of that potential (if indeed they do make such a distinction). This arises from the fact that the Deleuzian affirmation of a quasi-optimistic account of politics arises not so much from an analytical assessment of the current conjuncture, but, rather, from a set of ontological postulates about the abundance of life. In this sense, the political optimism of the Deleuzians derives less from reference to the current conjuncture, and more through the sheer performative force of their claims about the abundance of life, creativity and political possibilities. Consequently, the texts themselves – brimming with energy, vitality and life – come to embody that which is being affirmed. As McRobbie points out in a critique of Braidotti, the latter's

> exuberant, joyful, exciting writing has, arguably, its own performative effect and her configuring of what it is to be a woman is decisively non-victim based, non-essentialist, de-gendered, desiring

and productive, brimming with potential as to what this new kind of body (beyond girlhood) can do. Braidotti takes a stand against left-ist pessimism, and her work pushes her readers towards new, rather than established forms of radical activism.

(McRobbie, 2009: 163)

This is of course a commendable aim, and there can be no doubt that Deleuzian insights have brought some challenging issues to the table. For instance, Jane Bennett's work poses difficult questions about what it might mean for political theory to characterise 'things' as having a certain agency and vitality. However, in this regard, it seems that while such perspectives encourage a commendable set of *ethical* dispositions, they do not provide us the resources for the more *analytical* and *sociological* questions of how progressive political formations come into being, and how we might conceptualise them in their located contexts. Thus, while the persistent, affirmative, joyful affirmation of life and political possibility that we find in Deleuzian writing has a certain appeal during times of overt or implied political pessimism, such approaches strike me as of limited use for the empirical analysis of current forms of radical activism, and risk drifting away from optimism towards uncritical naivety.

However, a more conjuncturally oriented and politically engaged Deleuzianism can be found in Hardt and Negri's account of contemporary radical politics, articulated in their influential books *Empire* (2000) and *Multitude* (2004). Unlike the Deluzians described above, Hardt and Negri provide a theoretical account of contemporary oppositional politics explicitly grounded in the empirical emergence of new forms of transnational oppositional political mobilisation, which they characterise as the 'multitude'. For Hardt and Negri (2004: 138), the multitude is paradoxically both singular and multiple *at the same time*, in that it consists of a diversity of forms of resistance, but is united in its revolutionary capacity to dismantle the structure of global capital. However, the Deleuzian influence in their work arises in their rejection of the constitutive role of articulation and representation. They argue that the 'multitude' arises spontaneously rather than through political articulation (Hardt and Negri, 2000: 410–15), whereby struggles against 'Empire' are not – as in Laclau's account of hegemony – articulated horizontally, but, rather, 'jump' vertically in a cycle 'not defined by the communicative extension of the struggle' (ibid.: 58). Again, this is a problematic theoretical basis for a (cautious) political optimism. Their appeal to a Deleuzian notion of immanence to explain the spontaneous emergence of the 'multitude' as a unified oppositional political subject ignores the complex and difficult forms of articulation and representation that are necessarily involved in the construction of the radical political subject (see Laclau, 2005a: 239–44, 2005b; Mouffe, 2005: 107–15; Dean and Passavant, 2004: 327). So while Hardt and Negri at first glance seem to rectify some of the problems with Deleuzian theory noted above, their approach seems ill-equipped to account analytically for the emergence of new forms of feminist politics, by virtue of its lack of engagement with the complex negotiations of political subjectivities, so integral to current and previous forms of feminist action.

The (re)turn to Gramsci

Despite the various problems identified above with Deleuzian interventions, the Deleuzians have been much more consistent than contemporary post-Marxists in their emphasis on the role of popular culture in the construction of counter-hegemonic political practices. In a useful article in an edited collection on the abundance/lack division in political theory, Jon Simons draws some interesting parallels between the debates described above, and the longstanding debate in cultural studies between cultural pessimists and cultural populists (Simons, 2005; see also Fiske, 2006; Webster, 2006; Frith, 2006). While I disagree with Simons' conclusions, this is a helpful way of framing the debate, not least because it opens up fruitful lines of enquiry between political theory and cultural studies. He argues that Lacanian theorists of lack – such as Laclau and Žižek – adhere to a 'cultural pessimism' that lacks the theoretical resources necessary for taking account of the political possibilities of popular culture (Simons, 2005: 149). Deleuzian theorists of abundance, by contrast, see the popular cultural realm as a site of 'abundant creative forces for radical democracy' (ibid.: 154). Consequently, Simons reinforces analogous binaries between optimism/pessimism, abundance/lack and Deleuze/Lacan. My sense is that this framing of the debate relies on a specific genealogy of post-Marxist thought, one in which the Lacanian influence is emphasised at the expense of Gramsci's. Reflecting this, Simons tends to treat Žižek's Lacanian cultural pessimism as representative of lack-based perspectives *in toto*.

While Simons ultimately endorses a Deleuzian cultural populism which – for the reasons outlined above – we might consider problematic, he does nonetheless helpfully signal some ways out of the Deleuzian monopoly on political optimism. He writes that 'the adoption of [the Gramscian notion of] hegemony in British cultural studies, especially by Stuart Hall, was designed to counter the cultural pessimism of the Frankfurt School thesis about the culture industry as an implacable tool of mass deception' (Simons, 2005: 157). Foregrounding the Gramscian notion of hegemony as a critique of political/cultural pessimism, I want to draw on the preceding chapters to argue for a reactivation of the affinities between Stuart Hall's cultural studies and Laclau's post-Gramscian political theory.

I do not pretend at this stage that I can offer anything resembling a comprehensive account of how we might go about rearticulating (in the sense of 'bringing back together') Hall's cultural studies and Laclau's post-Marxism. Rather, I simply want to highlight the shared *ethos* which motivated the initial formulation of both theoretical projects, and to suggest that a reactivation of that ethos might serve to alleviate the residual heroism – or even 'purism' – that one finds both in contemporary post-Marxist accounts of oppositional politics, and some accounts of the trajectory of late twentieth-century feminist politics. Most significantly, and as alluded to above, both projects were initiated in the very late 1970s and early 1980s at a time when, within the UK and some sections of the European left, there was widespread disorientation amidst the rise of Thatcherite neoliberalism, alongside strong challenges to the economistic strands of the left coming from new forms of political mobilisation not reducible to class struggle. While, for many on the left, this occasioned a narcissistic retreat into post-revolutionary melancholia (see, for example, Brown, 2000; Butler, 1998), for some the recent translation into English of Gramsci's *Prison Notebooks* opened up space for a productive rethinking of the role of the economy in Marxist theory as well as a reorientation of leftist politics more generally.

Here is not the place to give a comprehensive exhaustive account of the 'Gramscian moment', but it will suffice to say that one of its main contributions was to provide a theoretical basis upon which to argue that the failures of an economistic conception of left-wing theory and politics might occasion a cautious optimism. This 'failure' potentially made space for a more dynamic politics engaged in complex forms of articulation and negotiation with discursive tenets drawn from, for example, liberalism, feminism, post-colonialism and critical race theory. Both Hall's *The Hard Road to Renewal*, published in 1988, and Laclau and Mouffe's *Hegemony and Socialist Strategy*, first published in 1985, are characterised by a cautiously optimistic theoretical account of how the introduction of the Gramscian notion of hegemony – with its decentering of the economy and broadening of the terrain of potential political struggle – is not only 'good news' for the left, but is in fact the very precondition of a successful progressive politics (McRobbie, 1992; 1999: 105; Hall, 1992; Bowman, 2007: xii).[5]

This Gramscian investment in a *combination* of cautious political optimism and a decentring of dominant understandings of politics has, I would argue, been more resolutely adhered to in Hall-inspired cultural studies than in the more overtly political theory-oriented strands of post-Marxism. While, as we saw, Laclau's recent work continues to be grounded in a cautious political optimism, my concern is that this might risk being undone by his appeal – which he shares with Rancière – to a somewhat heroic notion of populist anti-system mobilisation as *the* political moment *par excellence*. While still undoubtedly operating within a post-Gramscian frame, my worry is that the conflation of politics and populism marks a shift away from the Gramscian emphasis on political articulation in and through popular culture, and across the state/civil society distinction. As Paul Bowman argues in a provocative analysis of the points of convergence and divergence between Laclauian post-Marxism and Hallian cultural studies, 'post-Marxist political theory in particular must now attend to the challenge and criticisms laid down by deconstruction and cultural studies if it is not, paradoxically, to disengage from the possibility of intervening politically in anything like the way that was its own initial *raison d'être*' (Bowman, 2007: xv–xvi). Thus, despite clear Post-Gramscian parallels between Ernesto Laclau and Stuart Hall's work, it is remarkable that there has not been more exchange between the research programmes inspired by these two thinkers.[6]

In this case, I suspect this lack of cross-disciplinary engagement may be linked to a (political) post-Marxist uneasiness with the incipient cultural populism of classic texts such as *Resistance Through Rituals* (Clarke et al., 1975) in which a Gramscian analysis was used to affirm the (alleged) political valence of a range of youth subcultural practices. *Resistance Through Rituals* (alongside Dick Hebdige's *Subculture: the Meaning of Style* (1979)) arguably overemphasised the politically subversive and/or resistant character of a range of subcultural practices,[7] and afforded a privileged (but, crucially, not static) status to class and, at least initially, gave insufficient attention to gender dynamics in youth subcultures (Garber and McRobbie, 1975). However, this should not detract from the significance of the *Resistance Through Rituals* intervention, and the 'turn to Gramsci' in cultural studies and left political theory more generally. The 'turn to Gramsci' provided theoretical space for an ethos of openness to the emergence of political practices which depart from conventional models of political action, as well as fostering a resolutely non-defeatist ethos of conjunctural political analysis. As Clarke et al. argue, the Gramscian notion of hegemony

> is a matter of the nature of the balance struck between contending classes: the compromises made to sustain it; the relations of force; the solutions adopted. Its character and content can only be established by looking at concrete situations, at concrete historical moments. The idea of 'permanent class hegemony' or of 'permanent incorporation' must be ditched.
>
> (Clarke et al., 1975: 40–1; see also Bennett, 1986)

While some feared that the affirmation of the potential political character of these subcultural practices might engender an overhasty 'politicisation' of a range of cultural practices (see Dean, 2000), the ethos of the initial 'turn to Gramsci' was one of engaged political responsibility, rather than naivety. In this sense, both the post-Marxist emphasis on the ontological primacy of the political, and post-Gramscian cultural studies' emphasis on the possible political valence of seemingly non-political cultural practices potentially rest on an engaged and responsible political optimism. In Oliver Marchant's words, which are imbued with a Gramscian spirit even if Gramsci is not explicitly referenced, 'the claim as to the primordial status of political ontology does not correspond to the commonplace notion of 'everything is political' – even though everything *is* political in the sense of being irresolvably subverted by the instituting/destituting moment of the political, as it is indicated in the play of the political difference' (2007: 169).

This approach – which emphasises the potential political *valence* of particular cultural practices – rather than (as with a Lacanian heroism) a 'theoretical *rarification* of the political event' (Marchant, 2007: 131) seems hugely preferable to either a Deleuzian immanentism (which offers no account of political negotiation/mediation) or a Lacanian heroism (which holds out for a sudden eruptive moment). Instead of a naïve optimism, such an approach fosters an openness to the emergence of (not always explicitly) political practices in a range of sites, in ways which disrupt and subvert the evenness of logics of feminist deradicalisation, depoliticisation or other forms of post-political and post-democratic logics. Such an approach might create space for a more rigorous theorisation of a range of feminist cultural practices such as Ladyfest and The F-word, without this necessarily entailing a drift into a complacent political naivety.

A similar ethos motivates several current strands of Arendtian feminist theory – which I drew on extensively in previous chapters – in that they refuse, perhaps more overtly than authors such as Laclau and Rancière, a heroic and/or 'purist' conception of political action. In some respects this is surprising, given that Arendt's *The Human Condition* (1958) can be read as a quintessential example of a purist, heroic and topographical account of politics, combined with a melancholic account of the fall of the public (political) realm. However, the radicalised reading of Arendt offered by Zerilli and Honig, particularly in relation to the Arendtian notions of judgement and imagination, offered helpful ways of reconceptualising contemporary feminist practices from a perspective that avoids a problematically purist or heroic conception of counter-hegemonic politics. Thus, despite Arendt's pessimistic account of the fall of the political realm, Honig and Zerilli's contemporary feminist appropriations of Arendt share with the Gramscian intervention a cautiously optimistic account of the possibility for new forms of political action that perhaps do not adhere to conventional liberal, Marxist (or even post-Marxist) conceptions of political action. While there will undoubtedly be tensions between the Gramscian and Arendtian traditions, these appropriations of Gramsci and Arendt nonetheless both provide possible ways of reclaiming the terrain of (cautious) political optimism from the Deleuzians. In contrast to the Deleuzian affirmation of immanent political possibilities, these reworkings of Arendt and Gramsci maintain a cautious optimism, which avoids the naivety of the Deleuzians, in that the question of the *specificity* of political action and modes of politicisation is explicitly addressed. The optimism thus inheres in the claim that – to borrow a phrase from Honig – *nothing is ontologically resistant to politicisation*, a claim which occasions a call to remain alert to the possible emergence of forms of political action in unpredictable and unexpected locations. The consequence of this optimism is not naïvety but responsibility. Both the Arendtian and Gramscian perspectives outlined here provide an antidote to 'left melancholia', that is, in Wendy Brown's words, '[Walter] Benjamin's unambivalent epithet for the revolutionary hack who is, finally, not serious about political change, who is more attached to a particular political analysis or ideal – even to the failure of that ideal – than to seizing possibilities for radical change in the present' (Brown, 2000: 22).[8]

However, in addition to the possibilities of reinvigorating the *ethos* of post-Marxist theory, a rearticulaton of post-Marxist political theory and post-Gramscian cultural studies might also serve to rejuvenate post-Marxist political analyses of a number of substantive issues central both to feminist politics and contemporary counter-hegemonic politics more generally. Let me provide two examples. First, I am concerned that the potential fruitfulness of post-Marxist accounts of politics for the analysis of political intervention in and against popular culture has been constrained by the bifurcation of post-Gramscian cultural studies and post-Marxist political theory and, as McRobbie argued some time ago, 'the role of 'culture' remains underdeveloped in Laclau's project of 'building a new left' (McRobbie, 1992: 725). I would not want to suggest that the responsibility is on Laclau himself to provide an account of the role of 'culture' in his theory but, as my analysis of aspects of contemporary feminist cultural politics in Chapter 5 suggests, political interventions 'in and against' discourses circulating within popular culture represent a crucial dimension of contemporary (feminist) political struggle. This suggests that it would be fruitful to reactivate the debate about political intervention in popular culture. This has been done by several authors within cultural studies: for instance, Paul Bowman (2007) has explored in detail points of convergence and tension between Laclau, Hall and Derrida, while Sean Nixon (2000) has drawn fruitful connections between Foucaultian and Gramscian understandings of political intervention within popular culture. The onus is therefore very much on those within the discipline of political theory to respond to the challenges posed by Stuart Hall-inspired cultural studies and contemporary feminist politics.

Second, an articulation of post-Marxist political theory and Gramscian cultural studies enables a reassessment of the relationship between 'the state' and contemporary oppositional politics. Throughout Chapters 3 and 4, I argued that the abandonment of a feminist anti-statism had not necessarily curtailed the radicalism of contemporary feminist practices: in fact, we saw that – with The Fawcett Society and Women's Aid – their radicalism often derives from complex forms of articulation across the state/civil society divide. A further contribution of the Gramscian intervention, recurrent throughout both *Hegemony and Socialist Strategy* and *The Hard Road to Renewal*, was the claim that a principled anti-statism could not be seen as an adequate response to the decentering of class struggle. Despite this, one detects a whiff of anti-statism in Laclau's account of populism as 'anti-system' (crucially, it hinges on the extent to which 'system' and 'state' converge), and Rancière is unambiguous in his claim that contemporary emancipatory politics must operate at a 'distance from the state' (as he put it at a recent London conference, 'On the Idea of Communism', Birkbeck College, 14 March 2009).[9] Consequently, a reactivation of the 'Gramscian moment,' with its emphasis on political articulation that cuts across and subverts the state/civil society divide might again equip

us with the theoretical tools to think about an emancipatory politics
that avoids the temptation of anti-statist purism (and, as we have seen,
certain neo-Arendtian insights may also be helpful).

I hope to have shown that the empirical (re-)emergence of a range
of progressive feminist practices entailing various forms of political
intervention 'in and against' both the state and popular culture pose a
number of challenges for contemporary political theory. However, I have
suggested that the appropriate response to these challenges – concerning
the role of the state, popular culture, and optimistic/pessimistic forms
of affect – consists not necessarily in the creation of a radically new set
of theoretical tools but, rather, in the reactivation of a range of debates
which have been lying dormant for a long time, in part due to retrenchment of disciplinary boundaries. In more general terms though, the
onset of the 'New Feminist Politics' reaffirms the profound unpredictability of political action, and should prompt us to maintain a cautiously
optimistic – yet not naïve – openness to the emergence of politics, and
a healthy but not dismissive scepticism of melancholic narratives of the
decline of radical politics.

Notes

Introduction

1. I define as feminist any organisation which, broadly speaking, is explicitly concerned with combating the ongoing subordination and inequality that continues to affect women in a diversity of contexts, and in which the gendered character of that inequality is emphasised. I thus prefer the term 'feminist' over 'women's movement', as the latter potentially includes women organising in the service of a non or anti-feminist agenda (see Freedman, 2001: 1; Ferree, 2006: 6–11).
2. See Appendix A of Predelli et al. (2008) for a helpful overview of established women's groups currently operating in the UK.
3. On the issue of my being a male researcher looking into feminism, I should mention that, for the most part, I didn't find this to be a major obstacle: almost all respondents were more than happy to help and the fact that I am male aroused curiosity rather than hostility or non-co-operation. One possible objection is that, in talking to a male researcher, certain viewpoints or pieces of information may have been withheld. However, there is no solid evidence for this and the information presented should be taken at face value.
4. This concerns the 2006 Equality Act which created a single UK equalities body – the Equality and Human Rights commission – which is partly intended to streamline equalities legislation enabling greater recognition of intersectionality and 'multiple discrimination'. The act also introduced a duty on public bodies to promote gender equality.
5. Here, the notion of a logic seeks to group together a series of disparate social and political practices that nonetheless share a set of characteristics. These are not essential characteristics, but merely overlaps such that a series of commonalities – 'family resemblances' in Wittgensteinian parlance – can be discerned and identified (see Howarth, 2005: 323). I describe the notion of 'logics' in more detail in Chapter 2.

1 Current Developments in Feminist Politics

1. As Fiona Mackay points out, the standard narrative about UK feminism is that 'after an initial flourishing in the 1960s and 1970s the movement fragmented, dissipated and de-radicalised, stymied by the cold climate of neoliberal Thatcherism and the unravelling of simple notions of universal sisterhood. Feminist activism continued largely by means of unobtrusive mobilisation within institutions and through distinctive service delivery' (Mackay, 2008: 17).
2. See also Phillips (1991: 120–7) for a vivid account of the dynamics of autonomy, participation and friendship in early second-wave feminism in the Anglo-American context.
3. For a theoretical critique of the racialised character of the notion of sisterhood, see Mohanty's 'Under Western Eyes' (2003: 19–42).

4. Walby (2002), for instance, sees the partial institutionalisation of feminist politics as a sign of success and maturation.
5. Ellie Levinson's (2009) recent book *The Noughtie Girl's Guide to Feminism* is another popular text about contemporary feminism. In its style and presentation, Levinson's book is aimed at the 'chick lit' market, and, like Walter, champions a highly individualised understanding of feminism. In addition, Levinson uncritically adopts a disidentificatory stance towards older, supposedly 'man-hating' incarnations of feminism.
6. Although as we shall see in the section on post-feminism, McRobbie now puts forward a more pessimistic account.
7. Similarly, Forna's (1999) brief reflections on contemporary feminism sit somewhere between Nash's micropolitics, and McRobbie's work on post-feminist depoliticisation, discussed in the following section.
8. Viner writes, '[S]uddenly feminism is all about how the individual feels right here, right now, rather than the bigger picture. The idea of doing something for the greater good – or, indeed, because the reasons behind the action might be dangerous or insecure or complex – has become an anachronism. It's almost as if we dare not admit that the personal is political because we know it would make people like us less' (Viner, 1999: 21–2). Similar concerns, related to the emergence of what she calls 'lifestyle feminism', prompted Germaine Greer to write *The Whole Woman* (1999), the sequel to *The Female Eunuch* which, apparently, she said she would never write.
9. Within some new strands of European feminist theory the notion of a 'third wave' has been deployed to signify new forms of materialist epistemology (van der Tuin, 2009). However, this approach also suffers from a similar set of problematic generational framings (Hemmings, 2009).
10. Similarly, Lise Shapiro Sanders, for one, seeks to distance herself from a reading of the 'third wave' as a conservative, anti-second-wave 'post-feminism', promulgating a conception of the 'third wave' as 'founded on second-wave principles', but with certain cultural and political differences (Sanders, 2007: 5. See also Dicker and Piepmeier, 2003: 5).
11. One example is Pender (2004), which makes a case for *Buffy the Vampire Slayer* as a quintessentially third-wave cultural production.
12. This is a term taken from J. L. Austin's speech act theory. Here, a 'constative' statement simply reports or describes a given state of affairs, in contrast to a 'performative' act that brings something into existence through the process of naming (Austin, 1975: 5–12).
13. For further work on young women's reluctance to identify as 'feminist', see Aapola et al. (2005), Pilcher (1998), Harris (2004), Jowett (2004), Tibballs (2000), Howard and Tibballs (2003), Levy (2005), Griffin (2001, 2004), Budgeon (2001), Sharpe (2001), Rudolfsdottir and Jolliffe (2008) and Scharff (2009).
14. I note that, in the main, I have not addressed the complex question of the relationship between feminist politics and feminism in the academy. For now, it will suffice to say that academic feminism may, at one level, be read as indicative of feminist success, and as a key site for the articulation of feminist demands. On the other hand, academic feminism – and the discipline of feminist theory more generally – has been widely read as indicative of a political defeatism, and a retreat into obscurantist theoretical reflection *in*

lieu of engaged political critique (see, for example, Hemmings, 2006; Pereira, 2008 and Wiegman, 2002, on these debates). While a detailed analysis of the possibilities for feminist political articulations within the academy is not forthcoming in this book, this should not be read as indicating a commitment to a strong academic/activist divide. Indeed, many feminist activists are aware of, and take on board, insights and critiques articulated within the academy, and many contemporary feminist activists come to feminism through the academy (indeed, this is McRobbie's key point). Thus, contemporary feminist political practices are characterised by movements of people and ideas across the porous and shifting borders between the academy and activism. The academy is a vitally, and perhaps increasingly, important site for the production of feminist articulations. However, I would hesitate to afford the academy the privileged status afforded to it by McRobbie.

15. I should point out that my distinction between temporal and spatial narratives is largely a heuristic one, in that all the narratives I describe deploy certain conceptions of space and time.
16. See also Bagić (2006) for an account of the more deleterious consequences of feminist 'NGOisation' in the post-Yugoslav context.
17. Kalpana Ram (2000) makes a similar argument concerning Indian feminist appropriations of rights-based discourse.
18. This alludes to how my separation of the literature on 'state feminism' and 'transnational feminism' is in many ways not as neat as it might seem. While they form two distinct sets of literatures, their concerns overlap considerably.
19. Having said that, although recent short pieces by Maddison and Jung (2008), Gray (2008) and Grey (2008), relating to Australia and South Korea, Canada and Australia and New Zealand respectively, all provide glimpses in this direction.
20. Indeed, as Wendy Brown (2000: 27–8) reminds us, the etymology of the word 'radical' derives from the Latin *radix*, meaning 'root'.

2 Rethinking Feminist Radicalism

1. As an example of this, Wendy Brown's critique of Laclau and Mouffe's 'radical democracy' asks the question of 'precisely where the radicalism lies' (Brown, 1995: 11), implicitly casting herself as 'more radical' than Laclau and Mouffe, while also implicitly linking 'radicalism' to anti-capitalism.
2. For Heidegger (1973: 28–35), the 'ontological' refers to the general question of 'being', the formal/abstract characteristics of all social and political configurations, whereas the ontic refers to the localised, regional and contextual dimensions of social and political configurations – that is, the question of substantive entities, in opposition to the abstract/formal qualities of 'being' in general.
3. I acknowledge that the manner of this reference to Lefort risks perpetuating what Marchant calls the 'sloganisation' of Lefort's work, whereby the complexity of Lefort's output is subsumed under a set of slogans drawn from his work (Marchant, 2007: 85).
4. For other 'post-foundational' articulations of politics, see Nancy (2000), Lefort (1988), Critchley (2007) and Mouffe (2005).

5. Although Stavrakakis (2007: 150–8) provides a reading of Badiou which places his account of radical politics more explicitly within the framework of the 'democratic revolution', thus moderating the account of Badiou's work as hard line and/or heroic. The recent work of Slavoj Žižek (2000; 2002) is more unambiguously heroic, although in equating the authentically political with struggles around class and the economy, he departs from non-topographical/post-foundational notions of radical politics.
6. I emphasise the notion of radicality in Laclau's work through the formal logic of equivalence rather than through the substantive normative project of 'radical democracy' as articulated by Mouffe (see Laclau and Mouffe, 2001; Mouffe, 1992, 1993). This is because 'radical democracy' is a conjunctural normative intervention rather than an analytical device, although, according to Laclau (2005b), its radicalism does derive at least partly from the construction of equivalential linkages.
7. What is crucial, however, is that these contradictions and instabilities, potentially at least, open space for fruitful political engagement at the level of the state, through, for example, the passing of anti-sexist legislation, or the provision of state-funded services for childcare.
8. Furthermore, in this vein they argue that 'in the case of the feminist struggle, the state is an important means for effecting an advance frequently *against* civil society, in legislation which combats sexism' (Laclau and Mouffe, 2001: 179–80).
9. For a comprehensive account of the politics of women's policy agencies, see Squires (2007).
10. Another theoretical strand which has addressed the role of creativity and imagination in counter-hegemonic politics is that taking inspiration from Deleuzian notions of creativity, abundance and immanence. I do not discuss these perspectives here, but offer an analysis and critique of Deleuzian political theory in the latter stages of the conclusion.
11. Alain Badiou (2005: 24), for instance, claims that Arendt's equation of politics with the 'plurality of opinions' restricts politics to the realm of parliamentary politics.
12. For sound attempts at dealing with the question of Arendt and feminism, see Honig (1995a and 1995b). For an extremely forthright feminist critique of Arendt, see Rich (1979, especially pages 211–12).
13. For example, in her rigid public/private distinction, rather narrow topographical conception of the political realm, and concomitant subsumption of plurality to the One. I would like to thank David Payne for some insightful discussions on this issue.
14. Indeed, Cavarero seeks to highlight the oxymoronic character of the expression 'political theory': 'theory', she argues, pertains to the otherworldly, the abstract and the universal, whereas 'politics' pertains to worldly processes of plural interaction and contestation.
15. This, of course, opens Arendt to the charge of romanticising an unambiguously 'masculinist' conception of doing politics (see, for example, Springborg, 1989). I would hope, however, that these tendencies are weakened within the context of the feminist interpretation of Arendt advanced here.
16. As Pitkin (1998: 14) points out, contrary to widespread opinion, the 'rise of the social', for Arendt, does not refer to 'private' issues becoming public.

Rather, it refers to issues such as survival, the needs of the body, biological necessity and economics – issues that Arendt claims were historically dealt with within the realm of the 'household' – becoming matters of collective concern. The social, for Arendt, is thus 'neither private nor public' (1958: 28) but, instead, is a 'curiously hybrid realm' (ibid.: 35).

17. Examples of 'figures of the newly thinkable' include, according to Zerilli (2005a), Judith Butler's much maligned drag artist (in its capacity as a demonstration of the 'hyperbolic instantiation of gender norms' (ibid.: 61)), the sex/gender distinction in second-wave feminist theory and the Milan Women Bookstore Collective's foregrounding of the figure of the 'symbolic mother' (as an imagined figure capable of fostering free relations between women).

18. Norval partly frames her discussion in Rancièreian parlance, claiming that Wollstonecraft's intervention 'marks the verification of equality, i.e. the place of a dispute within the existing order' (2007: 76).

19. Saul Newman makes a similar argument in *Unstable Universalities* (2007: 88–93). See Muñoz (1999) for an engaging account of the role of imagination and disidentification in Cuban and Latina/o American queer politics. Elsewhere, Glynos (2003) argues from a Lacanian perspective for a notion of radical politics that aims at altering the contours of the possible, by exposing society's 'fantasmatic underside'.

20. It is important to note that in invoking the notion of 'political imagination', I am not suggesting that political action consists of 'imaginative' and 'non-imaginative' acts. A consequence of a non-topographical conception of politics is that every political action has an imaginative dimension, in that a pure repetition of a practice is impossible. Thus, when I refer to moments of political imagination, strictly speaking, I mean 'moments in which the imaginative dimension of a political action is brought to the fore:' the more that dimension is brought to the fore, the more radical it is.

21. For instance, as Howarth points out, a forest in the path of a proposed motorway may represent 'an inconvenient obstacle impeding the rapid implementation of a new road system, or it might be viewed as a site of special interest for scientists and naturalists, or a symbol of the nation's threatened natural heritage' (2000: 102).

3   The Fawcett Society: The End of the Road for Equality Feminism?

1. At the time of writing, Fawcett are running six major campaigns: Sexism and the City, focussed on gender equality in the workplace; Seeing Double, focussing on ethnic minority women; Engendering Justice, focussing on women and the criminal justice system; the Equal Pay campaign; Keeping Mum – a campaign against pregnancy discrimination; and femocracy, which addresses ethnic minority women's exclusion from mainstream politics. Consequently, although I refer to the Fawcett Society – and indeed Women's Aid and the F-word – in the third person singular, this is simply to allow for grammatical consistency, and does not imply that I consider the groups studied to be singular and unitary.

2. This emphasis on professionalism was very apparent at the 2005 AGM, during which there was outrage when it transpired that the minutes for the previous AGM were incomplete and that the accounts were not circulated in advance. 'It's just not good enough!' said one member indignantly. Someone also pointed out that if the organisation is to modernise and be taken seriously then it needs to get these things right. The extent of the dissatisfaction with this seemingly rather minor bureaucratic point was rather bemusing to an outsider! However, I took it to be indicative of the importance that the organisation places on appearing professional and 'doing things right'.

3. Justifications for the distinctly staff-led nature of the organisation included this being the most efficient use of the organisation's resources, especially given its improved relationship with the government post-1997, and also that the views expressed at the AGM may not be representative of the membership as a whole (Fawcett staff members, interview, 31/10/05). At the 2006 AGM it was proposed that the organisation establish a database of members' key skills to enable greater participation in the organisation's activity on the part of the members, although to my knowledge, this hasn't been carried out.

4. Katherine Rake was director of Fawcett from 2002 until July 2009, when she left to become chief executive of the Family and Parenting Institute.

5. In this sense, a case could be made that The Fawcett Society is a textbook equality-based liberal feminist organisation. As Andrew Heywood points out, 'liberal feminists champion legal and political equality with men. They have supported an equal rights agenda, which would enable women to compete in public life on equal terms with men, regardless of sex. Equality thus means equal access to the public realm' (2003: 250).

6. I use the word 'system' rather hesitantly here: I do not intend to invoke an essentialist notion of a structured totality. Instead, I simply wish to point out how Fawcett's campaigning presupposes an acceptance of a series of more basic (that is, 'systemic') institutional configurations which are, of course, ultimately contingent. See also Fawcett Society, 2005c.

7. A 'floating voter' is a voter who doesn't identify strongly with one political party.

8. Rake commented as follows: 'Now, will it [Cameron's commitment to women's representation] deliver a revolution in terms of the number of women in parliament at the next general election? Well, no, but with one of the oldest parliaments in the world it's quite difficult to get revolutions, you've got to be in there for the long game really, and you have to constantly keep that issue on the agenda, but I think the days are kind of gone where people can dismiss it out of hand. I think that they've really understood the significance of it as an issue, both in terms of the party's electoral liability and also in terms of peoples' sense of connectedness and democracy and what have you and I think that that would be a huge victory really' (Katherine Rake, interview, November 2006).

9. Positive action measures are institutional guarantees aimed at increasing the number of women in representative institutions.

10. For a general account of the characteristics of Nordic welfare states, see Esping-Anderson (1990) and Kautto et al. (1999: 13–14). The latter point out the problems inherent in seeing the 'Nordic' model as a single, unitary

welfare model. For sound accounts of the role of gender issues in Nordic welfare states see Kjeldstad (2001) and Jónasdóttir and von der Fehr (1998). For a detailed, though now rather outdated, comparative study of gender and welfare in the UK and Sweden, see Ruggie (1984). For a radical feminist critique of Danish social democracy, see Schirmer (1982).

11. However, another recent document outlining the tenets of Fawcett's policy aims is more forthright. It talks about the need for a 'revolution' in men's lives, especially in terms of the domestic division of labour which in turn is linked to a project of placing greater value on care-work (Fawcett Society, 2005a: 12).

12. An OBE stands for 'Order of the British Empire', and is a British order of chivalry which, if a little anachronistic, is nonetheless taken seriously.

13. The fact that the reclamation of feminism has been personally spearheaded by Katherine Rake is perhaps demonstrative of the somewhat hierarchical nature of the organisation. However, this project of hers does seem to have widespread support within the organisation, as evidenced by the rest of the paragraph.

14. Of note is that, shortly after this, an article was published in the comment section of *The Guardian* of 22/08/06 titled 'In Praise of ... The Fawcett Society', much to Katherine Rake's delight, which praised Fawcett for campaigning 'insistently, pragmatically and never in a way that would allow it to be parodied as ludicrous or extreme'.

15. See Falkof (2007) for an extensive feature article in *Stop Gap* on the 'men in feminism' question.

16. See http://www.femconferences.org.uk.

17. This event was lively and well attended. The panel included the academic Haleh Afshar, Catherine Redfern (founder of The F-word) and Natasha Walter (author of *The New Feminism*). Here, Rake's enthusiasm for the debate about feminism was instantly palpable (indeed, infectious), and may well have been a motivating factor for her spearheading of a bold reclamation of feminism.

18. Katherine Rake chaired this event and speakers included Angela McRobbie and Kat Banyard (campaigns officer for Fawcett's Sexism and the City campaign), as well as a former lap-dancer.

19. Indeed, it prompted a feature article in *The Guardian* in which members of the public were asked to wear the T-shirt. See Levinson, 2006.

20. Signatories thus far include lawyers Vera Baird and Cherie Blair, politicians Dianne Abbott, Hilary Benn, Theresa May, Ken Livingstone, Harriet Harman and Oona King; human rights campaigner Shami Chakrabarti, author Traci Chavalier, singers Sophie Ellis-Bextor and Kate Jackson, TV journalists Kirsty Wark and Samira Ahmed, artist Tracey Emin and sportswoman Tanni Grey-Thompson.

21. Myspace is an extremely popular 'social networking' website. See http://www.myspace.com/fawcettfeministchallenge

22. According to a joint briefing by Fawcett and Object, 'the term 'lap dancing club' refers to venues where live entertainment is provided for the purposes of sexual stimulation of the customers. This includes routines referred to as lap dancing, table dancing, pole dancing, erotic dancing, stripping, and striptease' (Object and The Fawcett Society, 2009).

23. Although Object are quick to refute accusations both from other feminists and from the non-feminist public that the type of feminism they promote is in some way 'anti-sex' (see their FAQ at http://www.object.org.uk/index.php/the-facts/faq).

24. Similarly, in a feature article in *Stop Gap*, Christina Julios (2007) from the Ethnic Minority Foundation calls on mainstream white-dominated women's organisations to be far more representative of the concerns of women in all their diversity, so as to move away from the 'middle-aged, middle-class whitewash' that currently predominates.

25. Further concerns about the T-shirt were raised by journalist Deborah Orr (2007), on the pages of UK broadsheet paper *The Independent*. She deemed the whole exercise rather superficial and argued that it did not tell us a great deal about the substantive political changes which are behind the Fawcett Feminist Challenge. In response to this, Rake claimed that she could see why it might be perceived as superficial, were it not for the fact that 'underneath it is a whole set of very concrete demands and facts about the inequalities still faced by women. The Fawcett Society is campaigning to close the gaps between men and women as far as access to power, money and justice are concerned. Yesterday, we held an event with Gordon Brown, so we are speaking directly to the heart of power' (Rake, in Cochrane, 2007).

4   Women's Aid: Professionalised Radicalism?

1. It is worth mentioning that Nicola Harwin, Women's Aid's current director, came to the organisation as a result of helping to set up a community centre and a refuge in the early 1970s, and that such projects were very much governed by an ethos of self-help and self-empowerment (Nicola Harwin, interview, February 2007).

2. Following the split, the refuge in Chiswick was to provide the springboard for the formation of the national domestic violence charity Refuge, which, despite these initial tensions, now has strong co-operative links with Women's Aid (for instance, the national domestic violence helpline is run jointly by the two organisations).

3. While almost all of Women's Aid's campaigning efforts are UK-based, it has engaged in international partnership projects with domestic violence organisations in Russia and Uzbekistan (Women's Aid, 2004a: 26).

4. Services which Women's Aid provides for survivors of domestic violence include refuge accommodation, outreach services, 'floating support' for women who wish to remain in their own home, aftercare and resettlement for women and children after leaving refuges, support groups for women who have experienced domestic violence, activities and support services for children, provision of independent advocacy services and the provision of a freephone 24-hour Domestic Violence Helpline, run in co-operation with the organisation Refuge (Barron, 2005).

5. The key campaigning issues for Women's Aid at present are improved funding for services for survivors of domestic violence; improved measures to ensure safe child contact with parents following separation due to domestic violence and ensuring an exemption from the 'no recourse to public funds'

rule for women experiencing domestic violence who are under immigration control.

6. This is exemplified by Women's Aid's recent online consultation (based on an idea conceived by Margaret Moran MP, then chair of the All-Party Parliamentary Group on Domestic Violence) titled 'Womenspeak', in which domestic violence survivors were consulted in order for their priorities to be articulated (Women's Aid, 2002b). Similarly, in 2003, Women's Aid organised an international conference on approaches to preventing domestic violence, in which government legislation was discussed from the point of view of survivors' wishes and demands (Women's Aid, 2003a). In addition, Women's Aid hosted a Question Time Debate on the government's *Safety and Justice* paper in 2003 (Women's Aid, 2003b) and another on domestic violence and the justice system in 2002 (Women's Aid, 2002a).

7. In addition, as part of this national strategy, Women's Aid foregrounds the need to make available a 24-hour domestic violence support and advocacy services in every area as well as more comprehensive refuge provision (Women's Aid, date not specified, (b)).

8. As an example, Harwin mentioned Jo Richardson MP, who put forward the 1997 Domestic Violence Act as a private members' bill (Nicola Harwin, interview, February 2007).

9. This has the further consequence of imposing greater time constraints on refuge workers, an issue that comes to the fore in the following quote from a survivor of domestic violence: 'It would be good if refuges could talk to women and then pass on what we think. If it was done properly. But refuge workers don't have time to do it. They don't even have the time to go to meetings – how could they consult with women as well? They need time and resources if they are to do that. The other agencies need to realise' (Hague et al., 2003: 159).

10. Business in the Community is a UK membership organisation promoting socially responsible business practice.

11. Further examples of similar projects include a campaign with *Company* magazine called 'Tell a Friend', which received financial support from shoe retailer Faith (who for a period of time donated 5p from every pair of Japan flip flops sold in-store to Women's Aid), encouraging women experiencing domestic violence to talk to a friend about it, and to raise awareness of domestic violence more generally (Women's Aid, 2005b). Similarly, clothes retailer Topshop participated in a scheme whereby money from the sales of friendship bracelets was donated to Women's Aid (Women's Aid, 2005e). Department store House of Fraser also launched a commercially available personal alarm whereby 25p from every alarm sold was donated to Women's Aid (Women's Aid, 2003c).

12. As Nicola Harwin points out, 'the true extent and cost of domestic violence has been revealed and domestic violence has moved from the margins to the mainstream' (Women's Aid, 2004a: 5)

13. For instance, in the 'Domestic Violence FAQ' on their website, they draw attention to how 'access to culturally specific or specialised support may also be an important consideration for women from BME communities, lesbians, disabled women, asylum seekers and women with insecure immigration status. These women often face additional barriers to seeking help in the

first place – such as physical barriers, language, poverty and discrimination' (Women's Aid, 2005c).

14. This is cited as one of Women's Aid's key demands in Women's Aid, 2004b: 11.

15. In this regard, Women's Aid is particularly concerned by the government's assertion that 'repeat victimisation tends to be concentrated in disadvantaged communities' (Butler, 2003a).

16. In view of this, Women's Aid's enthusiasm for perpetrator re-education is qualified by the proviso that they 'need to be founded on gender analysis which tackles the belief system that convinces male perpetrators that they have a right to control women in intimate relationships. Failure to address this belief system means that men may simply switch from physical to emotional abuse, and women and children will continue to live in fear' (Butler, 2003a). This is a point which again emphasises the 'systemic' characteristics which make domestic violence possible. Similarly, Women's Aid argues that perpetrators, for the most part, are not 'mad', but that discourses of male ownership and superiority are such that 'they just believe they have a right to abuse "their" woman and often the children too' (Saunders, 2001).

17. In response to the question 'who is responsible for domestic violence?' the organisation writes, '[T]he abuser is. Always. There is no excuse for domestic violence. The abuser has a choice to use violence for which he is responsible and for which he should be held accountable. They do not have to use violence. They can choose, instead, to behave non-violently and foster a relationship built on trust, honesty, fairness and respect' (ibid.).

18. Of course, that is not to say Women's Aid were the only feminist group to politicise domestic violence: such a claim would be absurd given the wide-ranging forms of activism against domestic violence across geographical contexts.

19. The phrase 'new corporatism' in this context could be seen as synonymous with the term 'new public management' which has come to play a key structuring role in recent debates around public sector governance in the UK. See Osborne and McLaughlin (2002), Exworthy and Halford (1999) and Walker et al. (2005) for general overviews of the question of new public management and 'new managerialism'. Generally speaking, the dominant aspects of these changes in public sector governance cohere around a shift towards greater decentralisation, more intense audit regimes, measurement and monitoring of outputs, competition, entrepreneurship and the adoption of private-sector styles of management. Clearly these are very general trends and vary greatly across different contexts. Indeed, a problem with much of the existing literature on these changes is that they frequently exaggerate the scale of these trends, and tend to focus on policy and practice rather than the ways in which changes are discursively framed, justified and articulated.

20. The 'new corporatism' has been particularly problematic for Women's Aid in terms of the provision of services in refuges. For instance, a report by Women's Aid has highlighted how National Standards for Under 8s Day Care have had a restrictive effect on the ability of Women's Aid refuges to provide services for children. For child day care to be provided for more than two hours per day, specific government standards must be met, and the financial constraints on refuges are such that often it is difficult for these standards

to be met. In Women's Aid's words, 'as a result many refuges are having to limit play sessions for children to less than two hours a day. In other words, Government measures are actually reducing vital support services for children who have experienced domestic violence' (Saunders, 2003, see also Dahms, 2004). Furthermore, Nicola Harwin has pointed out how constant pressures to reduce costs can have a deleterious effect on the quality of service provision. She mentioned that many local Women's Aid organisations have difficulty competing with large housing corporations, and that 'will have a consequence for service provision because what you are getting is three providers saying right, we're running a range of services, we'll put a manager in place to run them all, whether it's the domestic violence ones or the single homeless ones or whatever. You will end up getting staff who are less qualified, less knowledgeable, reducing down to housing base services as opposed to a much wider holistic range of support' (Nicola Harwin, interview, February 2007).

5   The F-Word: Cultural Politics and Third-Wave Feminism

1. Liza Tsaliki writes, 'cyberspace has been compared to a new public sphere, comparable to the seventeenth-century coffee houses and salons in Britain and France, and the eighteenth-century press in Britain and the US – the realms wherein, as Jürgen Habermas has noted, participatory democracy was shaped through rational public debate [apparently]. Cyberspace ... becomes the forum of a new public sphere through its various IRC groups, Usenet groups, listserves and other subscriber bulletin boards which serve as institutionalised forums for public debate and exchange on a variety of issues' (Tsaliki, 2001: 85).
2. Redfern was editor of The F-word until 2007, when Jess McCabe took over the editorship (Redfern, 2007).
3. The features are divided into sections which include activism, body and health, culture and media, fashion and image, men, politics and current affairs, sex and relationships, violence and work and play. The bulk of my analysis focusses on the 'feminism' and 'activism' sections, although references are made to articles in other sections.
4. See http://www.feministing.com.
5. See http://uk.groups.yahoo.com/group/london3rdwave and http://uk.groups.yahoo.com/group/londonfeministnetwork.
6. See http://uk.groups.yahoo.com/group/ukfeministaction.
7. The term 'interpellation', in the strictly Althusserian sense, refers to a process whereby an individual assumes their identity within a social structure as a consequence of being addressed by the dominant ideological apparatus (Althusser, 1971: 162–3). In this context, however, I use the term in a less ideologically loaded sense to refer to the process by which an individual's subjectivity is called into existence.
8. However, whether or not this diversity includes men has proved to be a major bone of contention. While The F-word welcomes contributions from men (including one from myself), a discussion took place in 2003 on the London Thirdwave mailing list over the issue of whether men should

or should not be allowed to join the group. After some extremely heated exchanges, it was decided that men would be allowed to join the group but would not be allowed to attend the meetings. From a radical separatist perspective, the fact that the possibility of men joining the group was even entertained could be taken as indicative of a loss of purity and thus of deradicalisation. Indeed, this was the perspective put forward to some members in the 'no men' camp.

9. In this respect, the F-word shares certain resemblances with the Milan Women's Bookstore Collective, championed by Zerilli as an example of a freedom-centred feminist space (Zerilli, 2005a: 93–123).

10. For analyses of the relationship between the Spice Girls, girl power and feminism, see Taft, 2004 and Fritzsche, 2004.

11. This is the only reference to The F-word I have been able to find in any academic literature.

12. However, she also described how an email she sent to Womenspeakout about a misogynistic contestant on *Big Brother* led to her being ridiculed for engaging with such a 'trivial' matter (email from F-word contributor).

13. Maxine Carr was the girlfriend of Ian Huntley when he murdered two young girls in Soham, Cambridgeshire in 2002. She provided a false alibi for Huntley and was convicted of perverting the course of justice. However, she was cleared of assisting an offender given that the court concluded that she had believed Huntley's claims of innocence.

14. See, for example, Allen (2002, 2003), Smith (2003b), Lyster (2004) – which highlights the pernicious effects of men's magazines on heterosexual relationships – and Redfern (2005a), which highlights representations of normative femininity in advertising.

15. It should be noted, however, that the views expressed on The F-word around these issues are by no means consensual. Indeed, an article by Natasha Forrest (2002b) titled 'Whose Slut?' provoked a very heated debate around issues of female sexuality and objectification in which no semblance of a consensus emerged. See also Various Authors (2002a, 2002b).

16. For more on this see Chidgey (2003). In addition, see Bailey (2006) and Bell (2002) for accounts of post-2000 feminist events/festivals.

17. Furthermore, the debates around 'raunch culture' (inspired by American journalist Ariel Levy's *Female Chauvinist Pigs*) also represents an instance of transatlantic feminist cultural traffic.

18. Notably, another prominent feminist activist group, the Feminist Activist Forum, is specifically concerned with reclaiming the history of post-1970s UK feminism in a spirit of problematising dominant 'post-feminist' and 'wave' based feminist temporalities.

Conclusion: The Consequences of Optimism

1. Although the results of the June 2009 European elections might suggest this cautiously optimistic analysis is a little premature.

2. For instance, Women's Aid has set up co-operative links with similar organisations overseas, and The F-word blog, in particular, frequently draws attention to feminist practices and items of feminist interest overseas.

3. That said, one might reasonably argue that it is problematic and more than a little disingenuous to overplay the transnational dimension in the manner done so here. Such a line of argument risks reifying the 'transnational' and presupposing that any transnational feminist articulation is by definition more radical, transformative and progressive than an intranational articulation. Furthermore, if one works with a notion of the 'transnational' as linked to feminist activism around issues of race and migration (rather than cross-border co-operation between feminist groups), then the current UK context stands up more favourably.

4. The lack of engagement with feminism – and indeed male dominance – of a recent conference organised by Žižek and Badiou at Birbeck College, London ('On the Idea of Communism', 13–15 March 2009) arguably gives further credence to the rather masculinist thrust of Lacanian heroism.

5. As Butler points out, 'my understanding of hegemony is that its normative and optimistic moment consists precisely in the possibilities for expanding the democratic possibilities for the key terms of liberalism, rendering them more inclusive, more dynamic and more concrete' (2000: 13).

6. In many respects, I think this is a reflection of what Wendy Brown has called the 'professionalisation' of political theory (2005: 70), the tendency for political theory to have itself as its main referent. Within post-Marxism, there is a tendency to regard 'politics' as something that needs to be delineated, protected and affirmed. This is a worthwhile enterprise to some extent, but my sense is that it leads to a defensiveness that undermines the potential richness of our accounts of politics that might arise from dialogue with other academic disciplines.

7. Although this is not his direct concern, Gary Clarke's (1997) argument about the Birmingham School's overemphasis on the distinction between subcultures and 'straight society' points in this direction.

8. See Stavrakakis (2007: 274–6) for a compelling defence of productive leftist mourning, in contrast to narcissistic melancholia.

9. My position is therefore opposed to the anti-statist post- or neo-anarchisms affirmed in some recent texts informed by post-structuralist political theory (May, 2008; Day, 2005; Newman, 2007). While these texts are commendable in that they bring post-structuralism into productive dialogue with 'actually existing' contemporary radical politics, Day and Newman invest too heavily in the so-called anti-globalisation movement as the key agent in contemporary political struggle.

Bibliography

Aapola, Sinikka; Gonick, Marnina and Harris, Anita. 2005. *Young Femininity: Girlhood, Power and Social Change*. Basingstoke: Macmillan.

Adams, Melinda. 2006. 'Regional Women's Activism: African Women's Networks and the African Union', in Myra Marx Ferree and Aili Mari Tripp (eds). *Transnational Women's Activism, Organizing and Human Rights*. New York: New York University Press.

Ahmed, Sarah. 2004a. *The Cultural Politics of Emotion*. London: Routledge.

Ahmed, Sarah. 2004b. 'Affective Economies', *Social Text* 22 (2): 117–39.

Allen, Kate. 2002. 'Diet Grrrl – Feminism and Women's Magazines'. http://www.thefword.org.uk/features/2002/08/diet_grrrl_feminism_and_womens_magazines. Accessed 20/04/07.

Allen, Kate. 2003. 'Page 3 – Ban It!' http://www.thefword.org.uk/features/2003/03/page_3_ban_it. Accessed 28/03/07.

Allwood, Gill and Wadia, Khursheed. 2001. 'Gender and Class in Britain and France', *Journal of European Area Studies* 9 (2): 163–85.

Althusser, Louis. 1971. *'Lenin and Philosophy' and Other Essays*. London: NLB.

Annesley, Claire. 2001. 'New Labour and Welfare', in Steve Ludlam and Martin J. Smith, (eds). *New Labour in Government*. Basingstoke: Palgrave Macmillan.

Arendt, Hannah. 1958. *The Human Condition*. Chicago: Chicago University Press.

Arendt, Hannah. 1963. *On Revolution*. London: Faber and Faber.

Arneil, Barbara. 1999. *Politics and Feminism*. Oxford: Blackwell.

Aune, Kristin. 2002. 'Big Brother, Virgins, and Female Singleness'. http://www.thefword.org.uk/features/2002/06/big_brother_virgins_and_female_singleness. Accessed 28/03/07.

Austin, J. L. 1975. *How to Do Things With Words* (2nd edition). Oxford: Oxford University Press.

Bacchi, Carol Lee. 1999. *Women, Policy and Politics: The Construction of Policy Problems*. London: Sage.

Badiou, Alain. 1992. *Manifesto for Philosophy*. New York: SUNY Press.

Badiou, Alain. 2005. *Metapolitics*. London: Verso.

Bagguley, Paul. 2002. 'Contemporary British Feminism: A Social Movement in Abeyance', *Social Movement Studies* 1 (2): 169–85.

Bagić, Aida. 2006. 'Women's Organising in Post-Yugoslav Countries: Talking About "Donors"', in Myra Marx Ferree and Aili Mari Tripp (eds). *Transnational Women's Activism, Organizing and Human Rights*. New York: New York University Press.

Bailey, Glencora. 2006. '"Backlash: The Hidden War on Women in the UK" – 1st Nov 2006, London'. http://www.thefword.org.uk/reviews/2006/11/backlash_nov_2006. Accessed 28/03/07.

Banaszak, Lee Ann; Beckwith, Karen; and Rucht, Dieter. 2003. 'When Power Relocates: Interactive Changes in Women's Movements and States', in Lee Ann Banaszak, Karen Beckwith and Dieter Rucht (eds). *Women's Movements Facing the Reconfigured State*. New York: Cambridge University Press.

Barron, Jackie. 2005. *The Survivors' Handbook*. http://www.womensaid.org.uk/ domestic-violence-survivors-handbook.asp?section=0001000100080001. Accessed 28/03/07.

Bateman, Jessica. 2007. 'A Real Alternative?' http://www.thefword.org.uk/ features/2007/01/alternative Accessed 28/03/07.

Bateman, Jessica; Lemond, Marianne; O'Reilly, Abby; Plant, Sheryl; Combe, Holly; and Redfern, Catherine. 2007. 'Female Chauvinist Pigs'. http://www.thefword.org.uk/reviews/2007/02/female_chauvinist. Accessed 28/03/07.

Bauman, Zygmunt. 2000. *Liquid Modernity*. Cambridge: Polity Press.

Bauman, Zygmunt. 2001. *The Individualized Society*. Cambridge: Polity Press.

Baumgardner, Jennifer and Richards, Amy. 2000. *Manifesta: Young Women, Feminism and the Future*. New York: Farrar, Straus and Giroux.

Baumgardner, Jennifer and Richards, Amy. 2004. 'Feminism and Femininity: Or How We Learned to Stop Worrying and Love the Thong', in Anita Harris (ed.). *All About the Girl: Culture, Power and Identity*. New York: Routledge.

Beck, Ulrich and Beck-Gernsheim, Elizabeth. 2002. *Individualization: Institutionalized Individualism and its Social and Political Consequences*. London: Sage.

Bell, Amy. 2002. 'The Lowdown on Ladyfest'. http://www.thefword.org.uk/ features/2002/07/the_lowdown_on_ladyfest. Accessed 28/03/07.

Bell, Diane and Klein, Renate. 1996. 'Foreword: Radical Feminists Speak, Write, Organise, Enjoy Life and Never Forget', in Diane Bell and Renate Klein (eds). *Radically Speaking*. London: Zed Books.

Bell, Rachel. 2005. 'Leading Lady: Milicent Garrett Fawcett 1847–1929', in *Stop Gap*, autumn 2005: 4.

Bell, Rachel. 2006. 'Women Unite, Reclaim the Night'. http://www.thefword.org. uk/features/2006/01/women_unite_reclaim_the_night. Accessed 28/03/07.

Bell, Rachel. 2007. 'University Challenge'. http://education.guardian.co.uk/ higher/comment/story/0,,2009297,00.html. Accessed 28/03/07.

Bell, Vikki. 2007. *Culture and Performance: The Challenge of Ethics, Politics and Feminist Theory*. Oxford, New York: Berg.

Bellamy, Kate and Rake, Katherine. 2005. *Money, Money, Money: Is it still a rich man's world?* London: The Fawcett Society.

Benhabib, Seyla. 1995. 'Feminism and Postmodernism', in Seyla Benhabib, Judith Butler, Drucilla Cornell and Nancy Fraser. *Feminist Contentions: A Philosophical Exchange*. London: Routledge.

Benn, Melissa. 2000. 'Short March Through the Institutions: Reflections on New Labour's Gender Machinery', in Anna Coote (ed.). *New Gender Agenda: Why Women Still Want More*. London: IPPR.

Bennett, Jane. 2001. *The Enchantment of Modern Life: Attachments, Crossings and Ethics*. Princeton: Princeton University Press.

Bennett, Jane. 2009. 'Agency, Nature and Emergent Properties: An Interview with Jane Bennett'. *Contemporary Political Theory* 8 (1): 90–105.

Bennett, Natalie. 2007. 'A Post-Feminist Age? Think Again'. http://commentisfree. guardian.co.uk/natalie_bennett/2007/03/building_feminist_walls.html. Accessed 28/03/07.

Bennett, Tony. 1986. 'Popular Culture and the "Turn to Gramsci"', in Tony Bennett, Colin Mercer and Janet Woollacott (eds). *Popular Culture and Social Relations*. Milton Keynes: Open University Press.

Bergqvist, Christina; Blandy, Tanja Olsson; and Sainsbury, Diane. 2007. 'Swedish State Feminism: Continuity and Change', in Joyce Outshoorn and Johanna Kantola (eds). *Changing State Feminism*. Basingstoke: Palgrave Macmillan.

Blase, Cazz. 2004a. 'But What of Us? UK Riot Grrrl – Part 1'. http://www.thefword.org.uk/features/2004/09/but_what_of_us_uk_riot_grrrl_part_1. Accessed 28/03/07.

Blase, Cazz. 2004b. 'But What of Us? UK Riot Grrrl – Part 2'. http://www.thefword.org.uk/features/2004/11/but_what_of_us_uk_riot_grrrl_part_2. Accessed 28/03/07.

Blase, Cazz. 2005a. 'But What of Us? UK Riot Grrrl – Part 3'. http://www.thefword.org.uk/features/2005/01/but_what_of_us_uk_riot_grrrl_part_3. Accessed 28/03/07.

Blase, Cazz. 2005b. 'But What of Us? UK Riot Grrrl – Part 4'. http://www.thefword.org.uk/features/2005/04/but_what_of_us_uk_riot_grrrl_part_4. Accessed 28/03/07.

Borchorst, Anette and Siim, Birte. 2008. 'Woman-Friendly Policies and State Feminism: Theorizing Scandinavian Gender Equality', *Feminist Theory* 9 (2): 207–24.

Bouchier, David. 1979. 'The Deradicalisation of Feminism: Ideology and Utopia in Action', *Sociology* 13 (3): 387–402.

Bouchier, David. 1983. *The Feminist Challenge: The Movement for Women's Liberation in Britain and the USA*. London: Macmillan Press.

Bowden, Andrew. 2003. 'Real Men Drink Pints'. http://www.thefword.org.uk/features/2003/06/real_men_drink_pints. Accessed 28/03/07.

Bowman, Paul. 2007. *Post-Marxism Versus Cultural Studies: Theory, Politics, Intervention*. Edinburgh: Edinburgh University Press.

Braidotti, Rosi. 1994. *Nomadic Subjects: Embodiment and Sexual Difference in Contemporary Feminist Theory*. New York: Columbia University Press.

Braidotti, Rosi. 2006. *Transpositions: On Nomadic Ethics*. Cambridge: Polity Press.

Braidotti, Rosi. Date not specified. 'Cyberfeminism With a Difference'. http://www.let.uu.nl/womens_studies/rosi/cyberfem.htm. Accessed 28/03/07.

Brooks, Libby. 2003. 'Top Girls: Part Three'. *The Guardian* 30/09/03. http://www.guardian.co.uk/g2/story/0,,1052504,00.html. Accessed 28/03/07.

Brown, Wendy. 1995. *States of Injury: Power and Freedom in Late Modernity*. Princeton: Princeton University Press.

Brown, Wendy. 2000. 'Resisting Left Melancholia', in Paul Gilroy, Lawrence Grossberg and Angela McRobbie (eds). *Without Guarantees: Essays in Honour of Stuart Hall*. London: Verso.

Brown, Wendy. 2005. *Edgework: Critical Essays on Knowledge and Politics*. Princeton: Princeton University Press.

Browne, Sarah. 2008. 'The Personal is Political: The Women of the Women's Liberation Movement in Scotland 1967–1979'. Paper presented at Women's History Network Conference, University of Glasgow, 6/09/08.

Bryson, Valerie. 1992. *Feminist Political Theory: An Introduction*. Basingstoke: Macmillan.

Budgeon, Shelley. 2001. 'Emergent Feminist (?) Identities: Young Women and the Practice of Micropolitics', *European Journal of Women's Studies* 8 (1): 7–28.

Bulbeck, Chilla. 1998. *Re-Orienting Western Feminisms: Women's Diversity in a Postcolonial World*. Cambridge: Cambridge University Press.

Burgess, Adrienne. 2002. 'Fatherhood Today'. *Towards Equality*, summer 2004: 7–10.
Bustelo, Maria and Ortbals, Candice, D. 2007. 'The Evolution of Spanish State Feminism: A Fragmented Landscape', in Joyce Outshoorn and Johanna Kantola (eds). *Changing State Feminism*. Basingstoke: Palgrave Macmillan.
Butler, Eleri. 2002. *Women's Aid's Members Response to 'Justice for All.'* www.womensaid.org.uk/landing_page.asp?section=000100010009000300040008. Accessed 30/08/06.
Butler, Eleri. 2003a. *Women's Aid Full Consultation Response to the 2002 Criminal Justice White Paper – Justice for All.* http://www.womensaid.org.uk/landing_page.asp?section=000100010009000300040008. Accessed 28/03/07.
Butler, Eleri. 2003b. *Response to 'Safety and Justice': The Government Consultation Paper on Domestic Violence.* http://www.womensaid.org.uk/landing_page.asp?section=000100010009000300040006. Accessed 28/03/07.
Butler, Judith. 1993. *Bodies That Matter: On the Discursive Limits of 'Sex'.* New York: Routledge.
Butler, Judith. 1995. 'Contingent Foundations: Feminism and the Question of Postmodernism', in Seyla Benhabib, Judith Butler, Drucilla Cornell and Nancy Fraser. *Feminist Contentions: A Philosophical Exchange.* London: Routledge.
Butler, Judith. 1998. 'Merely Cultural'. http://www.brynmawr.edu/Acads/GSSW/schram/butlermerelycultural.pdf. Accessed 28/03/07.
Butler, Judith. 1999. *Gender Trouble: Feminism and the Subversion of Identity* (2nd edition). New York: Routledge.
Butler, Judith. 2000. 'Restaging the Universal: Hegemony and the Limits of Formalism', in Judith Butler; Ernesto Laclau and Slavoj Žižek. *Contingency, Hegemony, Universality: Contemporary Dialogues on the Left.* London: Verso.
Butler, Judith. 2004. *Undoing Gender.* New York: Routledge.
Byrne, Paul. 1996. 'The Politics of the Women's Movement', *Parliamentary Affairs* 49 (1): 55–70.
Castoriadis, Cornelius. 1997. *World in Fragments: Writings on Politics, Society, Psychoanalysis and Imagination.* Stanford: Stanford University Press.
Cavarero, Adriana. 2002. 'Politicizing Theory'. *Political Theory* 30 (4): 506–32.
Celis, Karen and Meier, Petra. 2007. 'State Feminism and Women's Movements in Belgium: Complex Patterns in a Multilevel System', in Joyce Outshoorn and Johanna Kantola (eds). *Changing State Feminism*. Basingstoke: Palgrave Macmillan.
Chakraborty, Mridula Nath. 2007. 'Waiving It All Away: Producing Subject and Knowledge in Feminisms of Colours', in Stacy Gillis, Gillian Howie and Rebecca Munford (eds). *Third Wave Feminism: A Critical Exploration* (2nd edition). Basingstoke: Macmillan.
Charles, Nickie. 2000. *Feminism, the State and Social Policy.* Basingstoke: Macmillan.
Chester, Gail. 1982. 'I Call Myself a Radical Feminist', in Mary Evans (ed.). *The Woman Question: Readings on the Subordination of Women.* Oxford: Fontana.
Chidgey, Red. 2003. 'Get Your Frock On: An Insight into Organising a Women's Community Event'. http://www.thefword.org.uk/features/2003/09/get_your_frock_on_an_insight_into_organising_a_womens_community_event. Accessed 28/03/07.
Chidgey, Red. 2008. 'Labours Left Unfinished: Third Wave Feminism'. http://www.thefword.org.uk/features/2008/03/labours_left_un. Accessed 13/05/09.
Clarke, Alison. 2008. 'The Women Behind the Struggle'. *Stop Gap*, spring 2008: 7–10.

Clarke, Gary. 1997. 'Defending Ski-jumpers: A Critique of Theories of Youth Subcultures', in Ken Gelder and Sarah Thornton (eds). *The Subcultures Reader*. London: Routledge.

Clarke, John; Hall; Stuart; Jefferson, Tony; and Roberts, Brian. 1975. 'Subcultures, Cultures and Class: a Theoretical Overview', in Stuart Hall and Tony Jefferson (eds). *Resistance Through Rituals: Youth Subcultures in Post-War Britain*. London: Hutchinson.

Cochrane, Kira. 2006. 'The Third Wave: At a Computer Near You'. http://www.guardian.co.uk/g2/story/0,1743520,00.html. Accessed 28/03/07.

Cochrane, Kira. 2007. 'Got it, Bought the T-Shirt'. http://www.guardian.co.uk/gender/story/0,,2030006,00.html. Accessed 29/03/07.

Cockburn, Cynthia. 1991. *In the Way of Women: Men's Resistance to Sex Equality in Organisations*. Basingstoke: Macmillan.

Coles, Romand. 2005. 'The Wild Patience of Radical Democracy: Beyond Žižek's Lack', in Lasse Thomassen and Lars Tønder (eds). *Radical Democracy: Politics Between Abundance and Lack*. Manchester: Manchester University Press.

Collins, Jane. 2002. 'Alien She?' http://www.thefword.org.uk/features/2002/12/alien_she. Accessed 28/03/07.

Connolly, William E. 2005. 'Immanence, Abundance, Democracy', in Lasse Thomassen and Lars Tønder (eds). *Radical Democracy: Politics Between Abundance and Lack*. Manchester: Manchester University Press.

Coote, Anna. 2000. 'Introduction', in Anna Coote (ed.). *New Gender Agenda: Why Women Still Want More*. London: IPPR.

Coote, Anna and Campbell, Beatrix. 1987. *Sweet Freedom: the Struggle for Women's Liberation* (2nd edn). Oxford: Basil Blackwell.

Coppock, Vicki; Haydon, Deena; and Richter, Ingrid. 1995. *The Illusions of Post-Feminism*. London: Taylor and Francis.

Cosh, Emma. 2006. 'Why Not Feminism?' http://www.thefword.org.uk/features/2006/10/why_not. Accessed 28/03/07.

Coward, Rosalind. 1999. *Sacred Cows: Is Feminism Relevant to the New Millennium?* London: Harper Collins.

Critchley, Simon. 2000. 'Beckett is My Hero (It's Alright): An Interview with Simon Critchley'. http://www.usyd.edu.au/contretemps/1september2000/critchley.pdf. Accessed 16/07/07.

Critchley, Simon. 2007. *Infinitely Demanding: Ethics of Commitment, Politics of Resistance*. London: Verso.

Dahms, Nina. 2004. *One Year On: The Status of Children's Services in Refuge Organisations Since the Implementation of National Standards for Under 8s Day Care*. http://www.womensaid.org.uk/landing_page.asp?section=000100010009 0005000500080002. Accessed 28/03/07.

Darraj, Susan Muaddi. 2003. 'Third World, Third Wave Feminism(s): The Evolution of Arab American Feminism', in Rory Dicker and Alison Peipmeier (eds). *Catching a Wave: Reclaiming Feminism for the 21st Century*. Boston: Northwestern University Press.

Day, Richard J. F. 2005. *Gramsci is Dead: Anarchist Currents in the Newest Social Movements*. Toronto: Between the Lines.

Dean, Jodi. 2000. 'Introduction: The Interface of Political Theory and Cultural Studies', in Jodi Dean (eds). *Cultural Studies and Political Theory*. New York: Cornell University Press.

Dean, Jodi. 2006. 'Political Theory and Cultural Studies', in John Dryzek, Bonnie Honig and Anne Phillips (eds). *The Oxford Handbook of Political Theory*. Oxford: Oxford University Press.

Dean, Jodi and Passavant, Paul. 2004. 'Representation and the Event', in Jodi Dean and Paul Passavant (eds). *Empire's New Clothes: Reading Hardt and Negri*. New York: Routledge.

Dean, Jonathan. 2006. 'Reasons to be Cheerful'. http://www.thefword.org.uk/ features/2006/04/reasons_to_be_cheerful. Accessed 28/03/07.

Dean, Jonathan. 2009. 'Who's Afraid of Third Wave Feminism? On the Uses of the "Third Wave" in British Feminist Politics', *International Feminist Journal of Politics*, 11 (3): 334–52.

Dean, Jonathan. 2010. 'Feminism in the Papers: Contested Feminisms in the British Quality Press'. *Feminist Media Studies* 10 (4): forthcoming.

Deleuze, Giles and Guattari, Felix. 1972. *Anti-Oedipus: Capitalism and Schizophrenia*. New York: Viking Press.

Deleuze, Giles and Guattari, Felix. 2004. *A Thousand Plateaus: Capitalism and Schizophrenia*. London: Continuum.

Derrida, Jacques. 1982. *Margins of Philosophy*. Brighton: The Harvester Press.

Derrida, Jacques. 1988. 'Signature Event Context', in *Limited Inc*. Evanston: Northwestern University Press.

Desai, Manisha. 2005. 'Transnationalism: The Face of Feminist Politics Post-Beijing', *International Social Science Journal* 57 (2): 319–30.

Dicker, Rory and Peipmeier, Alison. 2003. 'Introduction' in Rory Dicker and Alison Peipmeier (eds). *Catching a Wave: Reclaiming Feminism for the 21st Century*. Boston: Northwestern University Press.

Dobash, R. Emerson and Dobash, Russell P. 1992. *Women, Violence and Social Change*. London: Routledge.

Drake, Jennifer. 1997. 'Reviewing Third-Wave Feminisms', *Feminist Studies* 23 (1): 97–108.

Drew, Jennifer. 2003b. 'Dysfunctional, Moi? The Myth of Female Sexual Dysfunction and its Medicalisation'. Available at http://www.thefword. org.uk/features/2003/04/dysfunctional_moi_the_myth_of_female_sexual_ dysfunction_and_its_medicalisation. Accessed 28/03/07.

Dworkin, Andrea. 1981. *Pornography: Men Possessing Women*. London: the Women's Press.

Dyrberg, Torben Bech. 2004. 'The Political and Politics in Discourse Analysis', in Simon Critchley and Oliver Marchant (eds). *Laclau: A Critical Reader*. London: Routledge.

Eisenhauer, Jennifer. 2004. 'Mythic Figures and Lived Identities: Locating the "Girl" in Feminist Discourse', in Anita Harris (ed.). *All About the Girl: Culture, Power and Identity*. New York: Routledge.

Eisenstein, Zillah, R. 1981. *The Radical Future of Liberal Feminism*. New York: Longman.

Ellery. 2006. 'Pretending That Men Aren't Grown Ups'. http://www.thefword. org.uk/features/2006/02/pretending_that_men_arent_grownups. Accessed 29/07/08/

Elman, R. Amy. 2003. 'Refuge in Reconfigured States: Shelter Movements in the United States, Britain and Sweden', in Lee Ann Banaszak, Karen Beckwith and Dieter Rucht (eds). *Women's Movements Facing the Reconfigured State*. New York: Cambridge University Press.

Ertürk, Yakin. 2006. 'Turkey's Modern Paradoxes: Identity Politics, Women's Agency, and Universal Rights', in Myra Marx Ferree and Aili Mari Tripp (eds). *Transnational Women's Activism, Organizing and Human Rights*. New York: New York University Press.

Esping-Andersen, Gøsta. 1990. *The Three Worlds of Welfare Capitalism*. Cambridge: Polity Press.

EVAW. 2006. *Making the Grade? The Second Annual Independent Analysis of Government Initiatives on Violence Against Women*. http://www.endviolenceagainstwomen. org.uk/documents/making_the_grade06.pdf. Accessed 27/03/07.

Exworthy, Mark and Halford, Susan. 1999. 'Professionals and Managers in a Changing Public Sector: Conflict, Compromise or Collaboration?' in Mark Exworthy and Susan Halford (eds). *Professionals and the New Public Management in the Public Sector*. Buckingham: Open University Press.

Falkof, Nicky. 2007. 'Twenty-First Century Boys'. *Stop Gap*, autumn 2007: 8–9.

Faludi, Susan. 1992. *Backlash: The Undeclared War Against Women*. London: Chatto and Windus.

Fawcett Society. 2001a. *Fawcett Society Response to Consultation 'New Tax Credits – Supporting Families, Making Work Pay and Tackling Poverty'*. London: The Fawcett Society.

Fawcett Society. 2001b. *Fawcett Society Response to the Parents and Work Taskforce*. London: The Fawcett Society.

Fawcett Society. 2001c. *Fawcett Response to the Work and Parents Green Paper*. London: The Fawcett Society.

Fawcett Society. 2004a. 'A Manifesto for Equality', in *Towards Equality*, autumn 2004a: 7–10.

Fawcett Society. 2005a. *Are We There Yet? 30 Years of Closing the Gap Between Women and Men*. London: The Fawcett Society.

Fawcett Society. 2005b. 'Fawcett Responds to Parental Leave Proposals'. http://www.fawcettsociety.org.uk/index.asp?PageID=103. Accessed 28/03/07.

Fawcett Society. 2005c. 'Every Woman's Guide to the General Election'. London: The Fawcett Society.

Fawcett Society. 2005d. *Older Women: Your Future in Their Hands?* http://www. eurolinkage.org/AgeConcern/Documents/older_women_voters_report.pdf. Accessed 28/03/07.

Fawcett Society. 2009. 'Campaigns Update', *Stop Gap*, spring 2009: 4–5.

Ferguson, Kathy, E. 1984. *The Feminist Case Against Bureaucracy*. Philadelphia: Temple University Press.

Ferree, Myra Marx. 2006. 'Globalisation and Feminism: Opportunities and Obstacles for Activism in the Global Arena', in Myra Marx Ferree and Aili Mari Tripp (eds). *Transnational Women's Activism, Organizing and Human Rights*. New York: New York University Press.

Ferree, Myra Marx and Pudrovska, Tetyana. 2006. 'Transnational Feminist NGOs on the Web: Networks and Identities in the Global North and South', in Myra Marx Ferree and Aili Mari Tripp (eds). *Transnational Women's Activism, Organizing and Human Rights*. New York: New York University Press.

Fisher, Duncan and Rake, Katherine. 2004. 'A Common Vision', in *Towards Equality*, summer 2004: 3.

Fiske, John. 2006. 'The Popular Economy', in John Storey (ed.). *Cultural Theory and Popular Culture: A Reader*. Harlow: Pearson.

Forna, Aminatta. 1999. 'Sellout', in Natasha Walter (ed.). *On the Move: Feminism for a New Generation*. London: Virago Press.

Forrest, Natasha. 2002a. 'Where are the Radicals?' http://www.thefword.org.uk/features/2002/11/where_are_the_radicals. Accessed 28/03/07.

Forrest, Natasha. 2002b. 'Whose Slut?' http://www.thefword.org.uk/features/2002/07/whose_slut. Accessed 28/03/07.

Foucault, Michel. 1977. *Discipline and Punish: the Birth of the Prison*. New York: Vintage Press.

Foucault, Michel. 1978. *The History of Sexuality, Volume 1*. London: Penguin.

Fraser, Nancy. 1989. *Unruly Practices: Power, Discourse and Gender in Contemporary Social Theory*. Minneapolis: University of Minnesota Press.

Freedman, Jane. 2001. *Feminism*. Buckingham: Open University Press.

Frith, Simon. 2006. 'The Good, the Bad and the Indifferent: Defending Popular Culture from the Populists', in John Storey (ed.). *Cultural Theory and Popular Culture: A Reader*. Harlow: Pearson.

Fritzsche, Bettina. 2004. 'Spicy Strategies: Pop Feminist and Other Empowerments in Girl Culture', in Anita Harris (ed.). *All About the Girl: Culture, Power and Identity*. New York: Routledge.

Fuss, Diana. 1995. *Identification Papers*. New York: Routledge.

Gamble, Sarah. 2001. 'Postfeminism', in Sarah Gamble (ed.). *The Routledge Companion to Feminism and Postfeminism*. London: Routledge.

Garber, Jenny and McRobbie, Angela. 1975. 'Girls and Subcultures: An Exploration', in Stuart Hall and Tony Jefferson (eds). *Resistance Through Rituals: Youth Subcultures in post-war Britain*. London: Hutchinson.

Gelb, Joyce. 1989. *Feminism and Politics: A Comparative Perspective*. Berkeley: University of California Press.

Genz, Stephanie. 2006. 'Third Way/ve: The Politics of Postfeminism', *Feminist Theory* 7 (3): 333–53.

Giddens, Anthony. 1991. *Modernity and Self-Identity: Self and Society in the Late Modern Age*. Cambridge: Polity Press.

Gill, Rosalind. 2007. *Gender and the Media*. Cambridge: Polity Press.

Gillis, Stacy; Howie, Gillian; and Munford, Rebecca. 2004. 'Introduction' in Stacy Gillis, Gillian Howie and Rebecca Munford (eds). *Third Wave Feminism: A Critical Exploration*. Basingstoke: Macmillan.

Glynos, Jason. 2003. 'Radical Democratic Ethos, or, What is an Authentic Political Act?' *Contemporary Political Theory* 2 (2): 187–208.

Glynos, Jason and Howarth, David. 2007. *Logics of Critical Explanation in Social and Political Theory*. Abingdon: Routledge.

Gramsci, Antonio. 1971. *Selections from the Prison Notebooks* (Quentin Hoare and Geoffrey Nowell Smith, eds). London: Lawrence and Wishart.

Grant, Jane. 1999. 'The Fawcett Society: An Old Organisation for the New Woman'. *Women: A Cultural Review* 10 (1): 67–77.

Grant, Jane. 2003. *Past, Present and Future: Fawcett's Achievements and Visions*. London: The Fawcett Society.

Gray, Gwendolyn. 2008. 'Institutional, Incremental and Enduring: Women's Health Action in Canada and Australia', in Sandra Grey and Marian Sawer (eds). *Women's Movements: Flourishing or in Abeyance?* London: Routledge.

Greer, Germaine. 1999. *The Whole Woman*. London: Anchor.

Grey, Sandra. 2008. 'Out of Sight, Out of Mind: the New Zealand Women's Movement', in Sandra Grey and Marian Sawer (eds). *Women's Movements: Flourishing or in Abeyance?* London: Routledge.

Grey, Sandra and Sawer, Marian. 'Introduction', in Sandra Grey and Marian Sawer (eds). *Women's Movements: Flourishing or in Abeyance?* London: Routledge.

Griffin, Christine. 2001. 'The Young Women Are Having a Great Time', *Feminism and Psychology* 11 (2): 182–6.

Griffin, Christine. 2004. 'Good Girls, Bad Girls: Anglocentrism and Diversity in the Constitution of Contemporary Girlhood', in Anita Harris (ed.). *All About the Girl: Culture, Power and Identity*. New York: Routledge.

Guadagnini, Marila and Donà, Alessia. 2007. 'Women's Policy Machinery in Italy Between European Pressures and Domestic Constraints', in Joyce Outshoorn and Johanna Kantola (eds). *Changing State Feminism*. Basingstoke: Palgrave Macmillan.

Hague, Gill. 1999. 'The Multiagency Approach to Domestic Violence: A Dynamic Way Forward or a Face-Saver and a Talking Shop?' in Nicola Harwin, Gill Hague and Ellen Malos (eds). *The Multiagency Approach to Domestic Violence: New Opportunities, Old Challenges?* London: Whiting and Birch.

Hague, Gill and Malos, Ellen. 2005. *Domestic Violence: Action for Change* (3rd edition). Cheltenam: New Clarion Press.

Hague, Gill; Mullender, Audrey; and Aris, Rosemary. 2003. *Is Anyone Listening? Accountability and Women Survivors of Domestic Violence*. London: Routledge.

Halford, Susan. 1992. 'Feminist Change in a Patriarchal Organisation: The Experience of Women's Initiatives in Local Government and Implications for Feminist Perspectives on State Institutions', in Mike Savage and Anne Witz (eds). *Gender and Bureaucracy*. Oxford: Blackwell.

Hall, Stuart. 1988. *The Hard Road to Renewal: Thatcherism and the Crisis of the British Left*. London: Verso.

Hall, Stuart. 1992. 'Cultural Studies and its Theoretical Legacies', in Lawrence Grossberg, Cary Nelson and Paula Treichler (eds). *Cultural Studies*. London: Routledge.

Hall, Stuart. 1996. 'On Postmodernism and Articulation: An Interview with Stuart Hall', in David Morley and Kuan-Hsing Chen (eds). *Stuart Hall: Critical Dialogues in Cultural Studies*. London: Routledge.

Hallward, Peter. 2004. 'Introduction: Consequences of Abstraction', in Peter Hallward (ed.). *Think Again: Alain Badiou and the Future of Philosophy*. London: Continuum.

Haraway, Donna, J. 1991. *Simians, Cyborgs and Women: The Reinvention of Nature*. London: Free Association.

Hardt, Michael and Negri, Antonio. 2000. *Empire*. Cambridge: Harvard University Press.

Hardt, Michael and Negri, Antonio. 2004. *Multitude: War and Democracy in the Age of Empire*. London: Continuum.

Harne, Lynne. 1996. 'Dangerous Liaisons: Reasserting Male Power Through Gay Movements', in Lynne Harne and Elaine Miller (eds). *All the Rage: Reasserting Radical Lesbian Feminism*. London: Teachers College Press.

Harris, Anita. 2004. *Future Girl: Young Women in the Twenty-First Century*. New York: Routledge.

Harwin, Nicola. 1999. The Multiagency Approach to Domestic Violence: A Perspective from Women's Aid', in Nicola Harwin, Gill Hague and Ellen Malos (eds). *The Multiagency Approach to Domestic Violence: New Opportunities, Old Challenges?* London: Whiting and Birch.

Harwin, Nicola and Barron, Jackie. 2000. 'Domestic Violence and Social Policy: Perspectives From Women's Aid', in Jalna Hanmer and Catherine Hitzin with Sheila Quaid and Debra Wigglesworth (eds). *Home Truths About Domestic Violence: Feminist Influences on Policy and Practice.* London: Routledge.

Hawthorne, Susan and Klein, Renate. 1999. 'Introduction' in Susan Hawthorne and Renate Klein (eds). *Cyberfeminism: Connectivity, Critique and Creativity.* Melbourne: Spinifex Press.

Hebdige, Dick. 1979. *Subculture: The Meaning of Style.* London: Routledge.

Heidegger, Martin. 1973. *Being and Time* (John Macquarrie and Edward Robinson, trans.). Oxford: Basil Blackwell.

Hemmings, Clare. 2005. 'Telling Feminist Stories', *Feminist Theory* 6 (2): 115–139.

Hemmings, Clare. 2006. 'The Life and Times of Academic Feminism', in Kathy Davis, Mary Evans and Judith Lorber (eds). *Handbook of Gender and Women's Studies.* London: Sage.

Hemmings, Clare. 2009. 'Generational Dilemmas: A Response to Iris van der Tuin's "Jumping Generations": On Second- and Third-Wave Feminist Epistemology', *Australian Feminist Studies* 24 (59): 33–7.

Hemmings, Clare and Brain, Josephine. 2003. 'Imagining the Feminist Seventies', in Helen Graham, Ann Kalosi, Ali Neilson and Emma Robertson (eds). *The Feminist Seventies.* York: Raw Nerve.

Henry, Astrid. 2003. 'Feminism's Family Problem: Feminist Generations and the Mother-Daughter Trope', in Rory Dicker and Alison Peipmeier (eds). *Catching a Wave: Reclaiming Feminism for the 21st Century.* Boston: Northwestern University Press.

Hernes, Helga. 1987. *Welfare State and Woman Power: Essays in State Feminism.* London: Norwegian University Press.

Heywood, Andrew. 2003. *Political Ideologies: An Introduction.* Basingstoke: Palgrave Macmillan.

Heywood, Leslie and Drake, Jennifer. 2004. 'It's All About the Benjamins: Economic Determinants of Third Wave Feminism', in Stacy Gillis, Gillian Howie and Rebecca Munford (eds). *Third Wave Feminism: A Critical Exploration.* Basingstoke: Macmillan.

Hitzin, Catherine. 2000. 'Gendering Domestic Violence: The Influence of Feminism on Policy and Practice', in Jalna Hanmer and Catherine Hitzin with Sheila Quaid and Debra Wigglesworth (eds). *Home Truths About Domestic Violence: Feminist Influences on Policy and Practice.* London: Routledge.

Holli, Anna Maria and Kantola, Johanna. 2007. 'State Feminism Finnish Style: Strong Policies Clash With Implementation Problems', in Joyce Outshoorn and Johanna Kantola (eds). *Changing State Feminism.* Basingstoke: Palgrave Macmillan.

Hollows, Joanne. 2000. *Feminism, Femininity and Popular Culture.* Manchester: Manchester University Press.

Hollows, Joanne and Moseley, Rachel. 2006. 'Popularity Contests: The Meanings of Popular Feminism', in Joanne Hollows and Rachel Moseley (eds). *Feminism in Popular Culture.* Oxford: Berg.

Honig, Bonnie. 1993. *Political Theory and the Displacement of Politics.* Ithaca: Cornell University Press.

Honig, Bonnie. 1995a. 'Introduction: the Arendt Question in Feminism', in Bonnie Honig (ed.). *Feminist Interpretations of Hannah Arendt.* Pennsylvania: Pennsylvania State University Press.

Honig, Bonnie. 1995b. 'Toward an Agonistic Feminism: Hannah Arendt and the Politics of Identity', in Bonnie Honig (ed.). *Feminist Interpretations of Hannah Arendt.* Pennsylvania: Pennsylvania State University Press.

Howard, Melanie and Tibballs, Sue. 2003. *Talking Equality: What Men and Women Think About Equality in Britain Today.* London: The Future Foundation.

Howarth, David. 2000. *Discourse.* Buckingham: Open University Press.

Howarth, David. 2005. 'Applying Discourse Theory: The Method of Articulation', in David Howarth and Jacob Torfing (eds). *Discourse Theory in European Politics: Identity, Policy and Governance.* Basingstoke: Palgrave Macmillan.

Jónasdóttir, Anna G. and van der Fehr, Drude. 1998. 'Introduction: Ambiguous Times – Contested Spaces in the Politics, Organisation and Identities of Gender', in Drude von der Fehr, Anna G. Jónasdóttir and Bente Rosenbeck (eds). *Is There a Nordic Feminism? Nordic Feminist Thought on Culture and Society.* London: UCL Press.

Jowett, Madeleine. 2004. '"I Don't See Feminists as You See Feminists": Young Women Negotiating Feminism in Contemporary Britain', in Anita Harris (ed.). *All About the Girl: Culture, Power and Identity.* New York: Routledge.

Julios, Christina. 2007. 'A Middle-Aged, Middle-Class Whitewash', *Stop Gap,* autumn 2007: 14.

Jonsson, Terese. 2009. 'Piercing the Whitening Silence'. http://www.thefword. org.uk/features/2009/03/piercing_the_wh. Accessed 13/05/09.

Kantola, Johanna. 2006. *Feminists Theorize the State.* Basingstoke: Macmillan.

Katbamna, Mira. 2005. 'Shelf Awareness'. http://www.guardian.co.uk/g2/ story/0,,1453643,00.html. Accessed 28/03/07.

Kautto, Mikko; Heikkila, Matti; Hvinden, Bjørn; Marklund, Staffan; and Plough, Neils. 1999. 'Introduction: Nordic Welfare States in the 1990s', in Heikkila Kautto, Marklund Hvinden and Neils Plough (eds). *Nordic Social Policy: Changing Welfare States.* London: Routledge.

Kelly, Liz. 1999. 'What Happened to the "F" and "P" Words? Feminist Reflections on Inter-Agency Forums and the Concept of Partnership', in Nicola Harwin, Gill Hague and Ellen Malos (eds). *The Multiagency Approach to Domestic Violence: New Opportunities, Old Challenges?* London: Whiting and Birch.

Kirtley, JoJo. 2002. 'All About Eve'. http://www.thefword.org.uk/features/2002/ 11/all_about_eve. Accessed 28/03/07.

Kjeldstad, Randi. 2001. 'Gender Policies and Gender Equality', in Mikko Kautto, Bjørn Hvinden, Johan Fritzell, Jon Kvist and Hannu Uusitalo (eds). *Nordic Welfare States in the European Context.* London: Routledge.

Knowles, Jo. 2004. 'Crime and Punishment: Maxine Carr and Other "Evil Women"'. http://www.thefword.org.uk/features/2004/06/crime_and_punishment_ maxine_carr_and_other_evil_women. Accessed 28/03/07.

Krook, Mona Lee. 2008. 'Campaigns for Candidate Gender Quotas: a New Global Women's Movement', in Sandra Grey and Marian Sawer (eds). *Women's Movements: Flourishing or in Abeyance?* London: Routledge.

Laclau, Ernesto. 1990. *New Reflections on the Revolution of Our Time.* London: Verso.

Laclau, Ernesto. 1996. *Emancipation(s).* London: Verso.

Laclau, Ernesto. 2004. 'An Ethics of Militant Engagement', in Peter Hallward (ed.). *Think Again: Alain Badiou and the Future of Philosophy.* London: Continuum.

Laclau, Ernesto. 2005a. *On Populist Reason*. London: Verso.

Laclau, Ernesto. 2005b. 'The Future of Radical Democracy', in Lasse Thomassen and Lars Tønder (eds). *Radical Democracy: Politics Between Abundance and Lack*. Manchester: Manchester University Press.

Laclau, Ernesto and Mouffe, Chantal. 2001. *Hegemony and Socialist Strategy: Towards a Radical Democratic Politics* (2nd edition). London: Verso.

Lang, Sabine. 1997. 'The NGOisation of Feminism', in Joan W. Scott, Cora Kaplan and Debra Keates (eds). *Transitions, Environments, Translations: Feminisms in International Politics*. London: Routledge.

Lang, Sabine. 2007. 'Gender Governance in Post-Unification Germany: Between Institutionalization, Deregulation and Privatization', in Joyce Outshoorn and Johanna Kantola (eds). *Changing State Feminism*. Basingstoke: Palgrave Macmillan.

Leeds Revolutionary Feminist Group. 1982. 'Political Lesbianism: The Case Against Heterosexuality', in Mary Evans (ed.). *The Woman Question: Readings on the Subordination of Women*. Oxford: Fontana.

Lefort, Claude. 1988. *Democracy and Political Theory*. Minneapolis: University of Minnesota Press.

Levinson, Elie. 2006. 'Are You Afraid of The F-word?' http://www.guardian.co.uk/g2/story/0,,1888732,00.html. Accessed 28/03/07.

Levinson, Ellie. 2009. *The Noughtie Girl's Guide to Feminism*. Oxford: Oneworld.

Levitas, Ruth. 1998. *The Inclusive Society? Social Exclusion and New Labour*. Basingstoke: Macmillan.

Levy, Ariel. 2005. *Female Chauvinist Pigs: Women and the Rise of Raunch Culture*. London: Pocket Books.

Lovenduski, Joni. 1995. 'An Emerging Advocate: The Equal Opportunities' Commission in Great Britain', in Amy Mazur and Dorothy McBride Stetson (eds). *Comparative State Feminism*. Thousand Oaks: Sage.

Lovenduski, Joni. 2005. 'Introduction: State Feminism and the Political Representation of Women', in Joni Lovenduski (ed.). *State Feminism and Political Representation*. Cambridge: Cambridge University Press.

Lovenduski, Joni. 2007. 'Unfinished Business: Equality Policy and the Changing Context of State Feminism in Great Britain', in Joyce Outshoorn and Johanna Kantola (eds). *Changing State Feminism*. Basingstoke: Palgrave Macmillan.

Lovenduski, Joni; Campbell, Rosie; and Childs, Sarah. 2005. 'A Woman's Place – Still Not in the House', *Towards Equality*, spring 2005: 4.

Lovenduski, Joni and Randall, Vicky. 1993. *Contemporary Feminist Politics: Women and Power in Britain*. Oxford: Oxford University Press.

Lukes, Steven. 1974. *Power: A Radical View*. London: Macmillan.

Lyster, Samantha. 2004. 'A Perfect Delusion'. http://www.thefword.org.uk/features/2004/04/a_perfect_delusion. Accessed 28/03/07.

Mackay, Finn. 2004. 'Surf's Up! In Praise of the Second Wave'. http://www.thefword.org.uk/features/2004/04/surfs_up_in_praise_of_the_second_wave. Accessed 28/03/07.

Mackay, Fiona. 2008. 'The State of Women's Movements in Britain: Ambiguity, Complexity and Challenges from the eriphery', in Sandra Grey and Marian Sawer (eds). *Women's Movements: Flourishing or in Abeyance?* London: Routledge.

MacKinnon, Catherine. 1989. *Toward a Feminist Theory of the State*. Cambridge: Harvard University Press.

Maddison, Sarah and Jung, Kyungja. 2008. 'Autonomy and Engagement: Women's Movements in Australia and South Korea', in Sandra Grey and Marian Sawer (eds). *Women's Movements: Flourishing or in Abeyance?* London: Routledge.

Mahmood, Saba. 2005. *Politics of Piety: The Islamic Revival and the Feminist Subject.* Princeton: Princeton University Press.

Marchant, Oliver. 2007. *Post-Foundational Political Thought: Political Difference in Nancy, Lefort, Badiou and Laclau.* Edinburgh: Edinburgh University Press.

Marshall, P. David. 1997. *Celebrity and Power: Fame in Contemporary Culture.* Minnesota: University of Minnesota Press.

May, Todd. 2008. *The Political Thought of Jacques Rancière: Creating Equality.* Edinburgh: Edinburgh University Press.

Mazur, Amy. 2007. 'Women's Policy Agencies, Women's Movements, and a Shifting Political Context: Towards a Gendered Republic in France', in Joyce Outshoorn and Johanna Kantola (eds). *Changing State Feminism.* Basingstoke: Palgrave Macmillan.

Mazur, Amy and Stetson, Dorothy McBride. 1995a. 'Introduction', in Amy Mazur and Dorothy McBride Stetson (eds). *Comparative State Feminism.* Thousand Oaks: Sage.

Mazur, Amy and Stetson, Dorothy McBride. 1995b. 'Conclusion: The Case for State Feminism', in Amy Mazur and Dorothy McBride Stetson (eds). *Comparative State Feminism.* Thousand Oaks: Sage.

McBride, Dorothy and Mazur, Amy. 2006. 'Measuring Feminist Mobilisation: Cross-National Convergences and Transnational Networks in Western Europe', in Myra Marx Ferree and Aili Mari Tripp (eds). *Transnational Women's Activism, Organizing and Human Rights.* New York: New York University Press.

McCabe, Jess. 2006. 'Calling for a Third Wave'. http://www.thefword.org.uk/blog/2006/august. Accessed 28/03/07.

McManus, Susan. 2005. *Fictive Theories: Towards a Deconstructive and Utopian Political Imagination.* Basingstoke: Palgrave Macmillan.

McRobbie, Angela. 1992. 'Post-Marxism and Cultural Studies: A Postscript', in Lawrence Grossberg, Cary Nelson and Paula Treichler (eds). *Cultural Studies.* London: Routledge.

McRobbie, Angela. 1999. *In the Culture Society: Art, Fashion and Popular Music.* London: Sage.

McRobbie, Angela. 2000. *Feminism and Youth Culture* (2nd edition). Basingstoke: Macmillan.

McRobbie, Angela. 2004. 'Post-Feminism and Popular Culture', *Feminist Media Studies* 4 (3): 255–64.

McRobbie, Angela. 2007a. 'Top Girls? Young Women and the Post-feminist Sexual Contract', *Cultural Studies* 21 (4): 718–37.

McRobbie, Angela. 2007b. 'Illegible Rage: Young Women's Post-Feminist Disorders'. http://www.lse.ac.uk/collections/LSEPublicLecturesAndEvents/pdf/20070125_McRobbie.pdf. Accessed 16/03/07.

McRobbie, Angela. 2009. *The Aftermath of Feminism: Gender, Culture and Social Change.* London: Sage.

Meehan, Elizabeth. 1990. 'British Feminism from the 1960s to the 1980s', in Harold L. Smith (ed.). *British Feminism in the Twentieth Century.* Aldershot: Edward Elgar.

Mendoza, Breny. 2002. 'Transnational Feminisms in Question', *Feminist Theory* 3 (3): 295–314.

Middleton, Jo. 2007. 'Feminism 2.0'. *Stop Gap*, autumn 2007: 12–13.

Millett, Kate. 1977. *Sexual Politics*. London: Virago Press.

Missmogga. 2002. 'What's Up Baby?' http://www.thefword.org.uk/features/2002/10/whats_up_baby. Accessed 28/03/07.

Moghadam, Valentine, M. 2005. *Globalizing Women: Transnational Feminist Networks*. Baltimore: The Johns Hopkins University Press.

Mohanty, Chandra Talpade. 2003. *Feminism Without Borders: Decolonizing Theory, Practicing Solidarity*. Durham: Duke University Press.

Moosa, Zoohra. 2008a. 'Introduction', in Zoohra Moosa (ed.). *Seeing Double: Race and Gender in Ethnic Minority Women's Lives*. London: The Fawcett Society.

Moosa, Zoohra. 2008b. 'How Not to Sell Out', in Zoohra Moosa (ed.). *Seeing Double: Race and Gender in Ethnic Minority Women's Lives*. London: The Fawcett Society.

Mouffe, Chantal. 1992. 'Democratic Politics Today', in Chantal Mouffe (ed.). *Dimensions of Radical Democracy: Pluralism, Citizenship, Community*. London: Verso.

Mouffe, Chantal. 1993. *The Return of the Political*. London: Verso.

Mouffe, Chantal. 2000. *The Democratic Paradox*. London: Verso.

Mouffe, Chantal. 2005. *On the Political*. London: Routledge.

Mueller, Carol McClury and McCarthy, John D. 2003. 'Cultural Continuity and Structural Change: The Logic of Adaptation by Radical, Liberal and Socialist Feminists to State Reconfiguration', in Lee Ann Banaszak, Karen Beckwith and Dieter Rucht (eds). *Women's Movements Facing the Reconfigured State*. New York: Cambridge University Press.

Munford, Rebecca. 2004. 'Wake Up and Smell the Lipgloss: Gender, Generation and the (A)politics of Girl Power', in Stacy Gillis, Gillian Howie and Rebecca Munford (eds). *Third Wave Feminism: A Critical Exploration*. Basingstoke: Macmillan.

Muñoz, José Esteban. 1999. *Disidentifications: Queers of Colour and the Performance of Politics*. Minneapolis: University of Minnesota Press.

Murray, Jenni. 2003. 'A Vision of Equality', in *Towards Equality*, summer 2003: 3.

Nancy, Jean-Luc. 2000. *Being Singular Plural*. Stanford: Stanford University Press.

Nash, Kate. 2002. 'A Movement Moves ... Is There a Women's Movement in England Today?' *European Journal of Women's Studies* 9 (3): 311–28.

Newman, Janet. 2002. 'The New Public Management: Modernization and Institutional Change', in Kate McLaughlin, Stephen Osborne and Ewan Ferlie (eds). *New Public Management: Current Trends and Future Prospects*. London: Routledge.

Newman, Saul. 2007. *Unstable Universalities: Poststructuralism and Radical Politics*. Manchester: Manchester University Press.

Nixon, Sean. 2000. 'Intervening in Popular Culture: Cultural Politics and the Art of Translation', in Paul Gilroy, Lawrence Grossberg and Angela McRobbie (eds). *Without Guarantees: Essays in Honour of Stuart Hall*. London: Verso.

Norval, Aletta. 2007. *Aversive Democracy: Inheritance and Originality in the Democratic Tradition*. Cambridge: Cambridge University Press.

Nussbaum, Martha. 1999. 'The Professor of Parody'. *New Republic Online* 22/02/99. Available at http://www.qwik.ch/the_professor_of_parody. Accessed 30/03/07.

Object and The Fawcett Society. 2009. 'Campaign to Reform Lap Dancing Club Licensing: A Joint Briefing by The Fawcett Society and Object, February 2009'. http://www.object.org.uk/downloads/Object%20Fawcett%20%C9fing%20Feb%2009.pdf. Accessed 08/04/09.

O'Reilly, Abby. 2006. 'Declaration of Independence'. http://www.thefword.org. uk/features/2006/09/independence. Accessed 28/03/07.

Orr, Deborah. 2007. 'We Know What Modern Feminists Look Like, But Do We Know What They Now Believe?' http://comment.independent.co.uk/ columnists_m_z/deborah_orr/article2334883.ece. Accessed 29/03/07.

Orr, Lesley. 2008. 'Women's Aid in Scotland: Recording Feminism and Social Change'. Paper presented at 'Feminism and History: Rethinking Women's Movements Since 1800' conference, Bishopsgate Institute, London, 15/11/08.

Osborne, Stephen and McLaughlin, Kate. 2002. 'New Public Management in Context', in Kate McLaughlin, Stephen Osborne and Ewan Ferlie (eds). *New Public Management: Current Trends and Future Prospects.* London: Routledge.

Outshoorn, Joyce and Kantola, Johanna. 2007a. 'Changing State Feminism', in Joyce Outshoorn and Johanna Kantola (eds). *Changing State Feminism.* Basingstoke: Palgrave Macmillan.

Outshoorn, Joyce and Kantola, Johanna. 2007b. 'Assessing Changes in State Feminism Over the Last Decade', in Joyce Outshoorn and Johanna Kantola (eds). *Changing State Feminism.* Basingstoke: Palgrave Macmillan.

Panagia, Davide. 2006. *The Poetics of Political Thinking.* Durham: Duke University Press.

Patton, Paul. 2005. 'Deleuze and Democratic Politics', in Lasse Thomassen and Lars Tønder (eds). *Radical Democracy: Politics Between Abundance and Lack.* Manchester: Manchester University Press.

Patel, Pragna. 1999. 'The Multiagency Approach to Domestic Violence: A Panacea or Obstacle to Women's Struggles for Freedom from Violence', in Nicola Harwin, Gill Hague and Ellen Malos (eds). *The Multiagency Approach to Domestic Violence: New Opportunities, Old Challenges?* London: Whiting and Birch.

Pender, Patricia. 2004. 'Kicking Ass as Comfort Food: Buffy as Third Wave Feminist Icon', in Stacy Gillis, Gillian Howie and Rebecca Munford (eds). *Third Wave Feminism: A Critical Exploration.* Basingstoke: Macmillan.

Pereira, Maria do Mar. 2008. 'The Epistemic Status of Women's Gender, Feminist Studies: Notes for Analysis', *The Making of European Women's Studies* 8: 145–56.

Phillips, Anne. 1991. *Engendering Democracy.* Cambridge: Polity Press.

Phillips, Anne. 2000. 'Representing Difference: Why Should it Matter if Women Get Elected', in Anna Coote (ed.). *New Gender Agenda: Why Women Still Want More.* London: IPPR.

Pietilä, Hilkka. 2006. 'Women as Agents for Development: Learning from the Experiences of Women in Finland', in Myra Marx Ferree and Aili Mari Tripp (eds). *Transnational Women's Activism, Organizing and Human Rights.* New York: New York University Press.

Pilcher, Jane. 1998. *Women of Their Time: Generation, Gender Issues and Feminism.* Aldershot: Ashgate.

Pitkin, Hanna Fenichel. 1998. *Attack of the Blob: Hannah Arendt's Concept of the Social.* Chicago: Chicago University Press.

Plant, Sheryl. 2006. 'Men Are Back. But Where Did They Go?' http://www. thefword.org.uk/reviews/2006/03/men_are_back_bu. Accessed 9/07/08.

Pollock, Scarlet and Sutton, Jo. 1999. 'Women Click: Feminism and the Internet', in Susan Hawthorne and Renate Klein (eds). *CyberFeminism: Connectivity, Critique and Creativity.* Melbourne: Spinifex Press.

Predelli, Line Nyhagen; Perren, Kim; Halsaa, Beatrice; Thun, Cecile; Manful, Esmeranda. 2008. *Women's Movements: Constructions of Sisterhood, Dispute and Resonance: the Case of the United Kingdom*. FEMCIT, working paper no. 2.

Pringle, Rosemary and Watson, Sophie. 1992. '"Women's Interests" and the Poststructuralist State', in Michèle Barrett and Anne Phillips (eds). *Destabilizing Theory: Contemporary Feminist Debates*. Cambridge: Polity Press.

Projansky, Sarah. 2001. *Watching Rape: Film and Television in Postfeminist Culture*. New York: New York University Press.

Pugh, Martin. 2000. *Women and the Women's Movement in Britain, 1914–1999*. Basingstoke: Macmillan.

Rake, Katherine. 2003a. Untitled: published on *The Guardian* letters page, 3 July 2003. http://www.guardian.co.uk/letters/story/0,3604,989958,00.html. Accessed 28/03/07.

Rake, Katherine. 2003b. Untitled interview, BBC Radio 4. http://news.bbc.co.uk/media/audio/39416000/rm/_39416370_rake.ram. Accessed 10/11/06.

Rake, Katherine. 2004. 'Women's Votes: The Key to Electoral Success'. *Towards Equality*, summer 2004: 3.

Rake, Katherine. 2005. 'Politicians are Pursuing Women's Votes – but Are Women Convinced?' *Towards Equality*, spring 2005: 3.

Rake, Katherine. 2006a. 'Let's Reclaim the F-word'. *Stop Gap*, autumn 2006: 8–9.

Rake, Katherine. 2006b. 'The New Mass Women's Lobby Must Include Men'. http://www.guardian.co.uk/comment/story/0,1699966,00.html. Accessed 28/03/07.

Rake, Katherine. 2006c. 'Wither Feminism'. http://www.fawcettsociety.org.uk/index.asp?PageID=188. Accessed 10/11/06.

Rake, Katherine. 2006d. 'Editorial: Reclaiming The F-Word'. *Stop Gap*, autumn 2006: 3.

Rake, Katherine. 2007. 'Editorial'. *Stop Gap*, autumn 2007: 3.

Rake, Katherine. 2008a. 'Editorial'. *Stop Gap*, spring 2008: 3.

Rake, Katherine. 2008b. 'Editorial'. *Stop Gap*, autumn 2008: 3.

Rake, Katherine. 2009. 'Editorial'. *Stop Gap*, spring 2009: 3.

Ram, Kalpana. 2000. 'The State and the Women's Movement: Instabilities in the Discourse of "Rights" in India', in Ann-Marie Hildson, Vera Mackie, Martha Macintyre and Maila Stivens (eds). *Human Rights and Gender Politics. Asia-Pacific Perspectives*. New York and London: Routledge.

Rancière, Jacques. 1995. *On the Shores of Politics*. London: Verso.

Rancière, Jacques. 1999. *Dis-agreement: Politics and Philosophy*. Minneapolis: University of Minnesota Press.

Rancière, Jacques. 2006. *Hatred of Democracy*. London: Verso.

Randall, Vicky. 1998. 'Gender and Power: Women Engage the State', in Georgia Waylen and Vicky Randall (eds). *Gender, Politics and the State*. London: Routledge.

Redfern, Catherine. 2001a. 'Pick 'n' Mix Feminism'. http://www.thefword.org.uk/features/2001/05/pick_n_mix_feminism. Accessed 28/03/07.

Redfern, Catherine. 2001b. 'Is This Website Discriminating?' http://www.thefword.org.uk/features/2001/12/is_this_website_discriminating. Accessed 28/03/07.

Redfern, Catherine. 2001c. 'Rebranding Feminism'. http://www.thefword.org.uk/features/2001/12/rebranding_feminism. Accessed 20/06/09.

Redfern, Catherine. 2002a. 'The Freedom Trashcan 2002'. http://www.thefword.org.uk/features/2002/03/the_freedom_trashcan_2002. Accessed 28/03/07.

Redfern, Catherine. 2002b. 'A Third Wave?' http://www.thefword.org.uk/features/2002/09/a_third_wave. Accessed 28/03/07.

Redfern, Catherine. 2003a. 'Is this Website Discriminating? Responses'. http://www.thefword.org.uk/features/2003/03/is_this_website_discriminating_responses. Accessed 28/03/07.

Redfern, Catherine. 2003b. 'The F-word: Contemporary UK Feminism'. http://www.thefword.org.uk/features/2003/06/the_fword_contemporary_uk_feminism. Accessed 28/03/07.

Redfern, Catherine. 2005a. 'Ordinary Ads, Everyday Images'. http://www.thefword.org.uk/features/2005/11/ordinary_ads_everyday_images. Accessed 28/03/07.

Redfern, Catherine. 2007. 'Changes at The F-word'. http://www.thefword.org.uk/blog/2007/february. Accessed 28/03/07.

Redfern, Catherine. Date not specified (a). 'About The F-word'. http://www.thefword.org.uk/general/about_the_fword. Accessed 28/03/07.

Redfern, Catherine. Date not specified (b). 'FAQ'. http://www.thefword.org.uk/general/frequently_asked_questions#whatiscontemporary. Accessed 28/03/07.

Rich, Adrienne. 1979. *On Lies, Secrets and Silence: Selected Prose 1966–1978*. New York: Norton and Co.

Richards, Amy and Schnall, Marianne. 2003. 'Cyberfeminism: Networking on the Net'. http://www.feminist.com/resources/artspeech/genwom/cyberfeminism.html. Accessed 28/03/07.

Rogers, Anna. 2008. 'The Problem of Feminist Generations: Insights into Intergenerational Feminist Consciousness'. Unpublished paper.

Rowbotham, Sheila. 1989. *The Past is Before Us: Feminism in Action Since the 1960s*. London: Pandora Press.

Rowbotham, Sheila. 1997. *A Century of Women: The History of Women in Britain and the United States*. London: Viking.

Rowe, C. J. 2008. 'Cyberfeminism in Action: Claiming Women's Space in Cyberspace', in Sandra Grey and Marian Sawer (eds). *Women's Movements: Flourishing or in Abeyance?* London: Routledge.

Rowe, Marsha (ed.). 1982. *Spare Rib Reader*. Hammondsworth: Penguin.

Rudolfsdottir, Annadis, G. and Jolliffe, Rachel. 2008. 'I Don't Think People Really Talk About It that Much: Young Women Discuss Feminism', *Feminism and Psychology* 18 (2): 268–74.

Ruggie, Mary. 1984. *The State and Working Women: A Comparative Study of Britain and Sweden*. Princeton: Princeton University Press.

Sanders, Lise Shapiro. 2007. 'Feminists Love a Utopia: Collaboration, Conflict and the Futures of Feminism', in Stacy Gillis, Gillian Howie and Rebecca Munford (eds). *Third Wave Feminism: A Critical Exploration* (2nd edition). Basingstoke: Macmillan.

Sauer, Birgit. 2007. 'What Happened to the Model Student? Austrian State Feminism Since the 1990s', in Joyce Outshoorn and Johanna Kantola (eds). *Changing State Feminism*. Basingstoke: Palgrave Macmillan.

Saunders, Hilary. 2001. *Making Contact Worse? Report of a National Survey of Domestic Violence Refuge Services into the Enforcement of Contact Orders*. http:/ www.womensaid.org.uk/landing_page.asp?section=0001000100090005000500090011. Accessed 28/03/07.

Saunders, Hilary. 2003. *Whatever Happened to Safety and Justice for Children? The Women's Aid Briefing Paper on Children's Issues in Safety and Justice: the Domestic*

Violence Consultation Paper – July 2003. http://www.womensaid.org.uk/landing_
page.asp?section=0001000100009000300030007. Accessed 28/03/07.

Scharff, Christina. 2010. *Repudiating Feminism*. London: Ashgate (forthcoming).

Schirmer, Jennifer, G. 1982. *The Limits of Reform: Women, Capital and Welfare.*
Cambridge, Massachusetts: Schenkman Publishing Company.

Segal, Lynne. 1999. *Why Feminism? Gender, Psychology, Politics*. New York:
Columbia University Press.

Sharpe, Sue. 2001. 'Going for It: Young Women Face the Future', *Feminism and
Psychology* 11 (2): 177–81.

Simons, Jon. 2000. 'Knowing and Doing, Skepticism and Coherence'. *Political
Theory* 28 (2): 273–8.

Simons, Jon. 2005. 'The Radical Democratic Possibilities of Popular Culture', in
Lasse Thomassen and Lars Tønder (eds). *Radical Democracy: Politics Between
Abundance and Lack*. Manchester: Manchester University Press

Smith, Lorraine. 2003a. 'Ball Breaking? Coming Out of the Feminism Closet'.
http://www.thefword.org.uk/features/2003/07/ball_breaking_coming_out_of_
the_feminism_closet. Accessed 28/03/07.

Smith, Lorraine. 2003b. 'Body Image'. http://www.thefword.org.uk/
features/2003/03/body_image. Accessed 28/03/07.

Smith, Lorraine. 2003c. 'The Feminist Minefield?' http://www.thefword.org.uk/
features/2003/12/the_feminist_minefield. Accessed 28/03/07.

Snyder, Margaret. 2006. 'Unlikely Godmother: The UN and the Global Women's
Movement', in Myra Marx Ferree and Aili Mari Tripp (eds). *Transnational
Women's Activism, Organizing and Human Rights*. New York: New York University
Press.

Southall Black Sisters. 2004. 'Domestic Violence, Immigration and No Recourse to
Public Funds'. http://www.southallblacksisters.org.uk/research.html. Accessed
17/06/09.

Spalding, Anna. 2009. 'Whose Feminism is it?' http://www.thefword.org.uk/
features/2008/09/feminism_of_tod. Accessed 13/05/09.

Springborg, Patricia. 1989. 'Hannah Arendt and the Classical Republican
Tradition', in Gisela T. Kaplan and Clive S. Kessler (eds). *Thinking, Judging,
Freedom*. Sydney: Allen and Unwin.

Squires, Judith. 2007. *The New Politics of Gender Equality*. Basingstoke: Palgrave
Macmillan.

Stacey, Judith. 1992. 'Sexism by a Subtler Name? Postindustrial Conditions and
Postfeminist Consciousness in the Silicon Valley', in Dorothy O. Helly, and
Susan M. Reverby (eds). *Gendered Domains: Rethinking Public and Private in
Women's History*. Ithaca: Cornell University Press.

Staten, Henry. 1985. *Wittgenstein and Derrida*. Lincoln: University of Nebraska Press.

Stavrakakis, Yannis. 2007. *The Lacanian Left: Theory, Politics, Psychoanalysis*.
Edinburgh: Edinburgh University Press.

Stetson, Dorothy McBride. 2001. 'Conclusion: Comparative Abortion Politics
and the Case for State Feminism', in Dorothy McBride Stetson (ed.). *Abortion
Politics, Women's Movements and the Democratic State: A Comparative Study of
State Feminism*. Oxford: Oxford University Press.

Taft, Jessica. 2004. 'Girl Power Politics: Pop Culture Barriers and Organisational
Resistance', in Anita Harris (ed.). *All About the Girl: Culture, Power and Identity*.
New York: Routledge.

Tasker, Yvonne and Negra, Diane. 2007. 'Introduction: Feminist Politics and Post-feminist Culture', in Yvonne Tasker and Diane Negra (eds). *Interrogating Post-Feminism: Gender and the Politics of Popular Culture*. Durham: Duke University Press.

Thurgood, Ben. 2003. 'Sexual Healing'. http://www.thefword.org.uk/features/2003/09/sexual_healing. Accessed 28/03/07.

Tibballs, Sue. 2000. *The Sexual Renaissance: Making Sense of Sexual Difference in a New Era*. Kingston: the Women's Communication Centre.

Tibballs, Sue. 2005. 'Representation is the Key'. *Towards Equality*, summer 2005: 3.

Torfing, Jacob. 2005. 'Discourse Theory: Achievements, Arguments and Challenges', in David Howarth and Jacob Torfing (eds). *Discourse Theory in European Politics: Identity, Policy and Governance*. Basingstoke: Palgrave Macmillan.

Toynbee, Polly. 2002. 'The Myth of Women's Lib'. http://www.guardian.co.uk/g2/story/0,728017,00.html. Accessed 30/03/07.

Tripp, Aili Mari. 2006. 'The Evolution of Transnational Feminisms: Consensus, Conflict, and New Dynamics. Global Feminism', in Myra Marx Ferree and Aili Mari Tripp (eds). *Transnational Women's Activism, Organizing and Human Rights*. New York: New York University Press.

Tsaliki, Liza. 2001. 'Women and New Technologies', in Sarah Gamble (ed.). *The Routledge Companion to Feminism and Postfeminism*. London: Routledge.

Van der Tuin, Iris. 2009. 'Jumping Generations: On Second and Third Wave Feminist Epistemology', *Australian Feminist Studies* 24 (59): 17–31.

Various authors. 2002a. 'Response to "Whose Slut?"' http://www.thefword.org.uk/features/2002/08/response_to_whose_slut. Accessed 28/03/07.

Various authors. 2002b. 'More Responses to "Whose Slut?"' http://www.thefword.org.uk/features/2002/10/more_responses_to_whose_slut. Accessed 28/03/07.

Viner, Katharine. 1999. 'The Personal is Still Political', in Natasha Walter (ed.). *On the Move: Feminism for a New Generation*. London: Virago Press.

Wadsworth, Laura. 2004. 'Feminine Feminism'. http://www.thefword.org.uk/features/2004/03/feminine_feminism. Accessed 28/03/07.

Walby, Sylvia. 1990. *Theorising Patriarchy*. Oxford: Basil Blackwell.

Walby, Sylvia. 1997. *Gender Transformations*. London: Routledge.

Walby, Sylvia. 2002. 'Feminism in a Global Era', *Economy and Society* 31 (4): 533–57.

Walker, Richard; Kirkpatrick, Ian and Ackroyd, Stephen. 2005. *The New Managerialism and Public Service Professions: Change in Health, Social Services and Housing*. Basingstoke: Palgrave MacMillan.

Walter, Natasha. 1998. *The New Feminism*. London: Virago Press.

Warwick, Alex and Auchmuty, Rosemary. 1995. 'Women's Studies as Feminist Activism', in Gabrielle Griffin (eds). *Feminist Activism in the 1990s*. London: Routledge.

Waylen, Georgia. 1998. 'Gender, Feminism and the State: An Overview', in Georgia Waylen and Vicky Randall (eds). *Gender, Politics and the State*. London: Routledge.

Webster, Duncan. 2006. 'Pessimism, Optimism, Pleasure: the Future of Cultural Studies', in John Storey (ed.). *Cultural Theory and Popular Culture: A Reader*. Harlow: Pearson.

Whelehan, Imelda. 2000. *Overloaded: Popular Culture and the Future of Feminism*. London: the Women's Press.

Whittle, Louise. 2005. 'Left Behind'. http://www.thefword.org.uk/features/2005/08/left_behind. Accessed 28/03/07.

Widder, Nathan. 2005. 'Two Routes from Hegel', in Lasse Thomassen and Lars Tønder (eds). *Radical Democracy: Politics Between Abundance and Lack*. Manchester: Manchester University Press.

Wiegman, Robyn. 2002. 'Academic Feminism Against Itself', *NWSA Journal* 14 (2): 18–37.

Wilding, Faith. Date not specified. 'Where is the Feminism in Cyberfeminism?' http://www.obn.org/cfundef/faith_def.html. Accessed 28/03/07.

Wittgenstein, Ludwig. 1958. *Philosophical Investigations* (G.E.M. Anscombe, trans.). Oxford: Basil Blackwell.

Women's Aid. 2002a. Press Release: *Women's Aid holds 'Question Time Debate' on Domestic Violence and the Justice System*. http://www.womensaid.org.uk/domestic-violence-press-releases.asp?itemtype=press_policy&section=0001000100150001&id=604. Accessed 28/03/07.

Women's Aid. 2002b. *Womenspeak*. http://www.womensaid.org.uk/landing_page.asp?section=00010001000900080001000S. Accessed 28/03/07.

Women's Aid. 2003a. *Press Release: Women's Aid Hosts International Conference: Approaches to Preventing Domestic Violence*. Bristol: Women's Aid.

Women's Aid. 2003b. *Women's Aid Consultation Response to Restorative Justice – the Government's Strategy*. http://www.womensaid.org.uk/landing_page.asp?section=00010001000900030004000S. Accessed 28/03/07.

Women's Aid. 2003c. *House of Fraser Launch Bella Valore Personal Alarm to Raise Funds for Women's Aid*. Bristol: Women's Aid.

Women's Aid. 2003d. *Press Release: Women's Aid and NSPCC Urge Government to Make Contact Arrangements Safe for Children*. Bristol: Women's Aid.

Women's Aid. 2003e. *Press Release: New Good Practice Guide for Employers*. Bristol: Women's Aid.

Women's Aid. 2004a. *Celebrating 30 Years of Women's Aid 1974–2004*. http://www.womensaid.org.uk/downloads/WA30th_brochure.pdf. Accessed 28/03/07.

Women's Aid. 2004b. *Until Women and Children Are Safe: Annual Review 2002–2003*. Bristol: Women's Aid.

Women's Aid. 2004c. *Press Release: Sarah and Gordon Brown Host 30th Birthday Reception for the National Domestic Violence Charity, Women's Aid*. Bristol: Women's Aid.

Women's Aid. 2005a. *Women's Aid – a Brief History*. Bristol: Women's Aid.

Women's Aid. 2005b. *Press Release: Women's Aid and Company Magazine Launch the 'Tell a Friend' Campaign with Faith Shoes to Encourage Young Women to Speak Out About Domestic Violence*. Bristol: Women's Aid.

Women's Aid. 2005c. *Domestic Violence – FAQ Factsheet*. http://www.womensaid.org.uk/downloads/FAQs.pdf. Accessed 28/03/07.

Women's Aid. 2005d. *Press Release: Mayor Backs London Cabbies' Domestic Violence Awareness Initiative*. Bristol: Women's Aid.

Women's Aid. 2005e. *Press Release: 'Shop and Support' – Topshop Supports the Freephone 24-Hour National Domestic National Domestic Violence Helpline*. Bristol: Women's Aid.

Women's Aid. 2006. *National Service Standards for Domestic & Sexual Violence*. http://www.womensaid.org.uk/downloads/National%20Service%20Standards%20-%20final.pdf. Accessed 27/03/07.

Women's Aid. 2007. *Celebrities Act to End Domestic Violence*. http://www.womensaid.org.uk/downloads/Celeb%20campaign%20press%20release.doc. Accessed 27/03/07.

Women's Aid. Date not specified (a). *Work With Perpetrators in the UK.* http://www.womensaid.org.uk/page.asp?section=00010001000900070001. Accessed 28/03/07.

Women's Aid. Date not specified (b). *Providing Services for Children Who Have Experienced Domestic Violence.* http://www.womensaid.org.uk/landing_page.asp?section=0001000100090005000500080005. Accessed 28/03/07.

Young, Iris Marion. 1990. *Justice and the Politics of Difference.* Princeton: Princeton University Press.

Yuval-Davis, Nira. 2006. 'Human/Women's Rights and Feminist Transversal Politics', in Myra Marx Ferree and Aili Mari Tripp (eds). *Transnational Women's Activism, Organizing and Human Rights.* New York: New York University Press.

Zerilli, Linda. 2000. 'Response to Jon Simons'. *Political Theory* 28 (2): 279–84.

Zerilli, Linda. 2004. 'This Universalism Which is Not One', in Simon Critchley and Oliver Marchant (eds). *Ernesto Laclau: A Critical Reader.* London: Routledge.

Zerilli, Linda. 2005a. *Feminism and the Abyss of Freedom.* Chicago: University of Chicago Press.

Zerilli, Linda. 2005b. 'We Feel Our Freedom: Imagination and Judgement in the Thought of Hannah Arendt'. *Political Theory* 33 (2): 158–88.

Zivi, Karen. 2008. 'Rights and the Politics of Performativity', in Terrell Carver and Samuel Chambers (eds). *Judith Butler's Precarious Politics: Critical Encounters.* London: Routledge.

Žižek, Slavoj. 2000. 'Class Struggle or Postmodernism? Yes, Please', in Judith Butler, Ernesto Laclau and Slavoj Žižek. *Contingency, Hegemony, Universality: Contemporary Dialogues on the Left.* London: Verso.

Žižek, Slavoj. 2002. 'A Plea for Leninist Intolerance'. *Critical Inquiry*, Winter 2002. Available from http://www.lacan.com/zizek-plea.htm. Accessed 20/06/08.

Zupančić, Alenka. 2000. *Ethics of the Real: Kant, Lacan.* New York: Verso.

Index

Abbott, Dianne   190 n20
abortion   29, 32, 90
abundance/lack distinction   167,
    172–174, 177
Adams, Melinda   23
Afshar, Haleh   190 n17
Age Concern   91
agency (conceptions of)   43, 51–52,
    61, 174–176
Ahmed, Samira   190 n20
Althusser, Louis   194 n7
Amnesty International   108
anti-globalisation   24, 196 n9
Arendt, Hannah   187 n13
    conception of politics   48, 180–181,
        187 n11, 187 n15
    and Laclau   57–58
    'the social'   47–52, 70, 71, 72, 82,
        86, 121, 168, 187–188 n16
    and the 'woman question'   48,
        187 n12
Aune, Kristin   146
Austin, J.L.
    constative/performative
        distinction   3, 18, 62, 93, 151,
        157, 185 n12

'backlash' (Susan Faludi)   19
Badiou, Alain   41, 42, 164, 170, 187
    n5, 187 n11, 196 n4
Bagguley, Paul   11–12
Bagić, Aida   186 n16
Baird, Vera   190 n20
Banaszak, Lee Ann   13–14
Banyard, Kat   89, 190 n18
Barron, Jackie   105
'battered women's movement'
    (origins)   101–2
Baumgardner, Jennifer   2, 17–18, 32,
    141, 151
Beauvoir, Simone de   85
Beckwith, Karen   13–14
Belgium   28

Bell, Rachel   70
Bellamy, Kate   69
Benjamin, Walter   163
Benn, Hilary   190 n20
Bennett, Jane   173, 175, 176
Big Brother (TV show)   195 n12
Blackman, Honor   111
Blair, Cherie   190 n20
The Blob (movie)   50
blogging   3, 4, 90, 129, 131, 149, 150
Blunket, David   69, 111
Body Shop   109
Bowden, Andrew   146
Bowman, Paul   179, 182
Braidotti, Rosi   129, 173–174, 175
Brown, Gordon   72, 191 n25
Brown, Wendy   47, 87, 163, 181, 186
    n20, 186 n1, 196 n6
Browne, Sarah   7
Bruce, Fiona   111
Buffy the Vampire Slayer (TV series)   2,
    3, 164, 185 n11
Business in the Community   109
Bustelo, Maria   30
Butler, Judith   2, 39, 41, 51–52, 55,
    60, 61, 158, 188 n17, 196 n5
Byrne, Paul   11, 165

Cameron, David   69, 75, 189 n8
Cameron, Rhona   111
Campbell, Menzies   69
Campbell, Rosie   75
Capitalwoman   90
Carr, Maxine   145, 195 n13
Castoriadis, Cornelius   53, 57
    (see also 'figure of the newly
        thinkable')
Cavarero, Adriana   48, 187 n14
Celis, Karen   30
Chakrabarti, Shami   190 n20
Charles, Nickie   32
Chavalier, Tracy   190 n20
Chidgey, Red   154–155, 162

Childs, Sarah 75
Chiswick Women's Aid 102, 191 n2
Clarke, Alison 84
Clarke, Charles 69
Clarke, Gary 196 n7
Clarke, John 179–180
Collins, Jane 161
Commission for Equality and Human
    Rights (UK) 29, 184 n4
Compass (pressure group) 88–89,
    132, 148, 149, 150
Connolly, William 173, 174
consciousness-raising 33–34, 102, 120
Conservative Party (UK) 69, 74–75,
    189 n8
constative v performative 3, 18, 62,
    93, 151, 157, 185 n12
Critchley, Simon 42
cultural studies 164, 168, 177–183,
    196 n7
Curtis, Richard 111
Cut (movie) 112
cyberfeminism 129–130, 194 n1

Dallaglio, Lawrence 111
Day, Richard 196 n9
Dean, Jonathan 145, 161, 165
Deleuze, Giles 164, 167, 172–177,
    180, 181, 187 n10
Denmark 78
depoliticisation
  of feminism 7, 9, 16, 24, 25,
    128–129, 135–141, 142, 143,
    160, 163, 166, 167, 169, 180,
    185 n7
  theories of 168–169
deradicalisation (of feminism) 5,
    9–15, 22, 23, 24, 25, 28, 31–35,
    36, 52, 58, 61, 63, 64, 100–1,
    105–113, 121, 122, 125, 127,
    128, 139, 143, 163, 166, 180,
    194–195 n8
Derrida, Jacques 59, 172, 173, 182
Desai, Manisha 24
discourse (definition of) 59–60,
    188 n21
disidentification 4, 50, 54, 70,
    83–84, 90, 96, 97, 98, 128, 137,
    142, 153, 157–160, 185 n5

Dobash, R. Emerson and
    Russell 101–2, 105
domestic violence (see also Women's
    Aid) 62
  activism around 100–126, 164
  as 'figure of the newly
    thinkable' 101, 115–121
  and immigration 4, 113–115
  'mainstreaming' 112–113, 192 n12
  perpetrator responsibility/
    re-education programmes 118,
    193 n16–17
Donà, Alessia 30
Drew, Jennifer 147
Duff, Anne-Marie 111

Ellis-Bextor, Sophie 190 n20
Elman, R Amy 32
Emin, Tracey 190 n20
End Violence Against Women
    Coalition (EVAW) 108, 124
empty signifier (Laclau) 43–44, 55,
    57, 62, 71, 81, 82, 93, 94, 95, 96,
    116, 151, 157
equivalence (Laclau) 23, 38, 43–47,
    58, 62, 65, 72, 93, 94, 95, 99, 116,
    126, 140, 162, 187 n6
equalities legislation 7, 13, 27, 29,
    32, 184 n4
Ertrk, Yakin 26
European Union 27

Falkof, Nicky 190 n15
Fathers Direct 79
fathers' rights 79–81
Fawcett, Milicent Garrett 65–66,
    70, 84
Fawcett Society 1, 2, 4, 5, 7, 30, 63,
    64–99, 100, 104, 106, 107, 111,
    113, 125, 126, 128, 133, 162,
    165, 182
  2005 rebranding and aftermath
    82–99
  campaigns 188 n1
  childcare (state provision of)
    77–78
  childcare and work-life
    balance 76–82
  democratic deficit 96–97

Fawcett Society – *continued*
  distancing from radicalism   66–67,
    70–71
  and 'equality feminism'   89
  fatherhood/paternity leave   78–80
  'Fawcett Feminist Challenge'   90,
    97–98, 191 n25
  feminism (relationship to)   83–88
  'femocracy' campaign   92
  'Future of Feminism' seminars   90
  historical background   65–66
  and Labour Party   68–69
  parenting and work   76–77
  'positive action' measures   75–76
  professionalisation   66–68, 124,
    189 n2
  race and ethnic minority women
    (campaigning around)   72, 91–93
  and radical feminism   66, 85–86
  'Seeing Double' campaign   92–93
  'Sexism and the City' campaign   91,
    190 n22
  and third-wave feminism   88–89,
    93–94, 96, 97, 151, 155–156, 157
  'this is what a feminist looks like'
    t-shirt   85, 90, 97–98, 190 n19,
    191 n25
  use of quantitative research   70
  women's political representation
    and participation   71–76
FEM conferences   3, 89
Feminism
  and academia   13, 24, 185–186 n14
  autonomy   12–13, 14, 20, 22–23,
    26, 31–35, 58–59, 64, 67, 80–81,
    102, 103, 105, 106, 109, 118, 119,
    122, 123, 125, 126, 184 n2
  decline   5, 7, 9–15, 16, 22, 23, 24,
    28, 29, 30, 31, 34, 35, 36, 52, 58,
    64, 98, 126, 167, 183
  definition of   184 n1
  depoliticisation   7, 9, 16, 24, 25,
    128–129, 135–141, 142, 143, 160,
    163, 166, 167, 169, 180, 185 n7
  deradicalisation   5, 9–15, 22, 23,
    24, 25, 28, 31–35, 36, 52, 58, 61,
    63, 64, 100–1, 105–113, 121, 122,
    125, 127, 128, 139, 143, 163, 166,
    180, 194–195 n8

  and femininity   17, 19–21, 136–141,
    145–148, 195 n14
  fragmentation of   9, 10, 13, 14, 24,
    29–31, 35, 163
  generational dynamics   17–18, 51,
    96, 97–98, 127–128, 130, 131, 139,
    141, 150–160, 164–165, 185 n9
  and housework   56
  and individualisation   16, 20,
    135–141, 142, 143, 144, 160,
    161, 162
  institutionalisation of   5, 9, 13, 14,
    29, 30, 31, 32, 35, 46, 50–51, 64,
    67, 101, 105–108, 113, 124, 163,
    169, 185 n4
  and the internet   3, 23, 129–130
    (see also blogging, F-word)
  and popular culture   12, 15–18,
    19–21, 90–91, 127, 135–141,
    145–148, 149, 151, 160–162,
    166, 182
  and race/anti-racism   4, 7, 13, 16–17,
    23, 29, 46–47, 72, 91–93, 113–115,
    125, 161–162, 165, 191 n24
  radical/liberal/socialist
    distinction   4, 52
  radical vs liberal feminism   33,
    119, 145
  and radicalism/radicality   4, 5,
    9–15, 17, 23, 24, 26, 27, 30, 31–35,
    36–63, 64–65, 67, 80–99, 100–1,
    105–113, 116, 119, 124–126, 128,
    135, 144–145, 151, 160, 161–162,
    164, 165, 186 n20, 186 n1
  're-emergence'/resurgence   5, 9–10,
    15–18, 22, 23, 25, 58, 63, 99,
    126, 128, 133, 150, 163,
    164–166, 183
  second-wave   5, 16, 17, 18, 20,
    21, 25, 40, 54–55, 62, 64, 80–81,
    100, 102, 103, 105, 109, 110,
    119, 120, 125, 128, 130, 138,
    139, 141, 142, 151, 152, 153,
    154, 157–160, 184 n2, 185 n10
  separatism   22–23, 26, 30, 34,
    46–47, 59, 58–59, 101
  'seventies' feminism   9, 10, 11–12,
    14–15, 22–23, 31–35, 39, 64, 67,
    101, 103, 126, 138–139

and the state 14, 26–35, 45–46,
   62, 66–67, 81, 98–99, 105–107,
   125–6, 166, 182–183, 187 n7–8
and socialism/anti-capitalism 12,
   14, 23, 24, 46, 109, 144, 149, 161
spatial dynamics 21–31, 34–35,
   45–47, 62
subjectivity 51–52, 127
temporal dynamics 7, 9–21, 25,
   34–35, 62–63, 126, 127, 195 n18
third wave 5, 10, 15, 16–19, 21,
   83, 88–89, 93–94, 96, 97, 128,
   131, 132, 134, 141, 150–160, 161,
   162, 185 n9, 185 n10,
   185 n11
and young women 16, 17, 19–21,
   130–135, 136, 137, 138, 142–144,
   149, 150–160, 185 n13
Feminist Activist Forum 3, 162,
   195 n18
Feminist Fightback 3, 4, 162
Feministing (website) 131, 161
Ferree, Myra Marx 25, 37
figure of the newly thinkable'
   (Castoriadis/Zerilli) 53, 57, 82, 101,
   115–121, 126, 141, 144, 188 n17
Finland 26, 28
Fisher, Duncan 79
Forna, Aminatta 185 n7
Forrest, Natasha 145
Foucault, Michel 40
France 28
French Revolution 40
Friel, Anna 111
Frock On 149
The F-word (website) 5–6, 7, 20, 90,
   93, 94, 96, 127–162, 165, 175, 180
aims and format 130–131, 194 n3
and female sexuality 145–151,
   195 n15
feminism (understanding of)
   133–135
feminism and popular
   culture 135–141
origins 130
role of activism 148–150
role of radical feminism 144–145
and third wave feminism 150–160
young women (role of) 130–135

Gelb, Joyce 32
Genz, Stephanie 21
Germany 28
'girl power' 136, 143,
   195 n10
'girlie feminism' 17, 131, 140
Glynos, Jason 42, 44, 60–61, 171,
   188 n19
Gramsci, Antonio 141, 164, 167,
   168, 177–183
Greater London Council (GLC) 13
Greer, Germaine 159, 185 n8
Grey-Thompson, Tanni 190 n20
Guadagnini, Marila 30
The Guardian 85, 86, 87, 88, 132,
   190 n14, 190 n19

Hague, Gill 122
Hall, Stuart 47, 58, 141, 168, 178,
   179, 182
Hardt, Michael 164, 176–177
Harman, Harriet 190 n20
Harwin, Nicola 103, 105, 107, 108,
   111, 117, 120, 121, 191 n1, 194 n20
Hebdige, Dick 179
hegemony (Gramsci/Laclau) 42–43,
   47, 58, 141, 167, 176, 177–178,
   180, 196 n6
Heidegger, Martin 39, 186 n2
Hellicar, Catherine 69
Hemmings, Clare 7, 14
Henry, Astrid 158–159
hermeneutics 60
heteronormativity 60–61
Heywood, Andrew 189 n5
Hollows, Joanne 12, 20–21
Honig, Bonnie 43, 48, 57, 181
housework 56
Hornby, Nick 111
Howarth, David 42, 44, 59–61, 171,
   188 n21
human rights 23, 26, 106, 114–115,
   119
Humphreys, John 111
Huntley, Ian 146, 195 n13

Imkaan 124
immanence/transcendence
   distinction 167

individualisation
  Beck/Giddens   162
  and feminism   16, 20, 135–141,
    142, 143, 144, 160, 161, 162
interest group pluralism   101,
  121–126, 168
interpellation (Althusser)   194 n7
intersectionality   7, 92, 184 n4
International Women's Day   90
intersex   53–54
Ireland   149

Jackson, Kate   190 n20
Jonsson, Terese   161
Julios, Christina   191 n24
Justice for Women   4, 149

Kantola, Johanna   28, 29–30, 35, 45,
  117, 125
Katbama, Mira   132
Kelly, Lorraine   111
Kennedy, Charles   72
King, Oona   190 n20
Kinnock, Neil   13
Knight, Beverley   111
Knightley, Keira   112
Knowles, Jo.   145–146
Krook, Mona Lee   23

Labour Party (UK)   13, 21, 43, 66
Lacan, Jacques   163, 164, 167, 168,
  170, 172, 173, 177, 180
Laclau, Ernesto   1, 35, 38, 40, 42–47,
  49, 56, 57–59, 71, 81, 93,
  186 n1, 187 n6
  articulation   42–47, 56, 58
  and cultural studies   177–183
  discourse   59–61
  empty signifier   43–44, 55, 57, 62,
    71, 81, 82, 93, 94, 95, 96, 116,
    151, 157
  equivalence   23, 38, 43–47, 58, 62,
    65, 72, 93, 94, 95, 99, 116, 126,
    140, 162, 187 n6
  hegemony   42–43, 47, 58,
    141, 167, 176, 177–178, 180,
    196 n6
  and imagination   55–59
  logic of difference   71
  nodal point   119, 123

and optimism/pessimism   167–168,
  170–172, 174, 177
and transnational feminism   46–47
uses for political analysis   59–61
and Linda Zerilli   57–59
Ladyfest   3, 20, 144, 149, 162, 175, 180
Laing, Eleanor   72
Lang, Sabine   30
lap-dancing clubs   90–91, 150, 190 n22
Latin America   24
Lefort, Claude   40, 186 n3
left melancholia   163–164, 178, 181,
  183, 196 n8
Levinson, Ellie   185 n5
Levy, Ariel   147, 195 n17
Liberal Democrats (UK)   69
liberal feminism   5, 29, 33, 54–55,
  65, 119, 126, 189 n5
Livingstone, Ken   190 n20
'logics' (Glynos and Howarth)   60–61,
  184 n5
London Feminist Network   3, 90,
  131, 138, 144, 148–149
London Radical Cheerleaders   149
London Thirdwave   127, 129–130,
  131–132, 134, 142, 148, 150, 151,
  152, 155, 156
  inclusion of men   194–195 n8
Lovenduski, Joni   29, 66–67, 75
Lukes, Steven   40

Mackay, Finn   138, 144,
  149, 154
Mackay, Fiona   28, 184 n1
Mahmood, Saba   61
Mallos, Ellen   122
Marchant, Oliver   38–39, 41, 168,
  180, 186 n3
Marxism   42, 46, 47 (see also post-
  marxism)
May, Theresa   74–75
May, Todd   168, 172
Mazur, Amy   26, 27, 28, 32
McBride (Stetson), Dorothy   26, 27,
  29, 32
McCabe, Jess   156
McRobbie, Angela   11, 16, 19–21,
  25, 26, 50–51, 133, 136, 144,
  159, 169, 175–176, 182, 185 n7,
  185–186 n14, 190 n18

Meier, Petra 30
Mendoza, Breny 24
methodology 6
  implications of male researcher
    studying feminism 184 n3
Middleton, Jo 90
Milan Women's Bookstore
  Collective 188n17, 195 n9
Mill, John Stuart 65
Million Women Rise 3, 90, 149–150, 162
Mind the Gap 149
Miss London University beauty
  contests 150
Missmogga 161
Mitchell, Michelle 86
Moghadam, Valentine 22, 23, 26
Mohanty, Chandra Taplade 24–26,
  35, 46, 49, 165, 184 n3
Moosa, Zoohra 92
Moseley, Rachel 12, 20–21
Mouffe, Chantal 38, 40, 42–25,
  59–61, 135, 168, 186 n1,
  187 n6
Muñoz, Jose Esteban 188 n19
Murray, Jenni 70, 111
Myspace 90

Nash, Kate 16, 185 n7
National Alliance for Women's
  Organisations (NAWO) 4
National Society for the Prevention
  of Cruelty to Children
  (NSPCC) 108
Negri. Antonio 164, 176–177
'New Feminist Politics' 2–4, 85, 148,
  163, 165, 167–168, 183
Newham Asian Women's Project 4
Newman, Saul 188 n19, 196 n9
NGOs 13, 24, 25, 29, 65,
  186 n16
Nietzsche, Friedrich 174
Nixon, Sean 182
Nordic welfare state 27, 77–78, 81,
  189–190 n10
Norval, Aletta 54–55, 188 n18

Oakeshott, Michael 41
Object 1, 3, 90–91, 94, 149–150, 162,
  190 n22, 191 n23
Oliver, Miquita 111

ontic/ontological distinction 39,
  186 n2
Opportunity Now 109
optimism (role in political
  theory) 169–183
Orr, Deborah 191 n25
Orr, Lesley 7
Ortbals, Candice 30
Outshoorn, Joyce 28, 29–30
Oxfam 91

Pankhurst, Emmeline 84
Patel, Pragna 122
patriarchy 33, 45, 66, 97, 103, 117,
  118, 137, 145, 149, 153
Patton, Paul 173
Pender, Patricia 185 n11
personal/political 34, 40, 43, 55, 62,
  103, 185 n8
Phillips, Anne 184 n2
Pietilä, Hilkka 26
Pilcher, Jane 11
Pitkin, Hanna Fenichel 50, 187–188
  n16
Pizzey, Erin 102
Plant, Sheryl 146
Poland 43
politics
  conceptions of 1–2, 38–63, 168,
    177–183, 187 n14
  and imagination 47–59, 62–63,
    188 n20
  and the personal (see personal/
    political)
  and popular culture 177–183
  and the social 47–52, 61
popular culture
  and feminism 12, 15–18, 19–21,
    90–91, 127, 135–141, 145–148,
    149, 151, 160–162, 166, 182
  and politics 177–183
'popular feminism' (McRobbie) 16,
  136
pornography 3, 4, 33, 88, 91, 95,
  147, 149, 151
positivism 60
'post-democracy' 168–169, 180
post-feminism 19–21, 50–51, 90, 95,
  133, 135, 139, 142, 143–144, 160,
  164, 185 n7, 185n10

post-foundationalism   38–42, 47, 48,
    58, 59–61, 166–183, 186 n4
post-marxism (see also Laclau, Ernesto
    and Mouffe, Chantal)
    conception of politics   1–2, 42–47,
        57–61, 196 n6
    and cultural studies   177–183
    optimism/pessimism   163–164,
        166–183
postmodernism   16
'post-politics'   166–169, 170, 180
poststructuralism   96
    conception of politics   1–2, 38–63
    critique of feminist subject   16–17
    and empirical research   59–61
    and feminist state theory   30–31,
        45–46
    and optimism/pessimism   163–164,
        166–183
    and radicalism   35, 37–38, 43–63
Predelli, Line Nyhagen   4, 67, 92–93,
    102–3, 115, 124–125, 184 n2
Pretty Woman (movie)   21
Pringle, Rosemary   45
Projansky, Sarah   20
public/private   34, 50
Pudrovska, Tetyana   36
Pugh, Martin   12–13, 31–32

radical democracy (Laclau and
    Mouffe)   186 n1, 187 n6
Radical Feminism (as body of feminist
    thought)   4, 33–35, 56, 51, 66,
    85, 119, 123, 144–145
Rake, Katherine   68, 69, 73, 74, 75,
    79, 82–83, 84, 85, 86–89, 90,
    94, 97, 99, 155–156, 189 n4,
    189n8, 190 n13–14, 190
    n17–18, 191 n25
Ram, Kalpana   186 n17
Ranciére, Jacques   1, 41, 54, 168,
    170–172, 174, 181, 182,
    188 n18
'raunch culture'   145–148, 195 n17
Reclaim the Night   1, 3, 90,
    148–149, 162
Redfern, Catherine   129, 130, 131,
    132, 133–134, 136, 148, 149, 150,
    155, 190 n17

Refuge   124, 191 n2, 191 n4
Reproductive rights   149 (see also
    abortion)
Richards, Amy   2, 17–18, 32, 141,
    151
rights (theoretical issues)   50–51,
    54–55
Rights of Women   4, 30
riot grrrl   131, 144, 151
Ripley, Fay   111
Robinson, Tony   111
Roddick, Anita   109
Rorty, Richard   41
Rowbotham, Sheila   11
Rucht, Dieter   13–14
'rule-following' (Wittgenstein)   60–61

Sanders, Lise Shapiro   185 n10
Schumpeter, Joseph   73
Scotland   7, 28
second-wave feminism   5, 16, 17,
    18, 20, 21, 25, 40, 54–55, 62,
    64, 80–81, 100, 102, 103, 105,
    109, 110, 119, 120, 125, 128,
    130, 138, 139, 141, 142, 151,
    152, 153, 154, 157–160, 184 n2,
    185 n10
Segal, Lynne   11
separatism   22–23, 26, 30, 34, 46–47,
    59, 58–59, 101
'seventies' feminism   9, 10, 11–12,
    14–15, 22–23, 31–35, 39, 64, 67,
    101, 103, 126, 138–139
Sex Discrimination Act (UK)   77
sex/gender distinction   62, 188 n17
sex workers' rights   4
sexual harassment   44–45, 57, 149
sexuality   4, 7, 33, 34, 146–148, 150,
    162, 164
Simons, Jon   55, 177
Snyder, Margaret   23
Solidarnosc (Poland)   43
Southall Black Sisters   4, 114, 115,
    122, 124
Spain   28
Spalding, Anna   161
Spare Rib   130, 131
Spice Girls   136, 195 n10
Squires, Judith   13, 14, 187 n9

Stavrakakis, Yannis 168, 187 n5, 196 n8
state feminism 26–31, 45, 51, 67, 166, 186 n18
state/civil society distinction 45, 98, 179, 182, 187 n8
Stetson, Dorothy (see McBride (Stetson), Dorothy)
Sweden 28, 32, 78, 79, 189–190 n10
Syal, Meera 111

Thatcherism 43, 178, 184 n1
third wave feminism 5, 10, 15, 16–19, 21, 83, 88–89, 93–94, 96, 97, 128, 131, 132, 134, 141, 150–160, 161, 162, 185 n9, 185 n10, 185 n11
Third Way (Giddens) 21
Thornton, Kate 111
Thurgood, Ben 146
Tibballs, Sue 72, 74–75
transnational feminisms 21–26, 34, 46–47, 129, 162, 165, 186 n18, 196 n3
transversality 23, 26, 34, 46–47
Tripp, Aili Mari 22, 25
Tsaliki, Liza 194 n1
Turkey 26

UK Feminist Action (email list) 3, 132, 148
United Nations 22, 23, 24, 28
Fourth World Conference on Women (1995) 22, 23

Viner, Katherine 185 n8
Violence against women 33
activism against 4, 138–139 (see also domestic violence, Women's Aid)

Wadsworth, Laura 140–141
Walby, Sylvia 23, 26, 185 n4
Walter, Natasha 2, 15–16, 190 n17
Wark, Kirsty 190 n20
Watson, Sophie 45
Whittle, Louise 161
Wilding, Faith 129
Wittgenstein, Ludwig 60, 143, 184 n5
Wollstonecraft, Mary 54–55, 188 n18

'woman friendly welfare state' (Hermes) 27
Women's Aid 5, 30, 100–126, 133, 165
aims 104, 191 n5, 192 n7
celebrity endorsement 110–112
corporate sector (co-operation with) 108–110, 192 n11
domestic violence (understanding of) 115–121
engagement with the state 105–107, 125–6, 192 n6–7
and human rights 106, 114
'multi-agency' work 107–8, 122–124
'new public management' (impact of) 121–6, 193 n19–20
organisational structure 103
origins 101–3
overseas projects 191 n3
professionalisation 100–1, 105–113, 124, 125
race and immigration issues 113–115, 125
'radical liberal' feminism 119, 126
services 191 n4
'victim' vs. 'survivor' 119, 126
Women's Budget Group 4
Women's Liberation Movement (UK) 1978 conference 10
Women's policy agencies 13, 27, 29, 46, 187 n9
Women's Resource Centre 4, 124
Women's Social and Political Union 84
Womenspeakout 144, 195 n12
Working Girl (movie) 21

Xena, Warrior Princess (TV series) 3

Young, Iris Marion 121, 168
Young, Will 111
Yuval-Davis, Nira 22–23, 35, 46–47, 49

Zerilli, Linda 1, 35, 47–63, 175, 181, 195 n9
figure of the newly thinkable' 53, 57, 82, 101, 115–121, 126, 141, 144, 188 n17
and Laclau 57–59

Zerilli, Linda – *continued*
    and political imagination 38, 52–57
    political/social 47–52, 70, 72, 121
    subjectivity/subject question 51–52,
        96, 128, 135, 155, 160

'zines' 3
Zivi, Karen 55
Žižek, Slavoj 164, 168, 170, 171,
    177, 187 n5
Zupanćić, Alenka 171